T0361182

Leadership Agility

Leadership is about influencing others to move in a certain direction and there are many ways of achieving this influence. Each of these leadership styles has its inherent qualities and pitfalls, and will be more suited to specific people and different circumstances. The more leaders understand their preferred leadership styles and are able to flexibly switch to the most suitable style given the situation, the more effective they will be. This book maps out ten sets of opposite leadership styles, giving readers the possibility to understand the strengths and weaknesses of both sides, and to identify their own current preference.

The ten leadership style dimensions cover the full range of leadership roles, from the leader as coach (interpersonal leadership), to the leader as organizer (organizational leadership), as strategist (strategic leadership), as sense-maker (leadership and mission) and as role model (leadership and self).

Readers are invited to draw up their own leadership development plans, which is supported by an interactive App. Readers are also challenged to reflect on how they would approach a number of cases, after which they can go to an interactive web-forum to read how others have responded and engage in a discussion with them. *Leadership Agility* is a useful tool for practitioners in the corporate world as well as business students and emerging leaders.

Ron Meyer is Professor of Strategic Leadership at the Tias School for Business and Society, Tilburg University and Managing Director at the Center for Strategy and Leadership. For years, Ron has been combining boardroom consulting with in-house management training and applied management research. Besides that, Ron gives speeches and presentations on topics such as leadership, corporate strategy, business innovation, change management, strategic thinking and organizational development. He has (co-)authored numerous articles and books, among which is the internationally leading textbook *Strategy: Process, Content, Context*.

Ronald Meijers is senior partner Leadership, Transformation and Governance at Deloitte. For years, Ronald has been engaged in boardroom coaching and consulting, while fulfilling various management roles in professional services firms, such as co-chairman of the executive board of Krauthammer. He sits on various supervisory and advisory boards, e.g. at Dunamare, an education group. He gives key-notes on topics such as corporate culture, organizational collaboration, change management, creative thinking, leadership and governance. He has (co-)authored numerous articles, books and columns, among others in *Management Team* and *Management Scope*.

"Ron and Ronald have done it again. A very readable book on leadership with a focus on the main characteristics of agility. With a world that is increasingly facing the dilemmas caused by the diversity of diversity we need a new paradigm of leadership that goes beyond situational leadership. And this well-written book helps you to get aware of your dominant style and how to go beyond it."

Fons Trompenaars, Partner KPMG Trompenaars Hampden-Turner Culture for Business and co-author of *Riding the Waves of Culture: Understanding Cultural Diversity in Business*

"Successfully navigating through the storms and swells of a major transformation effort requires a compass, map and that old and trusted notebook with the lessons we and other captains learned on earlier traverses. This book provides exactly and all that in a practical and pragmatic manner."

Harry Brekelmans, Member of the Executive Committee, Royal Dutch Shell

"Oh no. Not another book about leadership. Trees are too important to be turned into leadership books. Books that typically promote tricks, styles and interventions that will allow you to become Winston Churchill or Jack Welsh in a heartbeat. And in the process ignore the single most important requirement for good leadership: authenticity. Faking a leadership style that is not yours, or playing a leadership role that ignores your very nature, is a recipe for organizational disaster and personal frustration.

This book, you guessed it right, is different. It is descriptive rather than prescriptive. It does not advertise the one leadership style that will save the world, but describes different dimensions of a leadership style.

Why is that helpful? First, it helps you understand yourself. Along 10 different dimensions you can assess your own style, understand what your basic leadership is, and what it is *not*. It makes you realize what your environment observes, and what *not*. And in that way helps you execute and communicate your decisions and messages much more effectively, because you better realize their impact. Second, it helps you better understand the leadership of others. Of your peers, your team members, or your boss. You understand that the fact that their style is different from yours does not make them bad leaders; just, indeed, different! It helps you build your own team, in recognizing that leadership styles might complement each other and lead to a more diverse and complete leadership culture. For the fans of a federative leadership style, that is (right, one of the 10 dimensions).

And finally, because the book makes for an interesting and captivating read. The case studies are insightful, thought provoking and fascinating. I still feel sorry for the tree, but at least it has turned into something that is both entertaining and helpful!"

Roger Dassen, Global Managing Director, Deloitte Touche Tohmatsu

"Practice shows that there is a huge need to improve leadership as it turns out that too many leaders do not create an environment in which their employees feel engaged. Therefore, this book of Meyer and Meijers is well timed. It provides the reader with great insights and inspirations, which hopefully can be transformed into practice as this could improve leadership in action."

Flemming Poulfelt, Professor of Management and Strategy, Copenhagen Business School and co-author of *Managing the Knowledge-Intensive Firm*

"A book based on many years of practical experience. Very inspiring with a lot of food for thought."

Nils Herzberg, Global Lead Internet of Things, SAP SE

"This is immensely readable book on the need for leaders to be agile in an increasingly volatile, complex and uncertain world. But above all, the advice that it provides is accessible, practical and no-nonsense."

Jamie Anderson, Professor of Business Strategy, Antwerp Management School and co-author of *The Fine Art of Success: How Learning Great Art Can Create Great Business*

"Paradoxes in today's organizations are demanding for leaders. Leaders have to be able to learn, switch and sometimes combine different leadership styles. Stated differently, now and in the future, leadership agility is the meta-skill for leaders. If you want a book with an excellent conceptual body around this core idea, start here. Ron and Ronald offer you 10 paradoxes in a clear and very compelling way."

Jesse Segers and Koen Marichal, co-directors of The Future Leadership Initiative, Antwerp Management School

Leadership Agility

Developing Your Repertoire of
Leadership Styles

Ron Meyer and Ronald Meijers

Routledge
Taylor & Francis Group

LONDON AND NEW YORK

First published 2018
by Routledge
2 Park Square, Milton Park, Abingdon, Oxon OX14 4RN

and by Routledge
711 Third Avenue, New York, NY 10017

Routledge is an imprint of the Taylor & Francis Group, an informa business

British Library Cataloguing in Publication Data
A catalogue record for this book is available from the British Library

Library of Congress Cataloging in Publication Data
Names: Meyer, Ron, 1962- author. | Meijers, Ronald, author.
Title: Leadership agility : developing your repertoire of leadership styles / Ron Meyer and Ronald Meijers.
Description: Abingdon, Oxon ; New York, NY : Routledge, 2018. | Includes bibliographical references and index.
Identifiers: LCCN 2017013027 (print) | LCCN 2017030049 (ebook) | ISBN 9781315159980 (eBook) | ISBN 9781138065079 (hardback : alk. paper) | ISBN 9781138065109 (pbk. : alk. paper)
Subjects: LCSH: Leadership.
Classification: LCC HD57.7 (ebook) | LCC HD57.7 .M494 2018 (print) | DDC 658.4/092--dc23
LC record available at https://lccn.loc.gov/2017013027

ISBN: 978-1-138-06507-9 (hbk)
ISBN: 978-1-138-06510-9 (pbk)
ISBN: 978-1-31515-998-0 (ebk)

Typeset in Bembo
by Integra Software Service Pvt. Ltd.

*To Johanna, for your engaging empathy and elegant agility
and
To Cilya, for your assertive authenticity and supportive sovereignty*

Contents

Figures

Tables

Preface

With thousands of books already published on the topic of leadership, why one more? And with so many books on your desk waiting to be read, why should you read this one first? In this preface we'll explain why and we'll summarize the key points of this book, but allow us to start with a short detour to more vividly make our point.

A few years ago, we were invited to speak at a leadership conference in Amsterdam. Afterwards, the social program consisted of a canal tour through the city, ending with a dinner at the magnificent Rijksmuseum. As we boarded the tour boat, we were welcomed by Herman, who introduced himself as our guide to the city. After his warm reception, we set off down the Prinsengracht, listening to Herman explain about the rich history of the place. But within ten minutes Herman was finished with his quick background sketch and turned to his audience to ask them where they were from. Hearing that some were Belgian, he explained how Amsterdam had risen to prominence after the arrival of refugees from Antwerp in the 16th century and he pointed to the luxurious residences these business people had built along the canals. In the same way, Herman connected the city to the history of the Italians, Germans and Americans on board. Asked by a Brazilian professor whether there was any link to his home country, Herman stunned him with a story of the Amsterdam merchants who had financed a Dutch fort in Recife on the Brazilian coast, and he promised to show the professor their houses as soon as we passed.

When after an hour Herman sensed that interest in his tales was starting to wane, he again surprised us by sharing that he had done a bit of reading up on the topic of leadership, because he had been told he would be stuck with a boat-load of experts. He went on to describe how the VOC, the first multi-national company in the world, was run and he skillfully related this to what he had read about leadership. A fascinating debate unfolded, cut short by our arrival at the dinner location. As we disembarked and thanked Herman for the inspiring tour, two colleagues asked whether they could sail back to the hotel with Herman after dinner instead of taking a taxi back. Herman graciously agreed and, sure enough, two hours later we were all back on board.

That is leadership. No one appointed Herman as our leader; he stepped forward and we embraced him. *And that is leadership agility.* Herman didn't use a standard script, assuming it would fit; he sensed what was required to connect with this particular group of people and he attuned his guide behavior to their needs.

As this example of Herman shows, to be an agile leader requires three specific qualities. First, you must be *flexible*. Flexibility is the capacity to switch between behaviors and not be rigidly stuck in one particular mode. To be flexible, a leader needs to have a broad repertoire of ways to engage people and the ability to smoothly switch between them. So, just as an agile tour guide like Herman can engage others by switching between different stories and different ways of telling them, an agile leader also needs to be able to nimbly switch between different engagement styles, for example, changing over from being challenging to being encouraging. We call this *leadership style flexibility* – having easy access to a broad repertoire of leadership behaviors.

Second, you must be *adaptable*. Adaptability is the capacity to acquire and master new behaviors, to further strengthen the existing repertoire. Herman could have tried to wing it using his existing range of stories, but he realized ahead of time that his repertoire didn't exactly fit with the group he wanted to guide. So, he had to go to the trouble of reading up on leadership and coming up with new stories to complement his familiar ones. This not only required conscious effort, but also forced him out of his comfort zone, to explore unfamiliar leadership theory for the first time in his life. The same effort is required of leaders who want to exhibit *leadership style adaptability* – the ability to add new leadership styles to their current portfolio. They, too, must move beyond their comfort zone, to acquire new knowledge, build new skills and practice a way of behaving that is opposite to the routine they were used to.

Third, you must be *responsive*. Responsiveness is the capacity to be acutely aware of the situation you are in and rapidly react to it. That means being sensitive to the needs of the audience you are trying to influence and swiftly adjusting your behavior to what is required. Herman understood this art of connecting to the people in his group as no other. He was quick to figure out the different nationalities on board and tweak his story line to appeal to their interests. In a similar manner, he was attentive to the fading concentration after the first hour and shifted his storytelling approach to adapt to the unfolding situation. Leaders must do the same, exhibiting *leadership style responsiveness* – judging the situation and swiftly adjusting their leadership style to match, either by flexibly accessing an existing style or adaptively learning a new one.

So, could you be a good tour guide if all you knew was the script given to you by the canal boat company? We would argue that this limited repertoire would make you a "one trick pony" – you might be successful under very specific circumstances, but in all other situations you would be mediocre at best. Some tour groups might politely clap and even give you a small tip, but you would be memorable to few and no one would ask you for a ride back. For leaders, the same is true if you have a fixed style repertoire that you repeat over and over again – in some circumstances it might just work, but in all other cases there will be a misfit. It is for this reason that we believe that leaders need to be agile – *have the capacity to flexibly switch between leadership styles, and adaptively master new ones, in rapid response to the specific needs of the people and situation they want to influence.*

Entering the age of agility

As this example of a tour guide illustrates, the need to be agile is not limited to organizational leaders. In all areas where a person can't afford to be rigid, but needs to quickly adjust to the particular – and changing – needs of the environment, agility is essential. Darwin would immediately recognize this argument. It's actually "survival of the fittest" in different words. People, and all other life forms, prosper if they are best suited to the environment and have the ability to rapidly follow shifting circumstances. So, for example, mice and rats are very flexible when it comes to their dining repertoire, eating more or less anything they find, while panda bears are almost extinct, largely due to their dietary inflexibility. Mice and rats are also very adaptable, learning new behaviors to live side-by-side with humans, while polar bears have neither adjusted to humans nor to their dwindling Arctic habitat. In this sense, leaders are more like rats than like either type of bear – their agility allows them to swiftly adjust their behavior and effectively respond to the specific demands of the situation.

While the need for agility is not limited to leaders, neither is it new. Leaders have always had to quickly adjust to circumstances to be effective. Leadership researchers initially thought that some personal traits would make certain people great leaders under all conditions, but very soon these "trait theories of leadership"[1] were displaced by "situational leadership theories"[2] that recognized the importance of alignment between leadership behaviors and the specific circumstances. Central to all these theories is the Darwinian idea of "fit" – leaders must be aligned with their environment and must evolve along with it.

So, is there nothing new that justifies fresh attention to the topic of leadership agility? Why should we suddenly care more about leadership agility than before? It is because there is definitely something new going on, at a very fundamental level – we have entered the *age of agility*, in which Darwinian survival of the fittest has been shifted up a gear. Just as in the natural environment, where evolution has been turbocharged and millennia of changes now happen in decades, so too in the organizational environment has evolution gone into hyperdrive. The situational pressures on leaders have become exponentially more complex, as their environments have become faster changing, more diverse and more demanding. All this means that leaders must make a step change in their capacity to be agile, or accept living on an ever shrinking sheet of ice.

There are many factors shaping the age of agility, of which four megatrends stand out as crucial influences on the need for enhanced leadership agility. The first megatrend is the pressure towards more *organizational agility* – leaders need to be increasingly agile because their organizations also need to be. We all know about the fast pace of change in many markets, driven by factors such as digitalization, customer-centricity, the energy transition, urbanization, increased connectivity, the circular economy, demographic shifts and the like. It has been argued by many authors[3] that disruption is sweeping many industries, while no sector is immune to constant innovation and improvement, requiring continual organizational adjustment. This in itself would already pose quite an organizational change challenge, especially as the pace of industry evolution seems to have picked up. Yet, what complicates the ongoing organizational adjustment is the unpredictability of which business model changes will be successful. The more unpredictable the market, the more unpredictable will be the success of an innovation or improvement, which means that companies must experiment more and can execute less. We call this the need for *strategic agility* – the capacity to quickly shift along with the market, not on the basis of long-term forecasts and extensive business plans, but on the basis of rapid trial and error, and scaling up of what seems to work.[4] Such strategic agility (as opposed to strategic planning) requires an organization that is agile, quickly and flexibly reacting to an unfolding new reality, while also learning new skills and developing new ways of working, depending on the business model that seems to be superior. For leaders this means that their organizations are constantly changing in unpredictable ways and that they need to change along with them, sometimes driving the change, sometimes adjusting to it.

The second megatrend driving the age of agility is *organizational diversity*. Organizations are becoming internally increasingly varied, making it more and more difficult for leaders to take a "one size fits all" approach to leadership. This diversity is showing up in many ways. At the level of individuals, organizations are seeing growing variety in the type of people employed. More women are in the workforce and accepting jobs that were traditionally male-dominated. The cultural and ethnic background of employees is also broadening, as companies hire more people from minorities, recruit more people from abroad and often send employees out to foreign subsidiaries themselves. At the level of teams and units, organizations are also seeing growing variety, due to the differing environments in which each needs to operate. As globalization continues, organizations increasingly work across borders, but are also becoming more sensitive to differences in national environments, making units more distinct. At the same time, units are often moving at different evolutionary speeds and in different directions due to the required strategic agility mentioned above. All this means that leaders must deal with an increasing diversity of people and units, requiring them to nimbly adjust to each to achieve the best possible fit.

The third megatrend driving the age of agility is the rise of *employee empowerment*, or, stated differently, the withering of hierarchy. We are at the start of a paradigm shift from thinking of organizations as hierarchies to seeing organizations as groups of cooperating people. Josephine Green has coined the phrase "from pyramids to pancakes"[5] as a catchy way of summarizing this fundamental transition. For decades, organizational theorists have lamented the mechanistic view[6] that organizations are places where people work (more aptly, where they are human resources). Yet in practice most people accepted that organizations were some sort of apparatus, with systems and processes, into which people could be slotted as cogs into a machine, much as Charlie Chaplin depicted workers in his famous movie *Modern Times*. As cogs don't need to think, neither do human resources. They only need to be managed – told what to do and disciplined by those one step above them. Of course, these people in turn need to be managed, all on the basis of formal authority, leading to multiple layers of management and a pyramid-form hierarchy. In each position at each layer, the behavior of people was predictable and didn't need to be adjusted to specific individuals. In the new people-centric view, organizations are groups of people working together towards a common goal, with some systems and processes to support this. The fundamental assumptions are that employees need to take ownership of their work, need to find ways to collaborate productively and can be facilitated in this process. In other words, in such flat organizations it is about empowering employees, not controlling them. This shift to more flatness has a huge impact on the need for leadership agility. As employees start seeing themselves less and less as human resources, but more as individuals, they also expect leaders to treat them as such, creating even more diversity to which leaders must adjust. At the same time, employee empowerment will not move at the same pace across individuals, units, organizations and countries, again creating more diversity for leaders to handle and a higher need to be agile in adjusting to different speeds and directions of change.

The fourth and last megatrend driving the age of agility is *career diversity*. There are still people who work their way up the corporate ladder within one function in one company, but they are becoming ever more rare. It is far more common for people to hop between companies multiple times during their careers, but also across functions, across sectors and across borders. Career paths are also becoming less predictable, with people taking sabbaticals or career breaks, but also leaving to set up their own company or being acquired by another firm. Many people don't even have a fixed job, moving from "gig to gig," always on a temporary basis. All this adds to the earlier mentioned organizational diversity, but for the people making the switches it means that they will likely have to make several huge adjustments as leaders throughout their working lives. The more agile they are, the bigger the chance of a successful transition to a new environment.

All four megatrends together are making it impossible for leaders to rigidly hold on to one set of leadership styles and be successful. Moreover, these trends are not one-off changes that leaders only have to adjust to once. Organizational agility, organizational diversity, employee engagement and career diversity all require leaders to become permanently more flexible, adaptive and responsive. That is why we boldly speak of the age of agility. And that is why it is the intention of this book to empower leaders to further develop their leadership agility.

Developing leadership agility

Back to Herman. It is impossible to become an agile tour guide without a lot of practice and the same is true for leadership agility. But there are a few steps before extensive practice where this book can add value. It starts with giving an overview of all major leadership styles and mapping where your current preferences are. The core of this book consists of ten opposite pairs of leadership styles and on each one of these ten dimensions you probably already have a preferred style. We call these your *default leadership styles* – these are the styles that constitute your comfort zone. In each chapter one dimension will be explored, focusing on the two opposite styles at the ends of a continuum. You will quickly recognize at which pole of the continuum you like to hang out and how difficult you find it to cover the entire continuum of styles. In each chapter there will also be a discussion around the strengths of both opposite styles, as well as the potential downsides of each style, if it is used incorrectly. We suspect that you will recognize which strengths of each style you have been able to capture and where improvement is possible, but also where you have tumbled into the pitfalls of each style and will need to avoid them in future.

After mapping your current leadership styles and recognizing strengths and downsides, the last chapters of the book will guide you towards the styles you need to work on to develop your leadership agility. These "stretch" styles can be those you use but don't yet master, or they can be styles that are quite new to you. To support you, and to make it more interactive, you can also download the accompanying *Leadership LEAP* (Leadership Enhancement Action Plan) App for tablets.

Before starting on this journey, the first two chapters will stake out the terrain. Chapter 1 will dig more deeply into the question of what leadership truly is, which is not an unimportant issue, given the multitude of views and the inflation to which the term is subject. Chapter 2 will give an overview of the various styles and explain how they differ and are linked to one another. Based on the map of styles presented (the *"leadership style rose,"* with 10 dimensions and in total 20 styles) the next 10 chapters will subsequently review one set of opposite styles per chapter.

It is not necessary to read Chapters 3 to 12 in this particular order, nor is it necessary to read them all at one go. Using the leadership rose in Chapter 2 as a map, you can easily pick out the leadership styles that interest you most and read those chapters first.

Before you get started, one last thought. Some of you might be thinking: "Wait a minute, why did Herman have to be so agile? Why didn't he just specialize in one script and let the canal boat company match him to the right audience?" Fair point. The world is full of one trick ponies that are nicely align with a particular niche. Liver transplant surgeons are not very agile, specializing in one skill, but generally extremely good at it. Olympic figure skating champions are undeniably world class at what they do, but generally don't dabble in speed skating or ice hockey, not to mention table tennis or liver transplantation. Isn't it better to be an excellent "one trick pony" than a poor "jack of all trades?" Shouldn't we build on our strengths and specialize, instead of constantly adjusting to the outside world, attempting to do things we are not good at?

Maybe Herman should have focused on only guiding leadership experts through the canals of Amsterdam and let the audience be adjusted to him, instead of him having to do all the adjusting.

Do you recognize the two sides to this argument? On the one hand, there is advantage to specializing in one type of behavior and getting very good at it, particularly if it fits with your strengths and your identity. Yet, on the other hand, there is advantage to being highly agile, capable of quickly and effectively responding to a wide variety of situations. These are two opposite demands on people, pushing them in contradictory directions. We call such tensions between conflicting requirements "paradoxes" and you will encounter them at the heart of all of the chapters that follow. This particular one is *the paradox of authenticity and adjustment* – focusing on a few leadership styles that are close to the genuine you, as opposed to developing a broad repertoire of leadership styles to be able to adjust to a wide variety of situations.

So, what is the best avenue to take? How agile do you really need to be as leader? Do you need to be highly flexible, adaptable and responsive, or should you lean more over to the side of specialization, genuineness and predictability? It is a fundamental leadership issue to which – you shouldn't be surprised – there are two opposite leadership styles. Leaders who emphasize authenticity and limit their leadership agility, sticking to a fixed set of leadership styles, have what we call a *consistent leadership style* (actually it is a meta-style – a style for dealing with leadership styles). Leaders who stress the importance of adjustment to various circumstances and strive towards high leadership agility have what we call a *responsive leadership style*. This is such an important leadership issue that an entire chapter has been dedicated to discussing it. This will be Chapter 12, the last chapter reviewing opposite leadership styles.

Now, time to start the tour. Let's see if we can live up to the standard of engagement that Herman set.

Ron Meyer and Ronald Meijers

Notes

1 The classic example is Carlyle, T. (1849), *On Heroes, Hero-Worship, and the Heroic in History*, Boston: Houghton-Mifflin. But also see Galton, F. (1869), *Hereditary Genius*, New York: Appleton.
2 The first theory to be called "Situational Leadership" was by Paul Hersey and Ken Blanchard. See: Hersey, P. and Blanchard, K.H. (1977), *Management of Organizational Behavior: Utilizing Human Resources* (3rd ed.), New Jersey: Prentice Hall. But other theories at the time also suggested that effective leadership styles were dependent on the specific circumstances, such as contingency theory. See: Fiedler, F.E. (1967), *A Theory of Leadership Effectiveness*, New York: McGraw-Hill; Vroom, V.H. and Yetton, P.W. (1973), *Leadership and Decision-Making*, Pittsburgh: University of Pittsburgh Press.
3 Of course, this argument goes back to Schumpeter, J. (1942), *Capitalism, Socialism and Democracy*, New York: Harper and Brothers. Since then the argument has been further developed by authors such as D'Aveni, R. (1994), *Hypercompetition: Managing*

the Dynamics of Strategic Maneuvering, New York: Free Press; Hamel, G. (2002), *Leading the Revolution*, New York: Plume.

4   See Weber, Y. and Tarba, S.Y. (2014), "Strategic Agility: A State of the Art. Introduction to the Special Section on Strategic Agility," *California Management Review*, Vol. 56, No. 3, Spring, pp. 5–12; Lewis, M., Andriopoulos, C. and Smith, W.K. (2014), "Paradoxical Leadership to Enable Strategic Agility," *California Management Review*, Vol. 56, No. 3, Spring, pp. 58–77.

5   See https://vimeo.com/18669177

6   The term "mechanistic organization" was coined by Burns and Stalker, to refer to a specific type of organization that is hierarchical, structured and bureaucratic. See: Burns, T. and Stalker, G.M. (1961), *The Management of Innovation*, London: Tavistock. Since then the term has often been used to refer to organizations that behave "mechanistically" and to theorists that treat people as rational actors, such as supporters of transaction cost economics. For a famous example see Williamson, O.E. (1991), "Strategizing, Economizing, and Economic Organization," *Strategic Management Journal*, Vol. 12, Winter, pp. 75–94.

Acknowledgements

Courage is what it takes to stand up and speak; courage is also what it takes to sit down and listen.

Winston Churchill (1874–1965)
Former British Prime Minister

In the more than ten years we've spent developing this book, we've tried to be as "courageous" as possible, presenting our ideas and frameworks to a wide variety of groups around the world and asking for their comments and suggestions. We've shared earlier versions of our work with thousands of people, in executive leadership programs, coaching sessions and keynote speeches. There has been much for us to "listen" to, as we have received a constant stream of constructive feedback. Without the willingness of so many people to provide us with their insights and questions, this book would never be what it has become.

Yet, with so many supportive contributors it is impossible to acknowledge each individual's input without the acknowledgements becoming a chapter in themselves. Therefore, we are forced to pick out only a few people and groups for special mention, although we hope that all our colleagues, students and clients not specifically listed here will still feel our heart-felt appreciation.

The first group to specifically thank are all the people who pre-read chapters of this book and sent back their observations and pointers. Thank you Paul van Baren, Erik Bax, Marit van Bergen, Alexandra Blackman, Mathilde de Boer, Bill Collins, Geert van Deth, Victor Gilsing, Aart Goud, Bie de Graeve, Herbert Hoppener, Danaë Huijser, Simon Hunt, Paul Hunter, Joel Janssen, Edwin Kanis, Twan van de Kerkhof, Tjerk Lerou, Jeroen van Loon, Rens van Loon, Marcel van Marrewijk, Philip Melkman, Alex van Os de Man, Julieta Matos Castaño, Raj Patel, Stephen Pitt-Walker, Will Reijnders, Lisa Ross, Damian Ruth, Peter Schansman, Joep Stuijt, Rob van Tulder, Juan Garcia Vallejo, Casper van der Veen, Marc Verbruggen, Roemer Visser and Frank van Zanten.

Throughout the development process we have been supported by a number of interns at the Center for Strategy and Leadership, including Ilse van der Beek, Daniela Dodan, Carmen van den Hemel, Lotte Humme, Anton Leemhuis, Matija Marijan, Mariapia Di Palma, Melinda Schuurmans, Giancarlo Stanco,

Magda Stancioi and Georgi Stoychev. Special thanks go to our most recent intern, Thomas Meyer, Ron's son, who has been responsible for ensuring the quality of the endnotes (while in the meantime figuring out what his dad has been up to all of those years).

Furthermore, we would like to thank a number of long-time sparring partners at our respective organizations. Ron has worked together with his partner, Martijn Rademakers, at the Center for Strategy and Leadership for more than 15 years and has greatly benefitted from his feedback and unwavering support. At the same time, Ron has been greatly inspired by his colleagues of the Tias School for Business and Society at Tilburg University. Special mention goes to Jan de Vuijst and Filip Caeldries, with whom he has co-taught many executive programs over the past years that have incorporated the thinking written down in this book.

Ronald would like to thank his colleagues in the Human Capital practice at Deloitte, with a special word of gratitude to Roger Dassen, for his agile thinking and persistence in searching out inspiring ideas. Furthermore, Ronald is greatly indebted to his former colleagues at Krauthammer, in particular Daniel Eppling, Steffi Gande, Irene van Giezen, Thierry Stephan, Jos Velthuis and Thijs Westerkamp. They have been consistent supporters from the very beginning and have constantly contributed by asking "so what?," pushing for relevance to everyday leadership practice. Moreover, they have been brothers- and sisters-in-arms, applying the leadership concepts in numerous executive development projects, while also using them in the way Krauthammer has been organized and led.

Finally, we are extremely lucky to have had the best two sparring partners close at hand. Our wives, Johanna and Cilya, are both experts in leadership in their own right. Given their experience in coaching and training leaders, they have always been there to challenge, to question, to wonder and to suggest. They have proofread and proposed alterations, but more importantly, they have critiqued our logic and inspired us by their approach to leadership development. Ronald would like to thank Cilya for being his most affectionate adversary, competitive to the bone, unwilling to lead, unable to follow and yet an enthu- siastic practitioner of the leadership paradoxes. Ron would like to thank Johanna for demonstrating the power of combining leadership and followership in one and the same relationship, gracefully shifting from leading to following and back, intuitively sensing when to do which, without ego or hang-ups getting in the way. Elegantly agile…an ambition we can all strive towards.

Part I

Leadership

1   The nature of leadership

For centuries people have been fascinated by the topic of leadership, first in the realm of warfare and politics, and later in business and sports.[1] Not that this interest has been constant, as attention has waxed and waned over the years, often depending on the great successes and historic tragedies brought about by highly visible leaders. Especially after the Second World War, the concept of leadership seems to have suffered by its connection to "Great Dictators," such as Hitler, Mussolini and Stalin. To this day, the German word for leader, *führer*, is tainted by the memory of the slavish following of great evil. Unsurprisingly, few people take the phrase "Our Beloved Leader" to imply a compliment.

In business, too, an early interest in leadership gave way to a period of focus on technical management skills, such as finance, operations, marketing and strategy. Yet, during the last two decades, leadership has made a great comeback, in the thinking of business people, in the curricula of business schools and in the sales of books and Apps. Hordes of managers are sent off to leadership development programs, young people aspire to become "next generation leaders" and when things go wrong in companies, more often than not the media point to a lack of leadership as the root cause. It's clear, leadership is hot.

But what is leadership? That depends on who you ask. So many people have jumped on the leadership bandwagon, adding their own hopes, fears, biases and twists, that we are at risk of losing sight of the fundamental nature of leadership. On the one hand, the concept of leadership has been stretched to encompass a curiosa shop of phenomena, making it seem to mean a lot of different things. On the other hand, most speakers and writers employ their own narrow notion of what they believe leadership should be, making it seem like something very specific. Interestingly, almost no one makes an effort to define leadership and to distinguish it from other concepts.

So, as it is the intention of this book to explore the qualities and pitfalls of various leadership styles, our journey must begin with a clarification of what we believe to be the essence of leadership. While it might seem a bit academic to start a book with definitions, having a focused and realistic image of what leadership is all about will serve us well, as we map different leadership styles and investigate how you might improve your own.

What leadership is not

Convictions are more dangerous enemies of truth than lies.
Friedrich Wilhelm Nietzsche (1844–1900)
German academic and philosopher

As the word "leader" has collected so many layers of meaning over the years, coming to a clear understanding of the fundamental nature of leadership starts by stripping away the various coatings of varnish. So, with a nod to Michael Porter, who started his famous HBR article on *What is Strategy*[2] by explaining what it is not, we can identify five different concepts with which leadership should not be confused. These are five common misconceptions about leadership that have contributed most to the muddled view so prevalent in practice and in theory.

Misconception 1: The leader as boss

Open a random annual report and most likely it will present "the top leadership team." Ask a random HR manager to make a list of their business leaders and they will give you an org chart displaying all of their managers. Ask a random employee to name the leader of the organization and they will point to the highest-ranking manager. In all of these cases, the words leader and manager are used interchangeably. It has become increasingly fashionable to call managers leaders, probably because it sounds less technocratic, less 20th century. Just as someone with an MBA doesn't want to be called a "business administrator" anymore, so too the label "manager" seems to have become dated, suggesting much less *schwung* than "leader," prompting ever more people to migrate from the former label to the latter. Yet this is a confusing sort of inflation, mixing up a formal position with an informal authority. The two are fundamentally different.

To clarify the distinction between manager and leader, let us focus on the ultimate boss, the CEO, as example. Such a person undeniably fills a top management position, but does this automatically make the CEO a leader? Are people inclined to follow CEOs just because of the chair they are sitting in, or do CEOs need to bring more to the table to win people over and mobilize them to move in a certain direction? It is clear that CEOs can potentially command obedience using the formal powers of reward and punishment attached to their office. CEOs can appeal to their superior rank in the hierarchy and use "carrots" and "sticks" to get people to fall in line. In other words, being the boss gives CEOs the means to "buy" compliance. Under these circumstances, people will follow if it is in their economic interest to do so. In such a calculative relationship, people will do what the CEO demands if their return on investment of time and effort is high enough and/or if the potential punishment is too daunting. So, purely on the basis of their position, CEOs can get people to follow – call it followership via "wallets" and "whippings."

However, almost all CEOs know that to get the best out of people requires more than bonuses and thumb screws. To get people truly on board requires the winning of hearts and minds. If people "have to" follow, their performance will be mediocre at best, but if they sincerely "want to," their performance can be stellar. If CEOs can tap into people's beliefs, passions, hopes and dreams, they can trigger enormous drive to join the company's journey and contribute whole-heartedly to the company's efforts. If CEOs can connect with people's intrinsic motivation, they can build engagement and a resilience to overcome odds. Being the formal boss is not what sways people, but it is the CEO's ability to inspire, charm, challenge, support, cajole, convince and even seduce – all qualities that have little to do with their management position and have everything to do with what they as individuals bring to the relationship. Under such circumstances, people will follow, not because it is in their economic, but in their emotional interest to do so. But they will need to respect and have trust in such CEOs to genuinely embrace them as individuals to willingly follow. Call it followership via "connection" and "confidence."

So, if we start with a simple definition of leadership as the ability to get people to follow, very little of this ability will be rooted in a person's formal position, while most will be found in how a person builds relationships, confidence and authority with others. Having the job of manager can help to get people to follow, as there will often be implicit respect for hierarchy and a sensitivity for potential rewards and punishment. Yet, having a management position can also interfere with getting others to follow, as people might question a manager's motives – after all, as the old saying goes, where you "sit" determines where you "stand." Managers are often mistrusted because they are driven by their own agenda, their own performance measures and their own narrow worldview.

While individuals can be appointed manager, they need to be accepted as leader. To have the ability to sway, leaders need to step forward and seek the lead, while winning people's trust and approval to be allowed to do so. Whether CEO or first line supervisor, the formal appointment as manager somewhere in the hierarchy by no means ensures that someone will be embraced as leader. Every person who wants to lead will have to earn it. Leadership is relational, not positional.

Vice versa, being accepted as leader by no means suggests that one needs to be, or needs to become, the boss. Even without formal power, a person can have enormous informal influence and be accepted as a leader. This influence can be rooted in such elements as a person's expertise, charisma, warmth, experience or passion, and will have been built up over time.

In Table 1.1 a playful overview is given of the distinction between being a manager and being a leader. To be absolutely clear, the two do not constitute opposite categories, such as the dichotomy between hot and cold, but just differing concepts, such as the distinction between hot and red – two very different things that are easily muddled if you don't watch out.

Unfortunately, the confusing mix up between the terms manager and leader has a number of regrettable consequences. First, it lures managers into a false

Table 1.1 Comparing management and leadership

	The World of the Manager	*The World of the Leader*
What do you do?	I have a **JOB** with rights and responsibilities	I fulfill a **ROLE** with or without a formal position
How do you become one?	I am **APPOINTED** by higher level managers	I become **ACCEPTED** by others who wish to follow
Which means do you have?	I have **FORMAL POWERS** to assign, spend, reward and punish	I have **INFORMAL AUTHORITY** built on trust, ability, inspiration and persuasion
What is your approach?	I get people to **COMPLY** by using carrots and sticks	I get people's **COMMITMENT** by winning hearts and minds
How do people respond?	We have **CALCULATIVE** relations asking what's in it for me	We have **SYMBIOTIC** relations as both care about a common goal
What is the best result?	**ACCEPTABLE** performance based on extrinsic motivation	**EXCELLENT** performance based on intrinsic motivation
Rule of thumb conclusion?	**MANAGE THINGS** Make sure that they **HAVE TO**	**LEAD PEOPLE** Make sure that they **WANT TO**

conviction of what is required to become a successful leader, suggesting that an appointment and formal power will do the trick. Take the example of Stefan, a highly qualified engineer, who for years had the difficult task of being head of global quality assurance at a Swiss manufacturer of construction materials. Despite being one of the best engineers in his field and developing excellent corporate procedures, he was unable to get production managers at the various sites around the world to implement his quality assurance measures. For years, he pleaded with the CEO to give him formal authority to "knock some heads together" and push through the necessary measures. After a major quality issue at one of the US plants, the CEO caved in and gave Stefan the powers he sought. Now Stefan was the global leader, or at least that's what he thought. But instead of listening more attentively to Stefan, the regional production managers kept dragging their feet and poor quality remained an issue. Stefan was bewildered. So, he gradually went from commanding to threatening, punishing and manipulating, while quality standards hardly budged. It was only after a personal crisis and a run in with the disillusioned CEO that Stefan realized that he had sought more formal power so he could force people to comply instead of winning them over. It just hadn't occurred to him that his job as manager gave him formal powers he actually shouldn't use, because that would rub people the wrong way. Becoming the boss had seduced him into becoming bossy. So, although it felt uncomfortably vulnerable to stop sending instruction emails, he got on a plane and went out to listen to people. He found that some colleagues needed help and reassurance, others needed to be convinced, while yet others needed to be challenged. And it took time – as he put it himself: "As with my wife, the courtship took a while, and even now I have to keep working on our relationship." But the improvements were dramatic.

Besides finding out the hard way that leadership is about engagement instead of enforcement, Stefan also learnt about the second consequence of the manager–leader mix up – a misunderstanding of where leaders are to be found in an organization. While in Brazil, he discovered that the real leaders of quality improvement were not the highest-ranking managers, but some production experts in the factories, who were widely respected by employees. Stefan had been so fixated on the hierarchy, getting the plant managers to deploy his quality procedures, that he failed to see that the key opinion leaders whose backing he needed were lower level managers or not even managers at all. Once he had the acceptance of these leaders and they rallied people in the factories to implement upgraded procedures, the formal plant managers quickly offered their belated support. On the basis of this experience, Stefan went out to find the "real leaders" at all the plants, at whatever level they were. And where leadership was lacking, he encouraged passionate people to step up and take a leadership role in the quality assurance process, whatever their formal position.

As the example of Stefan shows, it is easy to slip into this widespread misconception of equating leadership to management, but it is extremely unhelpful, masking what leaders really do and where they can be found. Leadership is the distinct quality of getting people to follow and leaders do this by using their built-up authority to sway people. As such, leadership can be exercised by anyone in (and outside) an organization at certain moments and on certain subjects. Employees can lead their bosses on some topics, while bosses can lead on others. Colleagues can lead each other, while they can also lead outside their organization, in coalitions or in the broader community. It is in this context that it can be said that we "manage downwards" but can "lead 360" (see Figure 1.1).

Misconception 2: The leader as hero

Ask a room full of people to come up with names of some effective leaders and invariably the usual suspects are brought forward, such as Mahatma Gandhi, Nelson Mandela, Abraham Lincoln, Winston Churchill, Simon Bolivar and Alexander the Great, but also Lou Gerstner (IBM), Andy Grove (Intel), Ingvar Kamprad (IKEA), Richard Branson (Virgin), Steve Jobs (Apple) and Jack Welch (GE), sometimes followed by a famous football coach. Sometimes people will mention a local celebrity, or even a former boss. What all the examples have in common, is that they are leaders of truly heroic stature. The names that easily come to mind are those of exceptional people, who have achieved success against all odds. These are the leaders who, despite overwhelming difficulties and an array of adversaries, were capable of pulling together a team of people and reaching spectacular results. As individual humans,

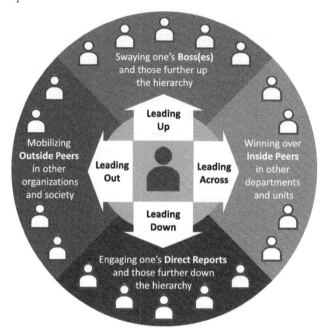

Figure 1.1 Leading whom? Leadership circle of influence

these are the leaders who have realized almost superhuman goals. They are people of exceptional competence, able to mobilize hundreds or thousands of people in an incomparable way.

Unfortunately, these heroes have often come to dominate our thinking about leadership. In the media – and in books like this one – the exploits of these extraordinary people are praised at length and they are held up as a benchmark of "true leadership," to which the rest of us should aspire. Implicitly, we tend to use these examples to raise the bar as to what constitutes a "real leader." As we start to equate leadership to being a hero, our expectations of what a leader should bring skyrocket – a leader needs to single-handedly be able to save the organization from a disastrous situation by being at the head of the troops, breaking resistance and persevering despite adversity. Leaders need to be of Hollywood movie size dimensions.[3]

But most organizations don't need a hero. They don't require the one superhuman to do it all single-handedly, which is fortunate, as there aren't that many of these superhumans around. Heroes are the exception, not the rule. Actually, clamoring for a hero is usually the wrong reaction to a lack of bread and butter leadership. What is generally needed is not one savior, but more widespread, day-to-day leadership by "ordinary" people in the organization, who set themselves the challenge to do "extraordinary" things. These leaders might not become the next generation of corporate movie icons, but they do make the difference between corporate excellence and mediocrity.[4]

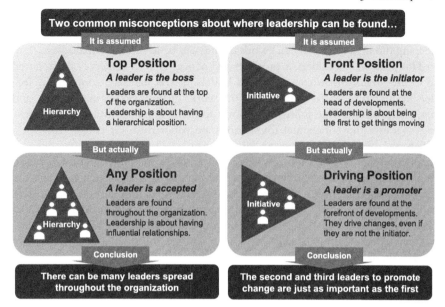

Figure 1.2 Leading where? Distributed leadership

So, avoiding the hero stereotype of leadership helps to make clear that leadership abilities are needed throughout the organization, not only in the hands of one person at the top, which is also referred to as distributed leadership (see Figure 1.2). At the same time, doing away with hero worship also makes it easier to see that leaders don't always have to be the first movers. Leaders don't always have to be in front, being the ones taking the initiative. Often, they can have much more impact by throwing their weight behind the initiative of a colleague and aiding developments already underway. Lending assistance and drumming up support to get things moving is much less heroic and headline-grabbing than being the instigator of a change, but it is an essential leadership role.

Misconception 3: The leader as prophet

One of the most stubborn misconceptions about leadership is that leaders are not concerned with the here and now, but only with the long run. As prophets, it is their role to divine the path that will lead their people "to the promised land," not to get involved in ordinary day-to-day concerns. They are charged with navigating a course through the uncharted waters of the future and transforming the old organization into a new one, fit for the changed world. They are not needed as caretakers of the current business, but as shepherds, to guide people through the wilderness of change. Their task is to ensure that the organization "does the right things," not so much to "do things right."[5] Similar to the distinction between politicians and statesmen, whereby statesmen differentiate themselves by taking a long-term perspective and standing above petty politics, leader also stand above the fray, keeping focus on the big picture transformation, not on the nitty-gritty transactions. The lowly task of keeping the organizational clockwork ticking can be left to mere managers.

This portrayal of leaders as prophets and managers as caretakers is also referred to as the "transformational view"[6] of leadership and has deep roots in the leadership literature. It has its origins in the works of Bass, Bennis and Kotter[7] and has a surprisingly wide following among academics and practitioners. "Surprising" because the conceptual foundations are paper thin. Of course, there is a difference between running an organization's existing business model and shepherding an organization towards a new business model (as will be discussed in Chapter 8), but it is purely whim to call the first task "management" and the second task "leadership." It reveals the preference of the authors, who seem much less fascinated by optimally running the current business than by what it takes to envision the future and transform the organization. Therefore, they only award the honorary title of "leader" to the role that they believe is of higher significance.

In reality, however, a leader who is only concerned with the long term and is oblivious to the short term is at best a daydreamer and at worst a nightmare. Just as there is no statesman who is not also a crafty politician, there is no successful leader in the long run who doesn't know how to mobilize people to at least get some results in the short run. The strategic challenge usually facing leaders is that organizations struggle to strike a balance between short-term stability and long-term change. People want to have guidance in the tricky trade-off between achieving short-term results in the going concern and investing in long-term developments. They want to know when evolutionary change is required and when a more revolutionary track is demanded. Therefore, to get people to follow, leaders must address people's entire agenda and not focus solely on dreamy prophecies or on the headline-grabbing transformational activities.

Misconception 4: The leader as guru

Some leaders instill organizations with a deep sense of purpose. To them, the organization has a fundamental mission to fulfill, a "manifest destiny," that is more than only making products or providing services. Their organizations serve a higher goal, making a contribution to the world, not just making money. The return on investment they seek is more than financial – they want to have an impact. Their purposes vary from advancing health to spreading happiness, inspiring learning, creating opportunity, alleviating need, supporting financial independence and enhancing the natural environment. All are "ends" for which money is only a means.

Behind their sense of purpose is usually a guiding philosophy, with strong beliefs and values, often translated into behavioral principles and a shared code of conduct. In the most purposeful organizations, leaders are more than missionaries, they are almost gurus, inspiring people with meaning, setting moral standards and providing answers to some of life's key questions. Think of such people as Ben Cohen and Jerry Greenfield (Ben & Jerry's), Anita Roddick (Body Shop), Yvon Chouinard (Patagonia) and Linus Torvalds (Linux) – they are like sages, to whom people can look up for truth, wisdom, justice and good. As gurus, they help us to understand "why," not only "what" and "how."[8]

It seems part of the *Zeitgeist* that many people are searching for purpose in their work and are not flying off to India to find a guru, but are looking for them in the workplace. While in the 1960s and 1970s social and ecological activists were countercultural and "dropped out" of school and business, now most people expect firms to be at least socially and ecologically sustainable. Increasingly, companies are the new activists, as can be seen in the rapid growth of companies certified as B-Corps (Benefit Corporations, with a central purpose of benefitting society).[9] Attention for the topics of purpose, business standards and ethical behavior have ballooned, matched by a blossoming of sustainability indexes and corporate social responsibility prizes. The perceived misbehavior of financial institutions and money managers during the financial crisis of 2008 seems to have only strengthened the growing appetite for "responsible leadership" and "meaning."

All this has fed a mounting belief that to be a "modern leader" one needs to exhibit more and more guru-like behavior. To be acceptable as a 21st century leader, one needs to have an inspiring philosophy and a higher purpose than only money-grubbing. "True leaders" are those with a rousing sense of mission and who adhere to the highest ethical standards. They should be the providers of meaning and moral guidance, and walk their own talk.

But we can't all be Mother Theresa, Desmond Tutu and Bono wrapped into one. As with hero worship, where unrealistically high abilities are expected of leaders, with guru worship unrealistically high moral authority is expected. "True leaders" are presumed to be close to a sage in their philosophy and close to a saint in their behavior. But it is useless to set the bar so high and then be disappointed that no one can jump over it. As there aren't enough heroes to go around, there aren't enough gurus either. But there are plenty of decent people who are good enough. Many leaders' sense of purpose is not awe-inspiring, but motivating enough to get people to follow. These leaders' philosophy might not offer answers to all of life's tough questions, but still be engaging enough for people to come on board.

The conclusion is that purpose is important to people and that providing meaning is a powerful way to get people to follow, but that it is an exaggeration that every leader needs to be a missionary and a philosopher. Often, instead of playing the guru, it is enough to be a guide, helping people to make sense of the world, the organization and themselves, helping them to find their own meaning and satisfaction in what they do.

Misconception 5: The leader as idol

You might have already seen a pattern emerge over the past few pages. Caricaturing leaders as heroes is an exaggerated expectation of their ability to get things done, caricaturing them as prophets is an exaggerated expectation of their focus on long-term developments and caricaturing them as gurus is an exaggerated expectation of their ability to create meaning for people in organizations. The common thread in all these misconceptions is that leadership has been inflated into something exalted, something extraordinary, at a higher level than mere mortals – to be found on Mount Olympus. "Leader" is an exclusive title, to be bestowed on only the very best. The examples of leadership that we use are almost picture perfect, with leaders achieving excellent results, while endearing themselves to their followers. These leaders embody the ideal that we enjoy to look up to. They are the gold standard by which all lesser individuals are measured.

So, the "meta-misconception" plaguing the topic of leadership is that our mental model of a "leader" is close to that of a deity. In our mind's eye leaders are truly of Herculean stature. To keep this illusion alive, the few people who seem to fit the bill of being "real leaders" have become idolized, often beyond all recognition, giving them something of a mega rock star status. We then turn around and use these "celebrities" as the norm against which we judge all the other imperfect "want-to-be leaders." And *voila*, when compared to the Botoxed and Photoshopped leadership "top models," most aspiring leaders come out looking clumsy and moderately effective.

Leadership needs to be knocked off this pedestal and brought back to human proportions. It's great to have role models, but they needn't be the top models, and they definitely shouldn't be idolized. Constantly comparing yourself to a corporate superstar is disheartening and disempowering, while it also promotes unrealistic expectations about norms that others around you should live up to.

In practice, leaders don't have to be perfect, they have to be respected. They need to have enough standing to inspire confidence and to sway people to follow them. And leadership is not something exclusive that is only used on special occasions by the high priests of the organization, but something ordinary that is used every day by people throughout the organization.

One of the major advantages of knocking leadership off its pedestal and bringing it back to human proportions is that most people will accept that such leadership is learnable. It is widely debated whether rock star leaders are born or bred and it is tempting to get involved in this discussion, but actually the point is largely irrelevant if heroes, prophets and gurus are the exception. If we focus on the leadership of the "mere mortal" variety, most would agree that this relationship building and influencing behavior is something that can be learnt. This realization is empowering. Too many people have convinced themselves not to work on their leadership abilities because they never will be an idol like Walt Disney, Freddy Heineken or Coco Chanel, just as many people don't dance because they will never move like their idol, be it Ginger Rodgers, Michael Jackson or Rudolf Nureyev. Bringing down expectations to the "good enough" level should inspire everyone to get on their feet and give it a whirl.

And that is exactly the intention of this book. Drop your idols, take a hard look in the mirror to see your style and let's see how we can help you improve your moves. We know for sure you'll also learn a few new steps along the way.

What leadership is

> *Leadership: the art of getting someone else to do something you want done because he wants to do it.*
>
> Dwight D. Eisenhower (1890–1969)
Former President of the United States

Having scraped off all the varnish, what is left is the bare timber of leadership – leading is about getting others to follow. An effective leader is someone who *is capable of influencing other people to move in a certain direction*. This simple definition can be divided into four elements, each further clarifying the fundamental nature of leadership:

- *"Other people."* A very important starting point in understanding leadership is to realize that it is not about the leader in isolation, but about the interaction between leader and follower – leadership is a relational phenomenon. Just as in communication, you need two sides – I don't communicate, we communicate. Leadership is not only about what the leader does, but also how the follower reacts. Therefore, understanding the needs and worldview of "other people" is crucial to effective leadership.
- *"Influencing."* In the interaction between leader and follower, a leader has a full spectrum of influencing methods. This ranges from using formal powers (that come with one's position), such as the power to hire, fire, reward, reprimand and reassign, all the way to informal powers such as the ability to convince, charm, inspire, support and challenge. However, using informal powers to play to people's intrinsic motivation is usually more effective and more lasting than using formal powers. Obviously, the better leaders understand the follower's mindset and motivation, the more effective leaders will be at influencing hearts, heads and hands.
- *"Is capable of."* In the interaction, leaders need to be willing and able to influence followers. As influence needs to be won, potential leaders must be willing to take the responsibility of a leadership role and invest in winning authority among potential followers. How leaders earn and exert this authority depends on their abilities and the profile of the followers. As will be described in following chapters, many different approaches can be effective.
- *"To move in a certain direction."* Ultimately, to be a leader means to lead somewhere. For a leader, the purpose of influencing other people is not to gain power as an end in itself, but as a means towards realizing other objectives. A leader mobilizes people to perform and achieve particular results.

Put this way, we lead all the time. Leadership can be heroic, charismatic, visionary and transformational, but it is also the stuff of everyday interaction with direct reports, colleagues, bosses, clients, suppliers, family members and team mates. If we want to influence people around us to move in a certain direction, we are leading.[10]

But although leading is an everyday activity, unfortunately it doesn't happen every day. It remains dreadful how many self-proclaimed leaders who want "to move in a certain direction" forget about "other people," "influencing" and "is capable of." A shocking number of managers actually don't see people, but only see "human resources," to be deployed to implement their plans. They implicitly draw on a highly mechanistic view of human beings – the *homo economicus* of their Economics 101 class – who they assume will respond rationally to key performance measures and linked bonuses. The very term "human resources"[11] is in fact dehumanizing and strengthens their belief that people can be treated as all other resources, to be bought and sold and to be deployed at will. Taking the time to understand the motivations, hopes and fears of the people around them is an alien concept. Taking even more time to build a relationship of respect, trust and authority with these people is seen as hopelessly wasteful. It is so much more efficient (and comfortably distant) to set objectives and then use carrots and sticks to enforce compliance.

If there is one thing core to the nature of leadership, it is that leading is relational, involving two or more willful beings. If you are not interested in people and don't like building relationships, get a dog and stay away from leadership. You can manage things, activities and processes, which don't have a heart and mind of their own. They can be rationally administered, run or taken care of – with or without a spreadsheet – but it is a logical fallacy to think that people can be run. To get people to follow requires more than a key performance indicator and a flick of the switch. People need to be persuaded, encouraged, energized and enticed – in short, lead.

Notes

1 Grint, K. (2011), "A History of Leadership," in Bryman, A., Collinson, D., Grint, K., Jackson, B. and Uhl-Bien, M. (eds.), *The Sage Handbook of Leadership*, London: Sage.
2 Porter, M.E. (1996), "What is Strategy?," *Harvard Business Review*, Vol. 74, No. 6, November–December, pp. 61–78.
3 This tendency to focus on an overly heroic view of leadership has been brought up before, e.g. Meindl, J.R., Ehrlich, S.B. and Dukerich, J.M. (1985), "The Romance of Leadership," *Administrative Science Quarterly*, Vol. 30, No. 2, pp. 78–102 and Yukl, G. (1999), "An Evaluation of Conceptual Weaknesses in Transformational and Charismatic Leadership Theories," *The Leadership Quarterly*, Vol. 10, No. 2, pp. 285–305.
4 Badaracco, J.L. (2001), "We Don't Need Another Hero," *Harvard Business Review*, Vol. 79, No. 8, pp. 120–126. The author laments the focus on heroic leadership, calling for more *quiet leadership*.
5 Bennis, W.G. (1989), *On Becoming a Leader*, Boston: Addison-Wesley. Bennis mentions this distinction as one of the twelve factors differentiating mere management from exalted leadership.
6 Bass, B.M. (1985), *Leadership and Performance Beyond Expectations*, New York: Free Press.
7 E.g. Bass, B.M. (1990), *Bass and Stogdill's Handbook of Leadership* (3rd ed.), New York: The Free Press; Bennis, W. and Nanus, B. (1985), *Leaders: The Strategies for*

Taking Charge, New York: Harper & Row; Kotter, J.P. (1990), "What Leaders Really Do," *Harvard Business Review*, Vol. 68, No. 3, May–June, pp. 103–111.

8 Sinek, S. (2009), *Start With Why: How Great Leaders Inspire Everyone to Take Action*, New York: Penguin.

9 See www.bcorporation.net

10 Many authors argue that leadership isn't that different from other interpersonal influencing such as strategizing and organizing. For example, Pye, A. (2005), "Leadership and Organizing: Sensemaking in Action," *Leadership*, Vol. 1, No. 1, pp. 31–49.

11 It is stunning and worrying how quickly the term "human resources" has spread around the world and is the dominant label to refer to people or personnel. We strongly support switching to "People and Organization" as a more correct and inspiring title for these activities and departments.

2 The practice of leadership

While the concept of leadership as discussed in Chapter 1 is straightforward, how to be an effective leader is much less obvious. Many books have been written by famous leaders[1] detailing their careers and explaining how they went about achieving their success, often containing the less than subtle message that we can learn from their example. Some books are even more explicit in proclaiming to give key insights into what it takes to be an effective leader.[2] Then there are bookshelves (and e-readers) full of works by theorists reflecting on the dynamics of leadership, who believe they have identified important aspects determining leadership impact.[3] Much of this work is excellent, perceptive and inspiring, but at the same time much of it is contradictory. Just as there are many different definitions of leadership, there seem to be many conflicting views on what type of behavior makes a leader effective.

So, maybe we haven't been looking hard enough and the secret recipe to successful leadership still needs to be found. Or, alternatively, we need to conclude that the holy grail of leadership does not exist. Maybe there are no "eight steps to successful leadership." Maybe there is not one particular approach or style that is superior to all others. No best practice. No formula that beats all others.[4]

In our view, the latter is the case. It is useless, and misleading, to formulate a "leadership script" that will be a hit under all circumstances. There is no ideal that we can take as our starting point. Talking about effective leadership is like talking about effective clothing – a Jamaican will probably give you a different answer than an Inuit. And you'll get a different answer in the summer than in the winter. And from a firefighter than from a belly dancer. And from an athlete than from a couch potato. You get the point, it depends on the situation, the time, the activities, the individuals…and even when these are all the same, "effective clothing" can be largely a matter of style and fashion. This doesn't mean that anything goes. A swimming suit will not be effective for an Inuit or a firefighter, and it is doubtful many couch potatoes would be happy wearing a sealskin coat. It's just that there are too many variables that need to be taken into consideration to arrive at some simple formula to calculate "optimal effectiveness."

This is good and bad news. The bad news is that we can offer you no magic potion that will transform you into a great leader. No snake oil that will cure all your ills. No diet that will turn you into Brad Pitt or Angelina Jolie. To a large extent, you need to figure out for yourself what works for you under your circumstances and how you can improve your leadership behavior. We can offer you insights, questions, suggestions and warnings, but you will need to make the translation to your own situation.

The good news is that there are plenty of different ways of being an effective leader and some of them might be much more suited to your personality, strengths and situation. There is no strait-jacket that you need to put on. Becoming a more effective leader means understanding your current way of building relationships and influencing people, and then stretching yourself to include neighboring styles, just outside of your current comfort zone. You don't have to master every possible leadership style, but just acquire the ones that work for you under your circumstances.

Leadership styles

> *He who knows others is clever, but he who knows himself is enlightened.*
>
> Laozi (5th–6th century BC)
> Chinese philosopher and poet

So, what type of leadership styles are there? In this book, we work with twenty archetypical leadership styles that line up along ten dimensions. In Table 2.1 an overview of these twenty styles is given in the form of a "leadership style pro-filer" that you can use to map your current style preferences. We suggest you fill it in, circling the number that best represents your current style along each of the axes (or use the Leadership LEAP App to do the same). Placing yourself somewhere along each of the separate dimensions doesn't necessarily mean you think you are good at a particular style, but merely that it is your preferred leadership approach – the default style that falls within your comfort zone.

If you feel sympathy for both sides of some of the dimensions, that is a good sign, because at both ends there are important advantages to be gained. At each of the opposite poles, the leadership style has particular strengths. The dimensions do not run from good to bad, but from one good to an opposite good. This means that your preferred style has potential benefits, but that there is an opposite style offering other advantages. The more your style focuses on one side of each dimension, the less you can tap in to the benefits of the opposite pole.

These ten dimensions are not the only ways in which leadership styles can differ, but they do represent many of the important balancing acts faced by leaders in their drive to effectively influence people around them. For this reason, these will be the ten dimensions that will be further explored in this book.

In each of the following chapters we will focus on one of these pairs of opposite leadership styles, exploring the qualities and pitfalls of both sides. Your initial "assignment" as reader is to assess whether you have fully captured all of the benefits of your preferred leadership style and to critically evaluate how

Table 2.1 Leadership style profiler

#		Scale	
1.	**Supervisory Leadership Style** I take hands-on control of key activities to ensure that people carry out the work correctly.	1....2...3....4...5....6	**Facilitative Leadership Style** I delegate key activities to the right people and ensure that they are well-equipped to carry out the work independently.
2.	**Demanding Leadership Style** I challenge people to do better by emphasizing the room for improvement.	1...2...3....4...5....6	**Encouraging Leadership Style** I show confidence in people by emphasizing their ability to do a good job.
3.	**Integrative Leadership Style** I build teams of like-minded people, creating a shared sense of identity and uniform ways of working.	1....2...3....4...5....6	**Federative Leadership Style** I build teams of people with a diversity of attitudes and views, giving them room to think and act differently.
4.	**Autocratic Leadership Style** I take responsibility for making decisions and ensuring speed and clarity.	1....2...3....4...5....6	**Democratic Leadership Style** I take responsibility for making sure the team takes decisions, ensuring quality and commitment.
5.	**Visionary Leadership Style** I set strategic goals that are very ambitious and broad, challenging people to find ways of achieving them.	1....2...3....4...5....6	**Pragmatic Leadership Style** I set strategic goals that are realistic and specific, guiding people's progress in achieving them.
6.	**Executive Leadership Style** I focus people on managing the current activities as efficiently and effectively as possible.	1...2...3....4...5....6	**Entrepreneurial Leadership Style** I focus people on renewing the organization, taking the risk to seek out new opportunities.
7.	**Value-Driven Leadership Style** I explain to people that our mission is to do well by making money for our shareholders and ourselves.	1....2...3....4...5....6	**Virtue-Driven Leadership Style** I explain to people that our mission is to do good by making a contribution to the well-being of our stakeholders.
8.	**Sovereign Leadership Style** I strive to fulfill my own objectives, mobilizing others to help me where possible.	1....2...3....4...5....6	**Servant Leadership Style** I strive to fulfill the group's objectives, offering others my help where possible.
9.	**Reflective Leadership Style** I think before I act, reflecting on leadership issues and options before moving into action.	1....2...3....4...5....6	**Proactive Leadership Style** I think while I act, reflecting on leadership issues and managing responses along the way.
10.	**Consistent Leadership Style** I approach each leadership situation in the same way, remaining predictable and authentic.	1....2...3....4...5....6	**Responsive Leadership Style** I flexibly adjust my approach to each leadership situation, depending on the specific circumstances.

often you tumble into the pitfalls inherent in each approach. The objective is to reflect on what you could do to improve your current preferred style. Your follow-up assignment is to open-mindedly consider whether you should try to stretch yourself and become more "fluent" in the opposite to your default style. You will want to consider under what conditions each of the unfamiliar styles might be a useful leadership approach for you and what you could do to practice and get better at it.

The ambition we have for you is to broaden your repertoire of leadership behaviors and for you to become more agile at employing these different styles. Most people have their favorite leadership styles and will use them over and over again, even where they are less appropriate or even downright counter-productive. We are animals of habit and will cling to our leadership routines, not because they are effective, but because they are familiar.[5] Especially where leadership styles have brought us success in the past, we will tend to repeat them endlessly, in the implicit hope that they will once again bring us success. Leaving this comfort zone of our well-worn behaviors and trying out alternative styles requires conscious effort and a certain measure of courage and persistence. But if it works and you get better at various opposite styles, with the flexibility to shift back and forth where fitting, then you will have achieved a higher level of *leadership agility*. You will have the capacity to flexibly switch between leadership styles, and adaptively master new ones, in rapid response to the specific needs of the people and situation you want to influence.

Along some of these ten dimensions, you might already be quite agile, being able to use both opposites interchangeably depending on the situation. Along other dimensions, however, there might be significant room for personal growth. In the last two chapters of this book we will come back to this question of developing as a leader and what you can do to accelerate your personal learning process.

Leadership roles

The greatest revolution of our generation is the discovery that human beings, by changing the inner attitudes of their minds, can change the outer aspects of their lives.

William James (1842–1910)
American philosopher and psychologist

Before diving full-length into the ten leadership style dimensions in the coming chapters, it is useful to recognize that each of the ten dimensions deals with a different leadership task and that the tasks differ in nature and scope. Some of the tasks have more to do with the individual interaction between leader and follower, while other tasks are at the level of organization, strategy and even mission (see Figure 2.1). We call these levels different *leadership domains* – different areas in which someone can exert leadership. So, influencing other people on a one-to-one basis is referred to as *interpersonal leadership* and comes with a set of tasks that one needs to address if one wants to play a role at this level. Influencing groups of people to work together effectively in teams is called

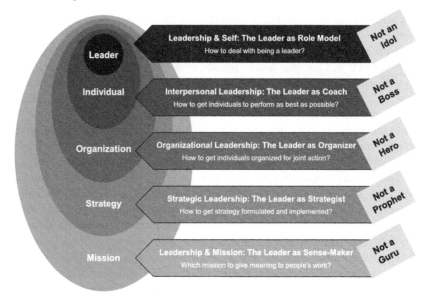

Figure 2.1 The five leadership roles

organizational leadership and playing a role in this domain entails taking on additional leadership tasks. Then there is the domain of *strategic leadership*, which is concerned with getting groups of people to successfully formulate and implement strategy. Again, taking on a leadership role in this domain comes with a complementary set of leadership tasks. Finally, there is also a domain that we refer to as *leadership and mission*, where the role of a leader is to get a group of people to embrace a shared reason for being.

In total, there are five different *leadership roles*, each aligned with one of the five leadership domains. Playing each leadership role comes with a set of specific leadership tasks. In this book, we will explore ten of the most important leadership tasks – two per leadership role. For each of these ten leadership tasks we will then reflect on the opposite leadership styles (these are the ten dimensions of the leadership style profiler in Table 2.1).

Have we lost you yet? In Figure 2.2 the leadership roles, tasks and styles have been brought together into one diagram, giving an overview of how they fit together into a consistent framework. Let's go through the leadership roles one by one, to gain a first insight into the underlying leadership tasks and styles.

Interpersonal leadership: The leader as coach

At the most basic level, leaders engage with other people on an individual basis. This is the domain of *interpersonal leadership*, where the one-to-one interactions are focused on influencing other individuals with the intention of achieving some type of result. The leader wants to get someone to move in a certain

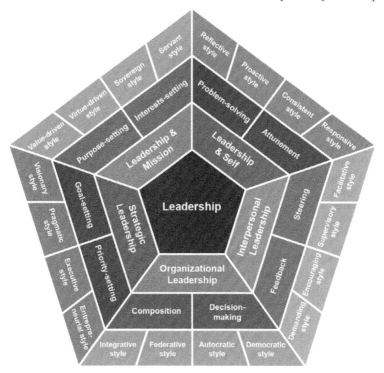

Figure 2.2 The leadership rose: Roles, tasks and styles

direction and uses a variety of influencing methods to realize this aim. These leader–follower "dyadic relationships" are the basic leadership "building blocks," found at the heart of all leadership situations, since in each case there will be interpersonal relationships that are involved in one way or another. Therefore, it should come as no surprise that interpersonal leadership is the most widely studied aspect of leadership and is sometimes implicitly seen as the only relevant leadership domain.

In such person-to-person relationships, the role of the leader is not to play the *boss*, as was pointed out in Chapter 1, but rather to be a *coach*. A coach doesn't command blind obedience, but attempts to influence desired behavior. A coach tries to direct, but does so sitting in the backseat. To accomplish this, a coach tries to understand what makes the other person tick and then tries to stimulate the best possible performance by engaging the other in the most effective way. A coach listens, challenges, supports, questions, lectures, praises…whatever is necessary to light the fire and get the other to excel.

In this role as coach, it could be said that a leader needs to decide "where to coach" and "how to coach." The question of "where to coach?" is about determining where to exert influence to get the other to move in the intended direction, while the question of "how to coach" is about determining the right tone of voice to get the other to move. The first is referred to as the task of *interpersonal steering* – influencing certain elements to direct behavior as required – while the second is referred to as the task of *interpersonal feedback* – communicating in a certain way to trigger the required behavior.

The task of interpersonal steering revolves around the issue of finding the optimal "buttons to push." What is it that leaders should try to influence to get the other to move as intended? Should leaders focus primarily on influencing which activities the other should undertake, or should leaders focus on creating the right conditions to enable the other? In other words, should leaders apply more direct steering via an emphasis on defining and checking up on specific *activities*, or indirect steering via an emphasis on ensuring facilitating *conditions*? Do you recognize the first dimension of the leadership profiler (in Table 2.1) here? Where leaders lean towards direct steering via activities, they will exhibit a *supervisory leadership* style. Where leaders favor indirect steering via conditions, they will exhibit a *facilitative leadership* style. The qualities and pitfalls of these two opposite styles will be the core topic in Chapter 3.

The task of interpersonal feedback, on the other hand, revolves around the issue of finding the optimal "voice to use." How should leaders touch hearts and minds to inspire others to move as meant? Should leaders be mostly challenging, pointing out what is wrong and/or lacking and needs to be improved, or should they focus on being supportive, showing confidence and appreciation for the abilities of the other? In other words, should leaders give critical feedback and *challenge* others to do better, or give supportive feedback signaling *appreciation* for the others' capability? This is indeed the second dimension of the leadership profiler in Table 2.1. Where leaders show a preference for challenging feedback, they will exhibit a *demanding leadership* style. Where leaders have a stronger inclination towards appreciative feedback, they will exhibit an *encouraging leadership* style. The qualities and pitfalls of these two opposing styles will be discussed in more detail in Chapter 4.

Organizational leadership: The leader as organizer

Leaders not only deal with individuals, but with groups of people who they would like to bring together into effective teams. Sometimes a leader's focus will be on a small group of people, such as the department of a company, the crew of a ship or a squad on the field. But a leader can also be focused on larger groups, such as an entire corporation, industry or country. Leaders can concentrate on formal organizations, such as a business unit, government agency or sports club, but also on informal groupings, such as young employees, concerned managers or the local community. And leaders can direct their attention to groups within their company, such as a foreign subsidiary, task-force, or cross-functional team, but also to groups across the company's boundaries, such as an alliance, industry association or lobby forum. In all cases, the leader's role is to help build and maintain an effective team of people. This is the domain of *organizational leadership*.

As was discussed in Chapter 1, it is an exaggeration to see the role of the organizational leader as that of the hero, single-handedly solving all of an organization's problems and guiding an organization in the right direction. A more realistic depiction of the role of the organizational leader is simply that of an *organizer* – someone capable of mobilizing and aligning a variety of individuals to achieve joint results. The organizational leader needs to be able to motivate people to work together, not only on their own. That means being able to build teams, to which people are willing to commit and give their best. This is a level more complex than just inspiring people on a one-to-one basis, as it is not always easy to establish mutual understanding, respect, trust and responsibility amongst individuals. As anyone interested in team sports will know, team dynamics can be tricky. Leaders need to be able to weld together a variety of individuals into more than the sum of the parts, finding ways to get them to fight *alongside* one another, instead of fighting *against* one another.

In their role as organizer, there are two key tasks that leaders need to take to hand – the building of teams and decision-making within teams. The question of "how to construct a team" is about determining who should be on board and how these people need to work together. It is referred to as the task of *organizational composition* – establishing who should be doing what and getting them aligned to perform joint activities. In football terms, who is on the field, playing which position, and how do they need to make the ball go around in order to score? In orchestra terms, who is playing which instrument and how can they be brought into harmony with one another? The second task of the organizer is to ensure that choices are made and carried out within teams. This is the task of *organizational decision-making* – establishing how a decision on a specific issue should be made and who should take responsibility for making the decision. If a football team is asked to play on artificial grass, how should this be decided and who determines whether they will? If an orchestra is offered the opportunity to perform a new rock opera, who calls the shots and makes the choice whether they go "heavy metal?"

Both organizational leadership tasks can be approached in very different ways. When it comes to organizational composition, leaders can take very different angles when determining the best way to put together an effective team. The core issue is how tightly leaders should pull together their teams. Should leaders form tightly-knit teams in which like-minded people have a strong sense of joint identity and work according to shared values, standards and procedures? Or should leaders assemble more loosely-knit teams, with more room for a diversity of perspectives and acceptance of different values and ways of working? In other words, should leaders emphasize *unity*, recruiting similar people and getting them strongly aligned around one identity, one culture and one way of working, or should leaders emphasize *diversity*, recruiting a variety of people and getting them to appreciate their differences and thrive on the occasional clash of views? This is the third dimension in the leadership profiler in Table 2.1. Where leaders have the tendency to lean over to the unity side of the spectrum, they will exhibit an *integrative leadership* style. Where leaders are more partial to the diversity side of the spectrum, they will exhibit a *federative leadership* style. The qualities and pitfalls of these two styles will be reviewed in more detail in Chapter 5.

When it comes to the task of organizational decision-making, the core issue for leaders is what their role should be in making sure that choices are made and implemented. Should leaders take the responsibility of making the decisions on their own, or should they make it a joint responsibility of the team to make the tough choices together? In other words, should leaders decide themselves, emphasizing speed and establishing a clear *direction*, or should leaders get the group to decide, emphasizing quality and commitment through *participation*? This is the fourth dimension in the leadership profiler. Where leaders have a clear preference for taking the decisions themselves, they will have an *autocratic leadership* style. Where leaders are inclined to get groups to make decisions together, they will have a *democratic leadership* style. In Chapter 6 the qualities and pitfalls of these two opposite styles will be explored in more depth.

Strategic leadership: The leader as strategist

While leaders are constantly at work running an organization, a more specific activity they are engaged in is the process of formulating and implementing strategy.[6] As leadership is about getting people to move in a certain direction, setting the strategic course of action is a crucial aspect of a leader's role. Leaders need to be intimately involved in the process of making strategic choices and mobilizing people to realize the intended strategy. This is the domain of *strategic leadership*.

But that is not to say that strategic leadership is limited to the boardroom. While CEOs will generally play an important strategic leadership role for their firm as a whole, business unit managers can take a lead in setting and deploying a business level strategy. But the same is true further down the hierarchy. For instance, a sales manager can take a leadership role in setting the strategic course of action for the sales department, while his/her head of direct sales can take the lead for the call center team.

It might even be that the head of direct sales has a strong opinion about the direction of the entire firm and plays an important role in setting the strategic agenda, focusing attention and dialogue within the company and even winning people over to experiment in new markets. In other words, strategic leadership is not confined to the top management team, nor to those with the formal authority and responsibility. Anyone concerned with the strategic direction of a group of people (their "circle of concern") and who tries to influence them (their "circle of influence") is engaged in strategic leadership.

What strategic leaders do not always need to do is come up with the strategy themselves. Strategic leadership is about setting strategy, not necessarily inventing it. As discussed in Chapter 1, it is a common misunderstanding that leaders are a type of lone prophet, spending all of their time on a mountain and then coming down with all of the answers. Some leaders might devise some or all of the strategy themselves, but they are exceptional cases. And few leaders have the luxury of ignoring the present and only thinking about the long term. In practice, the stereotype of the prophet is misplaced and it is better to see that the role of the strategic leader is simply to be a *strategist* – someone leading the process of creating the strategy and engaging the organization to move in the desired direction.

Guiding the strategy process presents leaders with many challenges, but two tasks stand out in particular. First, leaders need to determine what type of strategic aims need to be formulated to give people direction. Leaders must choose how ambitious and specific the strategic goals they want to set should be. Should they set strategic objectives that are broad, optimistic, long term and daring (abbreviated as BOLD goals), or should they be more specific, measureable, actionable, realistic and time-bound (abbreviated as SMART goals). This task is referred to as *strategic goal-setting* – should leaders focus more on *idealism* by projecting a stretching long run vision that will inspire people to think big, or should leaders focus more on *realism* by formulating more tangible plans that will motivate people to diligently implement? This is the fifth dimension in the leadership profiler. Where leaders have a preference for the idealistic pole of the continuum, they will have a *visionary leadership* style. If leaders like to hang out at the realistic pole of the continuum, they will exhibit a *pragmatic leadership* style. These two opposite styles will be examined in more detail in Chapter 7.

The second task confronting strategic leaders is determining what type of strategic focus needs to be given to people to ensure organizational continuity. Leaders must decide what kind of priorities need to be set to safeguard the sustainability of the organization. Should leaders focus people more towards building on the existing business and getting as much performance out of the current organization as possible, or should leaders focus people on disrupting the present organization and investing in innovative ventures? This is also referred to as the task of *strategic priority-setting* – should leaders get people to prioritize *exploitation* of the current business or *exploration* of new business opportunities? This tension can be found at the heart of the sixth dimension of the leadership profiler. Where leaders place much more emphasis on exploitation, they will exhibit an *executive leadership* style. But where leaders prefer to be the drivers of exploration, they will exhibit an *entrepreneurial leadership* style. The qualities and pitfalls of both styles will be at the center of attention in Chapter 8.

Leadership and mission: The leader as sense-maker

To get people to move in a certain direction, it helps to not only say "where" and "how" to get moving, but also more fundamentally "why." As *homo sapiens* – thinking "man" – people want to understand the reason and purpose of it all. Why do we need to go through a tough transformation? Why should I work hard? Why should I invest time, energy and emotions to give my best? Why should I get up and go to work in the morning at all? Is it only to get my salary? As people grapple with these deep-seated questions, they look around to others who can help them to find meaning in their work and even in their lives. Here many leaders come up short – they might have a great strategy, but they can't explain why anyone should care. They can't make clear to people why the strategy is important and what the fundamental purpose is that will be served. This is the domain of *leadership and mission*, from which many leaders shy away.

It's actually stunning how many organizations have mission statements that are little more than a string of interchangeable clichés seemingly downloaded from the internet. Behind these empty slogans are leaders who also seem incapable or unwilling to give a serious answer to the question "why?" If a sense of mission is so powerful and people look to leaders to help them find meaning in their work, why do so few leaders employ purpose to give people direction and supercharge their batteries? A compelling mission can sustain people during long hours of hard work, give them the strength to deal with uncertainty, bolster their courage to take on opponents and fortify their resolve to overcome setbacks – so, why wouldn't a leader pay attention to mission?

Maybe it is a lack of awareness, maybe a lack of practice, but maybe it is because leaders don't want to sound like a guru. Possibly the guru stereotype, in which the leader dons the robes of a sage and a saint, is much too wishy-washy for most down-to-earth leaders. It could be that many leaders feel uncomfortable with the unbusinesslike spirituality attached to the guru mold. But as discussed in Chapter 1, leaders don't have to be gurus, with deeply philosophical views on life and a world-changing mission for their organization. Leaders can have a much "smaller" answer to the question "why?" or just be a guide, helping people to find meaning in their work themselves. As such, we say the role of the leader is not to be a guru, but to be a *sense-maker*, literally helping people to make sense of it all.[7]

In this role of sense-maker, there are two key tasks that quickly come to the foreground – determining *which* purpose, and *whose* purpose, should be at the heart of the organization's mission. First, leaders need to clarify and communicate which type of purpose they believe the organization should pursue. They need to get across to people which fundamental good they want to achieve. As an organization is a "means to an end," leaders need to make clear what the ultimate benefit is of the organization's existence. This is the task of *purpose-setting* – establishing which purpose is at the core of the organization's endeavors. What is worthy and worthwhile?

Here, two very opposite types of purposes can be emphasized. On the one hand, leaders can focus people on the economic purpose of an organization, stressing the importance of winning the competitive game and creating financial welfare. On the other hand, leaders can draw people's attention to the social purpose of the organization, highlighting the importance of serving others and contributing to widespread well-being. So, the question is whether leaders should elevate the creation of economic *wealth* to be the raison-d'être of the organization, or put the creation of environmental, social, mental and physical *health* at the center of all activities? This tension can be found in the seventh dimension of the leadership profiler. Where leaders have a strong preference for promoting wealth creation, they will exhibit a *value-driven leadership* style. Where they lean more over to the health creation side of the continuum, they will exhibit a *virtue-driven leadership* style. These two contrary styles will be analyzed in more depth in Chapter 9.

The second task faced by leaders is not "which purpose" but "whose purpose" should be at the heart of the organization's mission. Whose interests should be served? This is the task of *interests-setting* – determining to whose benefit the organization should be run. Should leaders strive to fulfill their own needs and dreams, and recruit others to help them achieve this, or should leaders be humbler by helping a group to fulfill their shared objectives? In other words, should leaders promote their own *self-actualization* to the ultimate purpose of the organization and invite others to join in, or should leaders accept the purpose of the group and offer their *service* in its pursuit? This is the eighth dimension in the leadership profiler. Where leaders come down on the self-actualization side of the scale, they display a *sovereign leadership* style. Where they hang over to the service side of the scale, they demonstrate a *servant leadership* style. These two styles, with their inherent qualities and pitfalls, will be investigated in more detail in Chapter 10.

Leadership and self: The leader as role model

In looking at the various roles of leaders, we have constantly moved a "level" up, going from the domain of the interpersonal to the organizational, to the strategic, and finally to that of mission. At each level the leader's role was active – coaching, organizing, strategizing and sense-making – with the intention of deliberately trying to influence people to move in a certain direction. However, there is a fifth level, at which the leader isn't necessarily doing anything active towards followers, but is just being. In Table 2.1 it was actually the very first level, and we conveniently skipped over it for a few pages, because it is the most difficult role to see and explain. This is the domain of *leadership and self*, where the very person and day-to-day behavior of the leader impacts other people.

As was described in Chapter 1, at the basis of leadership lies people's will-ingness to accept someone as a leader and this acceptance hinges on confidence. Only where people have faith in someone will they willingly follow – only where they believe in the motives and abilities of the potential leader will they let themselves be won over. Therefore, a person's ability to lead depends wholly on other people's perception of their trustworthiness and credibility. If people don't have confidence in the aspiring leader, that's it, they won't willingly follow. In short, confidence is everything.

Yet, confidence is also fuzzy – it is not easy or straightforward how confidence can be built. Yes, playing the four earlier-mentioned leadership roles – coaching, organizing, strategizing and sense-making – in a constructive way can help to fortify one's believability, but gaining people's confidence is much broader. It is not only "what you say," but more "what you do," and even more "how both are perceived." In a sense, gaining confidence is like communication – the sender can actively broadcast, but it is key what the receiver hears, and that is a lot more than the consciously transmitted message. In communication, the sender can say "yes," but the intonation of the sender's voice, the blank look on their face and the crossed arms can all signal to the recipient that "no" is intended. Recipients listen on all "wave lengths" to discern what a sender really means. In leadership, the same is true. What a leader actively says and intentionally does is only a small part of what is picked up by others. Potential followers will tune in to all channels to find out what leaders "really mean" and who they "really are" – do they know what they are talking about, can leaders be trusted, are they credible and are they truly committed? In fact, leaders are always "on stage" and everything they do, and everything they are, will go into determining whether they still deserve the confidence granted to them.

So, being eternally in the spotlight, the most important ingredient for gaining followers' confidence is for leaders to live up to expectations, particularly the expectations they have created themselves. Leaders need to do what they promise and practice what they preach. Followers are very sensitive to leaders who seem to go back on their word and/or don't take their own medicine. In many languages, the saying is that confidence "comes by foot and leaves by horse," which goes to show that the speed at which confidence can crumble has been known to humanity for a long time. Therefore, leaders need to safeguard the faith that people have in them by acting in accordance with the expectations they have raised themselves – they need to "walk the talk" instead of only being the "sage on stage" who has all the wise words but exhibits few of the wise deeds.

But leaders can go further than *inspiring confidence*, by *inspiring self-confidence*. Followers need to have confidence in the leader, but they also need confidence in themselves to actually move. Followers need to believe that something can be achieved before they will take action. If they deem something to be too difficult or their capabilities too limited, their self-confidence will wither and nothing will be undertaken. This is where leaders can inspire self-confidence, by showing how it can be done. This is "leading by example" – showing direction by doing it oneself. By courageously going first and showing the way, leaders play the role of *role model*, encouraging others to follow in their footsteps.

Where leaders not only *talk* about change, but *are* the change, they will not only inspire confidence, but they will be strong role models on which others can fashion themselves. Where leaders not only advocate commitment, but show commitment, people will not only sense their sincerity, but will have a stimulating example to emulate. Where leaders not only preach about values, but live the values, enhanced believability of the leader will go hand in hand with having a motivating best practice for followers to latch on to.

This is the fifth leadership role, that of role model. While the other leadership roles all involve directly influencing others via interaction, being a role model is different, as the influence is indirect. By *being* a role model, someone else is inspired. This is why we speak of the domain of "leadership and self" – leaders need to start with themselves, shaping their own behavior and walking their talk, and only then might some people let themselves be influenced by their positive example.

When aspiring leaders start with themselves, pondering what type of person and leader they would like to be, two core topics often surface around which very different answers can be given. These two topics both have to do with how leaders relate to the outside world – "how to respond to external issues?" and "how to respond to different external circumstances?"

Behind the first question there is the fundamental task of the leader to resolve issues – the task of *leadership problem-solving*. On a daily basis, leaders need to grapple with hindrances and lead people to ways of dealing with challenges and opportunities. People look to someone as a potential leader if they sense that this person has the ability to confront issues and get things done. People's confidence in leaders will grow if these leaders successfully tackle difficulties and grab possibilities, while people's self-confidence will grow if leaders show them how trouble and potential can best be dealt with. Yet this task of problem-solving can be approached in very different ways. On the one hand, leaders can take a step back to carefully put issues into perspective and think options through, before implementing the necessary actions. On the other hand, leaders can also directly seize the bull by the horns, mobilizing people to try out some solutions, discovering what works best along the way. So, the question is whether *thought* should precede *action*, or whether the two should go hand in hand.

This is the tension found at the heart of the ninth dimension of the leadership style profiler. Where leaders believe that the best way for them to handle problems is to think before acting, they exhibit a *reflective leadership style*. Where leaders believe that acting and thinking need to be done simultaneously to trigger fast learning, they employ a *proactive leadership style*. In Chapter 11, the qualities and pitfalls of both styles will be reviewed, not only discussing what works for the leader, but also exploring how each style inspires confidence in followers in different ways.

Besides responding to specific problems, leaders also need to respond to differing circumstances. A crisis places different demands on leadership than when a situation is stable. Operating in an international environment challenges leaders in a different way than when they only work locally. Leading a production unit doesn't compare to leading a board of directors. Leading inexperienced people is a different cup of tea than leading experts. In all of these different conditions, leaders need to make a connection to the specific demands and needs, in a way that they feel comfortable and followers feel confident. To be successful at leadership, individuals need to "find the right fit" between themselves and the situation. This is the task of *leadership attunement* – aligning the behavior of leaders with the external requirements.

Here too, there are two opposite ways of achieving attunement. On the one hand, leaders can alter their behavior to meet the external demands. This means that leaders should focus on *adjustment*, modifying their approach – and to a certain extent even their current identity – to fit the situational requirements. In terms of "leadership supply and demand," it is demand that is dominant, determining the supply that is needed. On the other hand, leaders can stay much closer to their personally preferred behavior and get the environment to adjust to them. In such a case, leaders focus on *authenticity*, remaining close to their genuine self, and ask followers to accept them as they truly are. In practice, this means that attunement will happen by self-selection. Authenticity-minded leaders will select only those situations that suit them well, while only the people who fit with – or adjust to – the given leadership behavior will follow. In other words, along the lines of the previous metaphor, this is "supply-side leadership," where demand will realign to what is on offer.

So, the question is basically who should adjust to whom. Should leaders remain as authentic as possible, true to their core identity, and only lead in the situations that suit them well, asking followers to accept them as they are, warts and all? Or should leaders adjust as much as possible, sensitive to differing demands and capable of functioning under a variety of conditions? This tension between authenticity and adjustment is at the core of the last set of opposite styles in the leadership style profiler. Where leaders lean to the side of authenticity, believing they need to be genuine and predictable, they will exhibit a *consistent leadership style*. Where leaders hang over to the side of adjustment, believing they need to be sensitive, flexible and adaptable, they will exhibit a *responsive leadership style*. Both styles will be reviewed in more detail in Chapter 12.[8]

Leadership style determinants

> *The only way some of us exercise our minds is by jumping to conclusions.*
> Cullen Hightower (1923–2008)
> American writer

As you read through the coming chapters, assessing your currently preferred leadership style and asking yourself whether you should work on mastering other styles, the question will come up "when should I use which style?" This is not only a legitimate question, it is an essential one. As you further develop your repertoire of leadership behaviors, you will need to develop a sensitivity as to when which style fits best. Our ambition of increasing leadership style agility would be useless if we had no inkling of where to use which. Being a master carpenter doesn't only require someone to be able to use all possible tools, but also to know when to pull out a saw and when a hammer is more appropriate.

So, can we offer you a simple guide to which leadership style suits best where? Unfortunately, not. Despite extensive efforts by researchers to arrive at simple situational leadership frameworks[9] ("if A, use style 1, if B, use style 2"), none have proven to be more than a rough indication of what might work best. "If a nail, use a hammer, if a screw, use a screwdriver" sounds like sensible situational advice, but it breaks down quite quickly (and following this advice definitely disqualifies you as master carpenter). Some screws need to be hammered in a bit first, while to get a nail in you sometimes need to make a little hole with your screwdriver. And if your screw is crooked, you might need a hammer to straighten it, while if your nail is too long, you might need something totally different, like a saw, to cut it off. You get the point – most situations are too complex to work with simple rules, such as a 2x2 matrix. And this is particularly true for leadership. There are just too many factors influencing most leadership situations to come with "pre-baked" leadership advice.

In Figure 2.3, we have summarized a number of the key factors that might co-determine which leadership style is the most suitable at a certain moment. On the one side, the most effective leadership style will depend on characteristics of the leader and/or group of leaders. Much early research in the area of leadership focused on individual leadership traits, such as personality, appearance, competences and position, but contemporary research also studies group characteristics, such as leadership team composition, roles, culture and rivalries.[10] On the other side, effective leadership also depends on the characteristics of the followers, both individually and collectively. Individually, potential followers have their own personality, ambitions, views and experiences, together shaping their needs, expectations and "followership style."[11] It does not need belaboring that each person is different, posing quite a challenge for leaders who want to influence them. At the same time, groups of followers will react differently

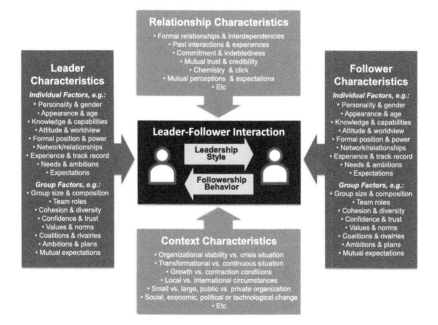

Figure 2.3 Determinants of effective leadership styles

than individual followers, depending on such factors as the size of the group (a "team" or a "mob"), their internal cohesion ("all for one" or "you're on your own"), their level of mutual confidence ("great faith in each other" or "bitter contempt") and their behavioral norms ("show respect" or "back-stabbing is part of the game"). As each group has its own dynamics, leaders will need to find ways of influencing those dynamics in the most effective manner possible.

Besides the characteristics of both sides of the leader–follower interaction, effective leadership also depends on the very nature of the evolving relationship. The relationship will have been influenced by such factors as past interactions, the level of dependency on each other, the mutual trust or distrust that has grown and the "chemistry" between the individuals (currently more often referred to as the "X-factor"). How one can best lead will depend heavily on how these factors have shaped the state of the relationship, the perceptions and expectations of each other, and what both sides feel is legitimate, sincere and useful interaction. Try putting that in a 2x2 matrix.

Finally, the most effective leadership style will depend on the context as well. Even when the people involved are the same, an altered setting can place different strains and demands on followers, and evoke different expectations, requiring leaders to win hearts and minds in a different manner. People need to be led differently in a crisis than during steady growth. They need different leadership while doing an acquisition than while being acquired. A product launch demands a different approach than a cost-cutting exercise. Each of these different business circumstances will challenge people in a different way, which in turn challenges leaders to consider adjusting their style. But the context can change in other ways as well. An international setting will pose different challenges than a national or local setting, an economic recession will require different guidance than during an economic upswing, and a social shift towards sustainability and corporate responsibility will raise different expectations of leaders than in places where these demands are already mainstream.

In short, leadership is indeed "situational," but every situation is unique. This places the burden on you to figure out what works best under your circumstances. Not easy, but intuitively you already knew that. What this book can offer you is a deeper understanding of your current preferred leadership style – your favorite tools, your rousing hit songs – and insight into some useful alternatives. The broader your repertoire is, and the better you can read your audience, the more likely you will be able to play the right tune at the right time and touch your audience's heart.

Leadership paradoxes

> *Not the violent conflict between parts of the truth, but the quiet suppression of half of it, is the formidable evil; there is always hope when people are forced to listen to both sides; it is when they attend to only one that errors harden into prejudices, and truth itself ceases to have the effect of truth, by being exaggerated into falsehood.*
>
> John Stuart Mill (1806–1873)
> British philosopher and political economist

One last note before starting on our journey. The opposite styles that will be discussed in the next ten chapters are all archetypes. They are the "pure" opposing poles along a continuum. These styles are so pure because they unabashedly emphasize only one of two underlying demands – the styles more or less ignore the "this-and-that" tensions described and simply choose one side over the other. Balancing "unity" and "diversity?" No, the integrative leadership style goes all out for unity, while the federative leadership style focuses single-mindedly on diversity. Mixing "idealism" and "realism?" No, the visionary leadership style whole-heartedly embraces idealism, while the pragmatic style is one and all realism.

But of course, in all ten cases these are only the two extremes. There are more than 50 shades of grey between the two extremes of black and white. The two archetypes are at the ends of a continuum, with plenty of mixed styles in between. You don't have to see yourself as one of the opposites and you don't have to apply one or the other – it is not digital. This is because the underlying tensions, such as unity and diversity, are not *dilemmas*, that force you to choose one or the other. They are much more like a *balancing act*, where you try to get the mix right, but doing more of the one necessarily leads to doing less of the other. Economists would call this a *zero-sum game* – if your style is "80% unity-focused," then you can only do "20% diversity," because the sum can never exceed 100%.

However, it would be too limiting to view the ten tensions as simple balancing acts. Yes, idealism and realism are opposites and seem to be on the two sides of a seesaw, but who says your style can't be a mix of 70% idealism and 50% realism? There are more ways of combining black and white than shades of grey along a continuum – a zebra isn't grey, but mixes black and white in a much more useful manner, while someone with a flashlight in the dark can send messages by alternating between black and white. In the same way, leaders can find their own approaches to blending such seemingly conflicting opposites as "direction" and "participation," or "authenticity" and "adjustment." In other words, leaders might be able to find fitting styles that combine the *best of both worlds*, not only styles that are muddled compromises between the two pure extremes.[12]

It is for this reason that we will refer to the ten tensions as *paradoxes* and not as simple balancing acts. A paradox is something that seems to be contradictory, but when looked at through a different lens is not so unsolvable as at first glance. "Direction" and "participation" together form a paradox, as they seem to be at odds with one another, with compromises in the middle as the only way of dealing with their opposite nature. "Seem to be," but if viewed differently, leaders might be able to find their own approaches to combining direction and participation in an effective manner.

So, in summary, we are arguing that there are many different possible hybrid styles between each set of black and white opposites. We offer you no formula for how to find your own hybrid styles. And on top of that, no fixed recipe for determining when to use which style. We never said that developing your leadership capabilities was going to be easy. But it should be fascinating.

And now it's time to open the "leadership style rose" presented in Figure 2.2 and pluck the first petal – interpersonal steering.

Notes

1 Some well-known examples are: Welch, J. and Byrne, J.A. (2001), *Jack: Straight from the Gut*, New York: Warner Books; Branson, R. (2006), *Screw It, Let's Do It: Lessons in Life*, Sydney: Random House Australia; Powell, C. (2012), *It Worked for Me: In Life and Leadership*, New York: HarperCollins; Hsieh, T. (2010), *Delivering Happiness: A Path to Profits, Passion and Purpose*, New York: Business Plus Hachette Book Group; Stewart, M. (2015), *The Martha Rules*, Emmaus: Rodale; Schultz, H. (2011), *Onward: How Starbucks Fought for Its Life without Losing Its Soul*, Emmaus: Rodale.

2 For example: Collins, J. (2001), *Good to Great: Why Some Companies Make the Leap…and Others Don't*, New York: Harper Business; Maxwell, J.C. (1998), *The 21 Irrefutable Laws of Leadership: Follow Them and People Will Follow You*, Nashville: Thomas Nelson; Rath, T. and Conchie, B. (2008), *Strengths Based Leadership: Great Leaders, Teams, and Why People Follow*, New York: Gallup Press; Goleman, D., Boyatzis, R. and McKee, A. (2003), *Primal Leadership: Unleashing the Power of Emotional Intelligence*, Boston: Harvard Business Review Press; Sinek, S. (2009), *Start with Why: How Great Leaders Inspire Everyone to Take Action*, New York: Penguin.

3 For example: Bass, B.M. and Bass, R. (2008), *Bass's Handbook of Leadership* (4th ed.), New York: Free Press; Day, D. and Antonakis, J. (2011), *The Nature of Leadership* (2nd ed.), Thousand Oaks: Sage Press; Schein, E.H. (2010), *Organizational Culture and Leadership* (4th ed.), San Francisco: Jossey-Bass; Conger, J. and Riggio, R. (2007), *The Practice of Leadership*, San Francisco: Jossey-Bass; Avolio, B.J. (2011), *Full Range Leadership Development* (2nd ed.), Thousand Oaks: Sage Press.

4 In the leadership literature, the basic idea that there is not one best leadership style, but that leaders need to respond differently to varied demands, has the catchy label *behavioral complexity*. See Denison, D., Hooijberg, R. and Quinn, R. (1995), "Paradox and Performance: Toward a Theory of Behavioral Complexity in Managerial Leadership," *Organization Science*, Vol. 6, No. 5, pp. 524–540.

5 Weick, K.E. (1996), "Drop Your Tools: An Allegory for Organizational Studies," *Administrative Science Quarterly*, Vol. 41, No. 2, pp. 301–313.

6 Cannella, A.A. Jr. and Monroe, M.J. (1997), "Contrasting Perspectives on Strategic Leaders: Toward a More Realistic View of Top Managers," *Journal of Management*, Vol. 23, No. 3, pp. 213–237; De Wit, B. and Meyer, R. (2010), *Strategy Synthesis: Resolving Strategy Paradoxes to Create Competitive Advantage* (3rd ed.), London: Cengage.

7 The foundational work on sense-making is Weick, K. (1995), *Sense-Making in Organizations*, Thousand Oaks: Sage.

8 Note that there is something special about this last tension, between "authenticity" and "adjustment," as was also pointed out in the Preface. Throughout this book we advocate leadership style agility, which seems to suggest that we argue that "adjustment" should prevail over "authenticity." If leaders can access the full repertoire of leadership styles, wouldn't this be the ultimate form of "responsive leadership?" There are two important points here. First, the two styles here, "consistent leadership style" and "responsive leadership style" are actually *meta-styles* – they are the styles of using styles. Consistent leadership means that someone uses their first 9 styles in a dependable and predictable way, while responsive leadership means that someone receptively and flexibly switches between styles on the first 9 dimensions. That is why this dimension is examined last in Chapter 12. The second important point here is that we don't argue that leaders should always be responsive, quickly adapting their styles to whatever is needed. It is truly a paradox to adjust yet remain

authentic. What we argue is that leaders should have the *capability* to adjust their style if they feel it is necessary, and not be forced into authentic consistency because that's all they are capable of doing. Agility is the potential to flexibly switch or even adapt, which we believe leaders need to have "up their sleeve." Whether they *want to* always adjust, and believe they should always adjust, is another matter (namely the topic of Chapter 12).

9　Situational leadership theory was originally developed by Paul Hersey and Ken Blanchard in 1969 under the label "life cycle theory of leadership," but was later relabeled. See Hersey, P. and Blanchard, K.H. (1977), *Management of Organizational Behavior: Utilizing Human Resources* (3rd ed.), New Jersey: Prentice Hall. Since then a number of empirical studies have been done that have not been able to corroborate the situational leadership theory framework. See for instance Fernandez, C.F. and Vecchio, R.P. (1997), "Situational Leadership Theory Revisited: A Test of an Across-Jobs Perspective," *The Leadership Quarterly*, Vol. 8, No. 1, pp. 67–84.

10　For a good overview of these leadership research streams see Yukl, G. (2009), *Leadership in Organizations* (7th ed.), Englewood Cliffs: Prentice-Hall.

11　It seems odd that libraries are full of books on leadership, but that little attention is paid to followership. It is as if followership is obvious and doesn't require any effort or learning. One of the first to speak of followership styles was Kelley, R.E. (1988), "In Praise of Followers," *Harvard Business Review*, Vol. 66, No. 6, pp. 142–148. Other interesting works on followership include Baker, S.D. (2007), "Followership: The Theoretical Foundation of a Contemporary Construct," *Journal of Leadership & Organizational Studies*, Vol. 14, No. 1, pp. 50–60, and Riggio, R.E., Chaleff, I. and Blumen-Lipman, J. (2008), *The Art of Followership: How Great Followers Create Great Leaders and Organizations*, San Francisco: Jossey-Bass.

12　For a thorough academic description of "paradox theory," see Smith, W. and Lewis, M. (2011), "Toward a Theory of Paradox: A Dynamic Equilibrium Model of Organizing," *Academy of Management Review*, Vol. 36, No. 2 (April), pp. 381–403. For a more accessible description see De Wit, B. and Meyer, R. (2010), *Strategy Synthesis: Resolving Strategy Paradoxes to Create Competitive Advantage* (3rd ed.), London: Cengage. Another recent book covers a similar approach to paradoxes: Martin, R. (2009), *The Opposable Mind: Winning Through Integrative Thinking*, Boston: Harvard Business School Publishing.

Part II
Interpersonal leadership

3 Interpersonal steering

The paradox of activities and conditions

The new App prototype looked fantastic. Stylish and professional, this was something you could proudly show to your business clients and not look like you were stuck in the 20th century. And the features were exactly what the insurance sales team needed – the App would be able to calculate the monthly premium that a client firm would need to pay for an insurance package precisely tailored to their needs. Putting this App in the hands of the insurance company's business-to-business sales people just might help them to reach their goal of achieving 10% sales growth in the coming year. No wonder that Ralph, the commercial director, had led the development of the App prototype and was now pushing for the App to be built in the coming months, using an external IT company to get the work done quickly.

Awkwardly, Belinda, the head of IT, had only recently heard about an App being developed by the commercial department and now finally got to take a look at the prototype. As she suspected, the App would not be as stand-alone as Ralph was suggesting. There would need to be significant integration between the App and back office systems to constantly upload the necessary information into the App and keep it up-to-date. To the question where he saw the App in two years' time, Ralph enthusiastically sketched a picture of the App moving beyond premium calculation, to real-time credit checks, quotations and deal-closing. Calmly listening to Ralph's vision, it was clear to Belinda that integration with the rest of the IT infrastructure was going to be inevitable.

As head of IT, Belinda realized that formally the App was in her domain and that practically she would need to do a lot to ensure its success. Therefore, her first instinct was to immediately take control of the App project. Clearly, Ralph had little understanding of IT architecture and limited experience in running IT development processes, so the whole project was a disaster waiting to happen. Moreover, when eventually things would go wrong, Belinda knew who would get the blame – more than once naïve business people in the company had eagerly started revolutions that got bogged down in IT reality, for which the IT department was then held responsible. By taking hands-on control of the App project, Belinda would be able to steer it in the right direction, keeping constant tabs on implementation progress and being able to troubleshoot where necessary. It would still be Ralph's project, but Belinda would head the Steering Committee, allowing her to closely supervise all necessary activities.

Yet, the more Belinda thought about it, the more she started to doubt whether tight control was the best way to get Ralph moving in the right direction. Ralph was passionate about the project and had a strong sense of ownership, so he would not be keen to give up control, especially because the IT department didn't have the reputation for getting things done quickly. Moreover, in many ways Ralph knew much better what needed to be done from a commercial perspective, making it difficult for Belinda to competently call the shots. Not to mention that it was a priority for Ralph, who was willing to make the time available, while Belinda already had her plate full and had little appetite for micromanaging yet another project.

Maybe Belinda needed to "nudge" instead of "shove" Ralph in the right direction. By creating the right conditions, maybe Ralph could make the App project a success on his own after all. Belinda would need to facilitate, ensuring that Ralph got the right support, had access to the necessary resources, was better informed about the overall IT strategy and was given timely feedback about IT issues. If all of these circumstances could be created, Ralph would be empowered to drive the App development process himself, with Belinda indirectly controlling direction in the background.

As she thought about it again, reflecting on whether she should take more direct control over the project, it struck her that the issue wasn't the project, it was Ralph. She shouldn't be thinking how much guidance the project required, but how much guidance Ralph could use. How could she best help him to succeed? This insight helped her to get the issue straight, but as she drove home she still wondered whether Ralph was best served by hands-on supervision or hands-off facilitation.[1]

The task of interpersonal steering

> *Though good might come of practice, this primal truth endures:*
> *The first time anything is done, it's done by amateurs.*
>
> Art Buck (dates unknown)
> American folk poet

Do you recognize Belinda's predicament? She has to work with Ralph, but deep down she would prefer to do the project herself. On IT, she's more knowledgeable than Ralph and has a better idea of where the project should be headed. But most importantly, if she did it herself, she would be fully in control. She's not a control freak, she just wants to make sure that projects in her area of responsibility are a success, which works best if she is not dependent on too many others.

Yet, alas, full control is impossible. Belinda is stuck with Ralph, who feels he owns the App and has significant knowledge vital to the project. Ralph is even reluctant to get Belinda involved at all, as her credibility has been tainted by past failures of the IT department, and Ralph wants a quick and clean implementation. Moreover, she doesn't have the time to get deeply involved.

While Belinda can't be in full control, the opposite option isn't realistic either – she can't ignore the App project and distance herself from Ralph, because her IT department will eventually be impacted. So, she is stuck between the opposite poles of full control and no control, with neither extreme being particularly attractive. She can linger around the pole of "no control" by leaving the initiative to Ralph, letting things happen and then hoping for the best, but "hope" is a sorry alternative for leadership.

Therefore, she needs to take the lead and steer Ralph in the right direction. Between "full control" and "no control," she can have "some control" over the behavior of Ralph, by exerting influence on him to follow a particular course of action. This is referred to as *interpersonal steering* – one individual being able to guide another to move in a certain direction. Interpersonal steering is about getting other people to do what you think is necessary. As such, this is the basic building block of leadership. Fundamentally, leadership is about deliberately influencing the behavior of other people – not leaving it up to chance or people's own fancy, but consciously directing their behavior towards a desired outcome. Leadership is about exerting control.

The word "control," like the word "power," has a bit of a negative connotation to many people. "I am seeking power to control you" sounds so much more ominous than "I am seeking influence to lead you," largely because the words "power" and "control" imply that it is done *to* you, not *with* you. "Influence" and "leading" suggest that followers have some say in the matter, *letting* themselves be influenced and led. Leadership is accepted and influence is permitted. Yet, strictly speaking, the concepts are not that distinct. If you influence, you have power, and when you lead, you exert control. Usually not absolute control, but some measure of steering along an intended path.

The question for Belinda is how best to control Ralph's behavior – how to steer him towards the best possible performance. To answer this question, it is useful to take a short detour to cybernetics (the study of steering systems[2]), for a quick peek at the basics of control. In Figure 3.1, a simple rendition is given of the relationship between a controller and the controlled system. If the controller only steers on the basis of plans, but does not monitor, this is called feedforward control or feedforward steering (only the forward arrow is used). But usually the controller steers and then monitors the performance of the controlled system so that constant adjustments can be made ("act"). This is called feedback control. So, if you (the controller) are riding a motorcycle (the controlled system), you open the throttle and race away, but check on the speedometer every once in a while, to see whether you are exceeding the speed limit too liberally. You literally move the steer of your bike left and right, monitoring the edge of the road and other traffic participants. So far, so good. The control system works and you understand the simple principles.

Now you get off your motorcycle and on to a horse. Not so different you might think. Instead of a throttle, you need to use your heels, and instead of a

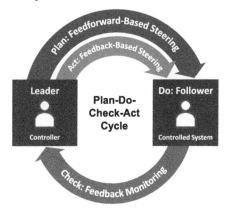

Figure 3.1 A simple control system
Note: This diagram blends two theoretical traditions, Cybernetics and Total Quality Management. In the cybernetic tradition (carried on into General System Theory), control systems are pictured by showing the controller, the controlled system, a forward arrow indicating the input and an output arrow looping back indicating the feedback (see Ashby, W. (1956), *An Introduction to Cybernetics*, London: Chapman & Hall). In Total Quality Management, the Deming circle is the central concept, with its four steps, plan-do-check-act (see Deming, W.E. (1982), *Out of the Crisis*, Cambridge: MIT Press). From a cybernetic point of view, act and plan are not distinct and sequential, but both control/steering activities, distinguished only on whether they are based on feedback or not. Therefore, in our diagram these two activities are placed next to each other instead of behind one another.

steer, you need to use the reigns. But as you put the horse "into gear," you notice that nothing happens. Maybe it's out of fuel or maybe it's broken…or maybe controlling a horse is fundamentally different than controlling a motorcycle. Of course, the latter is the case. The big difference is that a horse is willful. Just as with humans, horses are not soulless machines that can be controlled without consideration of their motivation. Controlling the behavior of a horse does not mean breaking its will and turning it into an automaton, but recruiting its will, finding ways in which it wants to do what you have in mind.

With a horse, you can get quite far tapping into its extrinsic motivation, literally using a carrot and a stick, to get it to move in the right direction (although anybody who rides horses or who's seen the movie *The Horse Whisperer* will know that connecting with a horse is also very important). Yet with humans, their will is even more complicated. People can be just as headstrong as horses, not liking to have someone "on their back" telling them what to do, but people's intrinsic motivation can be deeper and more diverse. Being able to tap into this intrinsic motivation offers enormous potential to unleash energy and achieve high performance.[3]

People's willfulness is important. People generally want to be self-steering, not steered. People want to be masters of their own destiny, not puppets on a string. They want to have the ability to make a difference and have the autonomy to do so in their own manner. In other words, people want to be empowered. People feel empowered when they have enough freedom to make their own decisions (room to maneuver) and enough resources and capabilities to implement the decisions they have made (sufficient means). To a certain extent, then, this can be at odds with a leader's desire to actually steer people in a particular direction. Therefore, the big challenge is how to steer behavior without squashing people's motivation. How can a leader, like Belinda, control performance without disempowering a person like Ralph?

The paradox of activities and conditions

> *A leader...is like a shepherd. He stays behind the flock, letting the most nimble go out ahead, whereupon the others follow, not realizing that all along they are being directed from behind.*
>
> Nelson Mandela (1918–2013)
> South African revolutionary and president

To better understand the challenge of controlling without disempowering, the analogy of controlling traffic at an intersection might be illuminating. There are basically two ways of guiding drivers to ensure that they don't crash into one another. The first way is to directly control the drivers' *activities*, which is commonly done by means of traffic lights. Putting an installation at an intersection influences traffic by regulating which activities should be carried out ("stop" or "go"). Drivers *have to* obey the lights, otherwise they will be fined, but generally they *want to* obey the lights, as they have been convinced of the efficiency and safety of the control system. They accept being told what to do as useful guidance and don't feel that their freedom to maneuver has been seriously impinged.

The second way of avoiding "intersection Armageddon" is to create the right *conditions* under which drivers will be able to self-regulate, deciding when to "stop" or "go" based on their own judgment. A common way to influence drivers to make the best choice themselves is by rearranging the intersection into a roundabout. On such a circular intersection, the design of the roads actually aids the driver to gather the necessary information to make an independent decision. So, while the driver determines which activities to undertake, the prearranged conditions "nudge"[4] the driver to do the right thing. The driver feels self-steering, but is indirectly controlled by the designers of the intersection. Or as Mandela puts it in the above quote, the drivers never realize "they are being directed from behind."

These two ways of controlling traffic – direct control by regulating activities and indirect control by arranging conditions – are not only opposites, but to a certain extent they are even at odds with one another. Who wants to have a roundabout with traffic lights? The same is true when we transfer these insights to the realm of leadership. Activities and conditions are two distinctive *levers of control* and it is questionable whether you want to pull both levers at the same time.

As became clear from the traffic example, activity-oriented control is very direct and straightforward. The controller steers by determining which activities need to be carried out and sometimes even the way by which they need to be done. After this initial steering, performance is monitored and adjustments are made. This is the closed "plan-do-check-act" cycle outlined in Figure 3.1. Most people will recognize this as a goal-setting, reporting and review cycle, by which agreements are made on what should be done (activities, broadly or narrowly defined), followed by reporting on performance (via performance indicators) and review meetings to discuss progress and potential corrective actions (i.e. additional activities). This direct control cycle can be carried out at very long intervals (yearly, quarterly or monthly plans and review meetings) or on a much shorter cycle time (weekly, daily or even continuously). The choice of how often to check up on performance will depend on the person being controlled and on the circumstances, but fundamentally the method of control is direct and activity-based (sometimes also called using *hard controls*).

Conditions-oriented control is indirect and literally "roundabout" (sometimes also called using *soft controls*). There is no closed "plan-do-check-act" cycle, but a looser "entrust-enable-engage" loop, that we call the *empowerment cycle* (see Figure 3.2). It starts with entrusting people with certain responsibilities and ensuring that they take true ownership of the tasks delegated to them. With this responsibility comes a measure of autonomy to carry out the tasks in the way people see fit themselves. Once entrusted with responsibilities and room, leaders need to determine the conditions that will enable people to make the right decisions themselves. People will need to have access to key *resources*, such as information, knowledge and connections, while being

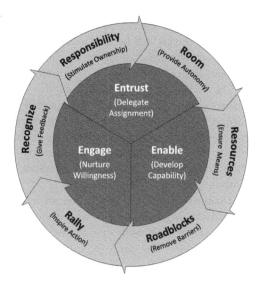

Figure 3.2 The empowerment cycle

competent in their use. Furthermore, *roadblocks*, such as rules, dependencies and competing objectives, will need to be removed, so people can forge ahead unimpeded. Besides these enabling conditions, that make people more *able* to self-steer, it helps to have engaging conditions, that make people more *willing* to steer in the direction preferred by the leader. Typical engaging conditions that "*rally* the troops" include a deep belief in the mission and strategy of the organization, a feeling of belonging to a community, a strong team spirit and sense of commitment to colleagues, an embrace of the shared values and culture of the organization, and having confidence in its leaders. Engagement can be further strengthened by getting *recognition* via constructive feedback from inside and outside the organization and witnessing the impact of one's own decisions and actions. With these enabling and engaging conditions in place, leaders can slowly start to let go, entrusting people with more responsibility and autonomy, while increasingly operating without the "plan-do-check-act" three-ring circus. Leaders can gradually further empower people as time goes by, while still retaining indirect control.

While these two levers of control – activities and conditions – are not entirely mutually exclusive, they are highly at odds with one another. "Holding on" and "letting go" don't blend very well. Each of the levers is based on a fundamentally different control philosophy – active steering vs. empowered self-steering – that represents opposite ways of influencing people to move in a certain direction. It is for this reason that we speak of the *paradox of activities and conditions* – focusing on activity-oriented steering conflicts with the use of conditions-oriented steering and vice versa. So, it should come as no surprise that leaders usually don't easily flip between the two, but exhibit a preference for one side over the other.

The supervisory leadership style

> *Never tell people how to do things. Tell them what to do and they will surprise you with their ingenuity.*
>
> George Patton (1885–1945)
> American general

Where leaders have an inclination to steer by directly controlling the activities people carry out, it is said that they have a *supervisory leadership style*. These leaders know what needs to be done and want to ensure that the required activities are executed correctly. They usually agree on a plan with the people they lead and then literally supervise ("oversee") implementation, monitoring whether the performance is according to expectations. By using this "plan-do-check-act" loop they can delegate work to others, while still being able to direct activities and get people to move in the direction they want.[5]

But if you remember Belinda, she struggled with the challenge of controlling performance without disempowering followers. For her the question would be how to supervise a person like Ralph, who might not be so keen on being directly controlled. Generally, supervisory leaders adhere to four guidelines to keep people motivated while still directly steering their behavior.

First, the "plan-do-check-act" loop shouldn't be made to feel like a noose – it should be loose enough to give people room to maneuver. As Patton suggests in the quote above, don't "tell people how to do things," but rather give them the autonomy to make their own decisions within a directional framework. The "plan" in "plan-do-check-act" shouldn't be too detailed, giving people plenty of leeway to "fill in the blanks" as they see fit. The amount of leeway necessary will then depend on each follower's experience, capability and learning ability. In the same fashion, the "check" in "plan-do-check" shouldn't be too frequent, giving people plenty of leeway to accomplish the activities in the order and speed they see fit.

Second, the plan should be something people can buy in to. If the leader can win hearts and minds, and followers embrace the set direction, then "do" and "check" will not feel like disempowering control, but as necessary activities to realize the shared plan. Some supervisory leaders are extremely talented at selling a plan to people, convincing them of its urgency and potential for success. Other supervisory leaders don't pitch the necessary activities to people, but develop the plan together with them, giving them a say on what the plan will be. This, too, can increase engagement, making plan deployment and performance reporting feel like an acceptable form of control.

Third, during the "doing" people should feel that the supervisory leader is with them, accompanying them in action, ready to support where required. Having the leader close by, informed and involved can give people a feeling of not being on their own, but being backed up by a committed and accessible leader, who cares about them and cares about the results they achieve. If people sense that the leader can be counted on to assist them, guide them and fight for them, then it is more likely that the hands-on supervision will not be seen as disempowering meddling, but as powerful backing, advice and "air cover."

Fourth and last, the "checking" shouldn't feel like an interrogation, with the leader looking to find fault and assign blame. If people feel that the "plan-do-check-act" cycle is a correctional instrument, intended to punish anyone who strays from the path set by the leader, then they will come to dread it and see it as a means of enforcing obedience. But if the supervisory leader uses the "checking" as a way of paying attention to the efforts of people and jointly learning what went well and what could be done better, then reviews can be highly motivational. Where leaders check in to see how they can help to improve performance, correct errors and solve problems, it is more likely that their hands-on supervision will not be seen as disempowering scrutiny, but as helpful coaching.

Adhering to these four guidelines can make the steering of willful people more successful, making it acceptable that supervisory leaders directly control the activities performed. But the underlying reason why supervisory leaders want direct control is usually not because the followers want it or accept it, but because it is necessary. Leaders supervise because results are needed. They take the lead and control activities because problems need to be solved, a certain level of performance is required and/or external stakeholders expect them to be in control.

The facilitative leadership style

> *When you find a man who knows his job and is willing to take responsibility, keep out of his way and don't bother him with unnecessary supervision. What you think is cooperation is nothing but interference.*
>
> Thomas Dreier (1884–1976)
> American editor and writer

Leaders more inclined to steer by indirectly controlling conditions, instead of directly controlling activities, have a *facilitative leadership style*.[6] These leaders don't want to regulate, but to stimulate – they don't tell a plant how to grow, but rather, they create the optimal circumstances under which a plant can grow by itself. They strongly believe that people should be self-steering, taking ownership of their work and responsibility for their performance, while the role of the leader should be to facilitate – literally "make easy" – that people take the best decisions and exhibit effective behavior. Instead of taking over and telling people what to do, the facilitative leader develops and equips people to be able to determine their actions themselves.[7]

At the basis of the facilitative leadership philosophy is the assumption that people will only be fully committed to the activities they carry out if they have bought into them by their own free will. Only when people have the feeling that they are deciding themselves will they become truly engaged and perform to their utmost ability. People's "will" is a source of great energy that should not be broken or harnessed, but should be nurtured and tapped into. Facilitative leaders respect people's yearning for self-determination and actively stimulate them to take control over their own destiny.

But unleashing people's energy through self-steering is only half of the facilitative leader's task – you can light a fire, but how do you keep it from going in all directions? The other half of the facilitative leader's work is to canalize people's energy, nudging it towards a certain course. As a canal guides water to flow in a certain direction, leaders can create conditions that will assist in letting people's energy flow along a set path. So, as mentioned earlier, besides "entrusting" (unleashing people's energy by giving them responsibilities and autonomy), leaders also need to "enable" and "engage." Facilitative leaders typically enable by making sure that people have all of the ingredients required to make an informed decision (i.e. strategic insight, up-to-date information, experience and the necessary education) and the means required to carry out the decision (i.e. budget, competent colleagues, connections and time). But enabling also means supporting people's decision-making by answering questions, acting as a sparring partner, offering advice, expressing confidence and helping to sell decisions to other stakeholders. Facilitative leaders typically engage by making sure that people feel part of the team (i.e. have a sense of community membership, team spirit and cultural affiliation), buy in to the same overall direction (i.e. embrace the mission, strategy and development objectives) and have confidence in the leaders of the organization.

Shaping all of these favorable conditions is actually a form of feedforward – the leader steers by pre-determining the circumstances under which followers will perform. This means that facilitative leaders need to do most of their work diligently up front, not quickly in response to feedback about people's performance and potential need for adjustment. Facilitative leaders have to think further ahead to develop most of the enabling and engaging conditions. Such conditions as a shared culture, strategic insight and confidence in the organization's leaders are not built up overnight, so facilitative leaders need to take a longer-term view before being able to "let go" and trust that people will make the right decisions themselves.

It should be noted, however, that facilitative leaders don't solely control by means of feedforward, but also actively promote feedback loops. Without feedback, there would be no learning and no adjustment in behavior along the way. Yet, instead of the leader being the one driving the learning and correction process, facilitative leaders encourage people to self-evaluate, going through a "plan-do-check-act" cycle themselves and asking for feedback from the people around them. Where people don't operate as independent self-steering individuals, but as self-steering teams, they can go through the "plan-do-check-act" cycle together, giving each other feedback, jointly learning and adjusting along the way. Sometimes facilitative leaders are asked for their feedback, or they proactively offer their feedback themselves, but they will always do such as input for other people's own decision-making, not as a direct control measure. As such, facilitative leaders discuss a lot with the people around them, but it is seldom in the form of checking up or reporting.

Table 3.1 Differences between the supervisory and facilitative leadership styles

	Supervisory Leadership Style	Facilitative Leadership Style
Emphasis on	Activities over conditions	Conditions over activities
Motivating people by	Accompanying them in action	Creating favorable circumstances
Control should be	Hands-on and directing	Arm's length and nudging
Orientation towards	Showing personal involvement	Giving freedom to act
Basic attitude	Trust is good, control is better	Control is good, trust is better
Core quality	Directly improving performance	Empowering people
Intended impact	Deliver as agreed	People take ownership
Underlying conviction	Stay close for the best results	Make way to bring out the best
Guiding principle/motto	You can count on me!	I'm counting on you!
Preferred tools	Real-time performance reports	Self-evaluation systems

Qualities and pitfalls of the supervisory leadership style

> *The best executive is the one who has sense enough to pick good men to do what he wants done, and self-restraint enough to keep from meddling with them while they do it.*
>
> Theodore Roosevelt (1858–1919)
> American politician and president

Neither the supervisory nor the facilitative leadership style is inherently superior. Each side has its own qualities. These distinctive strengths will appeal to different potential followers, under different circumstances and at different moments in time. Likewise, both opposite styles have their own looming pitfalls, into which the overly confident leader can easily tumble. These shadow-sides are typically due to the danger of overdoing a good thing (the threat of exaggeration), but can also be due to using a style at the wrong moment (threat of misfit) or in the wrong way (threat of misapplication).

When it comes to the qualities of the supervisory leadership style, there are many. First and foremost, this style is all about ensuring performance. Supervisory leaders are focused on getting results. They know what needs to be achieved and mobilize people to deliver. They set objectives, outline the activities needed to reach these goals and then work through people to realize them. People are the means, performance is the end. As such, supervisory leaders can be counted on to get things done, in the right way, on time, on budget.

Having a supervisory leader on top of things can be very powerful. When results *must* be delivered, when execution *must* be precise and then things *mustn't* go wrong, having someone in direct control is vital. Having a plan that externals can count on and then delivering on that plan, that is the key quality of the supervisory leader. Of course, the more specific the required output, the tighter the deadlines, the bigger the crisis, the more complex the coordination, the more crucial the performance and the more menacing the negative consequences, the more it is a relief to have someone in direct control making sure that everything works. Trust is good, but control is often better.

Supervision can also be efficient. Even the most experienced people might not always know which activities they need to undertake and how to complete these activities effectively and efficiently. Instead of letting these people muddle through, a supervisory approach can help them to structure their work, can give improvement advice and even show them how it can be done. By accompanying them around the "plan-do-check-act" cycle, the supervisory leader can help them to perform and trigger them to learn at the same time, in a master–apprentice type of way. By being involved and knowledgeable about their specific challenges, the supervisory leader can ask the right questions, reframe assumptions, offer feedback and give suggestions, all helping people to develop further while simultaneously jacking up results.[8]

The supervisory leader's impact on confidence should also not be underestimated. Having the impression that someone is in control can already boost morale, particularly if the supervisory leader is perceived as being competent and having a successful track record. Confidence can be further reinforced by having a hands-on leader willing to get in the trenches and fight when needed. Getting close to the action and showing how things should be done can be a powerful way for leaders to exhibit commitment and demonstrate that they care.

Yet, in their willingness to get their hands dirty, supervisory leaders might be tempted to go a step too far, pulling activities out of the hands of the people around them. In their drive to control performance, they often go off the deep end and become control freaks. Instead of listening to Roosevelt's advice in the above quote and having the self-restraint to let people carry out the defined activities themselves, many supervisory leaders constantly meddle in people's day-to-day execution. They descend into micromanagement, closely supervising every activity, constantly looking over people's shoulders, always knowing better, never trusting people to do it right. People start to feel like a dog on a very short leash.

As control-addicted micromanagers, feeling the burden of personal responsibility for delivering the results, many supervisory leaders work excessive hours and suffer from high stress.[9] Before they know it, they are caught up in the spiral of disempowerment – in their drive to ensure performance, they try to control people too tightly, people leave or become disengaged, results slump, leaders need to do more of the work themselves to compensate, financial incentives and punishments are brought in to motivate the disengaged, people learn to minimize their efforts and the leader needs to do yet more work to compensate.

Even where supervisory leaders are not outright micromanagers, the threat of disempowerment is constantly lurking. What the supervisory leader sees as necessary reporting, many people will experience as time-consuming bureaucracy or even Big Brother surveillance. What the supervisory leader intends as useful guidance, many people will view as useless disturbance or even as condescending interference. The supervisory leader might think that the "plan-do-check-act" cycle is not too tight, leaving plenty of room to fill in the "plan" details and abundant time between the "check" moments, but often the people being supervised will experience it as a straight-jacket. More "heavy-handed" than "hands-on." "People-sitting" as the grown-up version of baby-sitting.

Maybe the worst pitfall into which the supervisory leader can fall is to start treating people like human resources – only as means to an end. In severe cases, supervisory leaders even forget other people's needs and motivations, treating them as tools or "agents,"[10] to be used and discarded at will. With such a strong focus on results, the supervisory leader will want people to perform as needed and not make unnecessary mistakes, while worrying less about how people feel about the experience. Yet, people can't learn if they are only allowed to do what they are already good at and are not given leeway to try things out and make mistakes. Sometimes the supervisory leader needs to sacrifice short-term efficiency and effectiveness to let people develop, but this is a form of "letting go" that is often psychologically hard to accept for those in dire need of having a tight grip.

Qualities and pitfalls of the facilitative leadership style

Liberty means responsibility. That is why most men dread it.
George Bernard Shaw (1856–1950)
Irish playwright and critic

The facilitative leadership style, on the other hand, is all about growing people. The key quality of the facilitative leadership style is that people are helped and prepared to take responsibilities themselves. Facilitative leaders realize that they are just like football coaches – they can't score themselves, nor can they tell their players on the field which activities to do to score. Successful football coaches put almost all their effort into developing their players and their teams, so they can score themselves. Only if the players "own" the game and take responsibility for their play, will they win. The players need to be self-steering, as they can't be directed from the dugout. Yet, this doesn't mean coaches are powerless. Coaches can enable their players, by developing their skills, improving their tactical insight, practicing their moves and building their stamina. Coaches can also engage their players by strengthening team spirit, reinforcing trust in each other, engendering a winner's mentality and building self-confidence. And then they have to let the players learn, creating the right conditions to speed up their development, such as playing practice games, but also allowing them to try things out during a real match. Constantly, good coaches will nudge talents to grow in the right direction and only seldom will they shout from the sidelines what to do next.

The facilitative leadership style's emphasis on empowering people to self-steer is not only highly motivating for followers, but is also highly suited to the common situation that most leaders don't know which exact activities need to be carried out. Many of the people that leaders want to guide are specialists in their field and it is next to impossible for leaders to directly control them because of a lack of sufficient knowledge about their work. In the same manner, it is very difficult to supervise people who need to be inventive, creative or adaptive, because it is unknown in advance what these people should be doing. Leaders can't use a "plan-do-check-act" cycle when no plan can be drawn up and people need to flexibly respond to the context as it unfolds.

Empowering people to self-steer is also efficient. Initially, facilitative leaders need to invest time and effort into enabling and engaging people to be more self-steering. Yet, once people can work more autonomously, they can respond more quickly to issues themselves and require less face time with the leader.

Furthermore, while supervisory leaders are good at breeding confidence, facilitative leaders are good at breeding self-confidence. Supervisory leaders are present and interventionist, which under the right conditions can build confidence in the leader, while facilitative leaders are more entrusting and enabling, which can help self-confidence to grow among followers. Giving people a mandate to make their own decisions, learn from their own mistakes and, most importantly, realize their own successes triggers pride, increased commitment and a stronger belief in their abilities to succeed in future.

However, just as supervisory leaders can easily become over-the-top micro-managers, facilitative leaders can quickly fall into the trap of "macromanagement" – creating broadly positive conditions that don't really give any sense of direction, while at the same time abandoning people and letting them fend for themselves. The typical macromanager hangs back and lets things happen, preferring to stay at 30,000 feet, retaining a "big picture" overview, but not getting their hands dirty. In their belief that people should be entrusted to take ownership of their work themselves, macromanagers throw people into the deep end and then let them sink or swim.[11] Sometimes, this extreme hands-off attitude is rooted in the conviction that people need to have responsibility thrust on them and will self-steer and self-organize if pushed to do so. More often, this excessive level of *laissez faire* is due to leaders' lack of knowledge of what to do – they have little idea of how to influence people to move in the right direction, often missing vital insight into the people, the function, the company and the business. Many leaders who have moved to a new position, firm or even industry don't have sufficient understanding of which conditions will nudge people along the best course of action and therefore resort to macromanagement, hoping that people will be able to figure it out themselves.

The result of such a "you're on your own" approach is that people feel there is no leadership at all. They often feel *lost* (with no sense of direction) or *loose* (following their own direction).[12] As people start wandering off in different directions, an atmosphere of virtual anarchy can take hold, further undermining any confidence people still might have in the rudderless leader.

Qualities of Supervisory Leadership Style	Qualities of Facilitative Leadership Style
1. Leading from the front	1. Leading from behind
2. Directly steers behaviors	2. Indirectly nudges behaviors
3. Drives result-oriented activities	3. Creates supportive conditions
4. Ensures that people perform	4. Empowers people to perform
5. Disciplines people to deliver responsibly	5. Enables people to take responsibility
6. Steering allows leader to be in control	6. Self-steering allows follower to be in control
7. Guiding people increases their clarity	7. Growing people increases their potential
8. Accompanies people during learning	8. Supports people to learn themselves
9. Engages through sense of partnership	9. Engages through sense of ownership
10. Instills confidence in the leader	10. Instills self-confidence in followers
Pitfalls of Supervisory Leadership Style	**Pitfalls of Facilitative Leadership Style**
1. Disempowering micromanagement	1. Disorienting macromanagement
2. Demand for excessive reporting	2. Lack of sufficient interaction
3. Constant interference by know-it-all	3. General neglect by know-too-little
4. Feeling like errand boys for the boss	4. Feeling like lost boys without a boss
5. Insufficient room to experiment and learn	5. Insufficient feedback on learning situations
6. Quick to blame and punish for lack of results	6. Slow to evaluate and correct to get results
7. Direct steering degenerates to commanding	7. Self-steering degenerates into anarchy
8. Dependence grows on interventionist leader	8. Sense of abandonment grows thru absent leader
9. People misused as means by leader	9. Leader misused as means by follower
10. Lack of self-confidence among followers	10. Lack of confidence in leader's steering ability

Figure 3.3 Qualities and pitfalls of the supervisory and facilitative leadership styles

Even where facilitative leaders are not outright macromanagers, the threat of losing control remains ever present. In their willingness to sacrifice short-term performance for the long-term development of people, they sometimes run a high risk of not delivering the necessary results. They sometimes misjudge people's ability to learn quickly and fail to supervise them sufficiently, leading to lagging performance. Even worse, sometimes the mistakes made are difficult to correct and can damage confidence in the team.

In their willingness to trust people to do the right thing, facilitative leaders are also strongly susceptible to the threat of "moral hazard"[13] – people will be tempted to serve their own interests at the expense of the organization. By giving people autonomy and not regularly checking up on what they are doing, there is a significant risk that people will abuse the situation, doing what is best for themselves, even when it conflicts with the interests of the organization. Such misuse can range from simple free riding behavior to the more destructive undermining of other people and units. In some cases, people interpret the invitation to "take ownership" just a little too literally, varying from taking home office supplies to defrauding the company.

Finally, at a fundamental level, the question is whether facilitative leaders are right to assume that people prefer to be self-steering. Maybe George Bernard Shaw was right in the quote above, in observing that people dread the responsibility that comes with autonomy. What if the individuals who desire autonomy and responsibility make up a small minority, with a large majority of people inclined towards strong guidance? It just might be that the easiest pitfall for facilitative leaders to fall into is that of projection, assuming that others are motivated in the same way as they are. Facilitative leaders prefer to be facilitated and tend to treat others as they would prefer to be treated themselves.

Profiling your leadership style

> *The most dangerous leadership myth is that leaders are born – that there is a genetic factor to leadership. This myth asserts that people simply either have certain charismatic qualities or not. That's nonsense; in fact, the opposite is true. Leaders are made rather than born.*
>
> Warren Bennis (1925–2014)
> American scholar and consultant

While reading through this chapter, you were probably asking yourself which approach you generally take. Did you pick out typical behaviors that you exhibit and strengths that you have? Did you also recognize some of the pitfalls that you sometimes fall into?

It would be surprising if you exclusively use only one of the two styles. Most people will have at least occasionally employed both, but hardly ever equally well and equally comfortably. Most people will feel more at ease at one side of the style continuum than at the other. We refer to the style that is in your comfort zone as your "default style" – this is the style that you generally go to first and costs you the least effort. Moving to the opposite style feels less

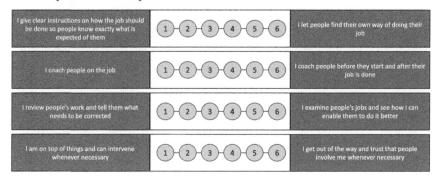

Figure 3.4 Profiling your leadership style: Interpersonal steering

agreeable, sometimes even awkward, and costs much more energy. More often than not, this is because you are less proficient at using that style productively.

At this moment, your first task is to identify your default style. As a quick aid to determining your current style preference, Figure 3.4 offers you four opposite statements, with a continuum between them. Set a mark along each of the four lines and then calculate the average. It's not rocket science, but this should give you a first indication of your leadership profile. You can also find this profiling tool on the App accompanying this book (*Leadership LEAP*).

It also helps to already ask yourself two further questions. First, how good do you think you are at your preferred style? Do you use it successfully under all circumstances and towards all people around you, and when do you experience some of the pitfalls? Second, how good are you at the opposite style and how easily can you switch over to it – how do you judge your leadership agility? These are the two areas for further personal growth that will be discussed in later chapters – how do I improve my current preferred style and how do I gain better access to its opposite?

As for Ralph's App, have you already decided what you would do if you were in Belinda's shoes? Would you lean over to the supervisory leadership side and take more direct control of the project, steering Ralph in the process? Or are you more inclined to hang out on the facilitative leadership side of the spectrum, empowering Ralph, while retaining indirect control? What type of conditions would you use as soft controls to nudge Ralph in the right direction? If you are interested to hear what advice other people would give Belinda regarding Ralph, you are invited to go to www.leadership-agility.com to read their views and maybe to share your own.

Notes

1 The names in all cases have been changed to protect the identity of the protagonists.
2 Beer, S. (1974), *Designing Freedom*, Chichester: Wiley.
3 Sprenger, R. (2010), *Mythos Motivation: Wege au seiner Sackgasse* (The Motivation Myth: Escaping from a Cul de Sac, in German), Frankfurt: Campus.

4 Thaler, R.H. and Sunstein, C.R. (2008), *Nudge: Improving Decisions about Health, Wealth, and Happiness*, New Haven: Yale University Press.

5 We prefer the term "supervisory leadership style" over the more commonly used label "directive leadership style" because the leader literally supervises along the way to achieve the intended direction. The term "directive" is fuzzy and can easily be misunderstood. One way in which it is confusing is that it suggests that there is also non-directive leadership. Yet all leaders are "directive" in the sense that they lead others in a certain direction. In the very definition of leadership lies the quality of giving direction, making "directive leadership" an oxymoron. Another way in which "directive leadership" confuses is that it muddles the *setting* of direction – i.e. decision-making – with the *steering* in a certain direction. Throwing these two leadership tasks on to one heap doesn't increase conceptual clarity. We prefer to separate the two and will deal with the setting of direction in Chapter 6. For the classic distinction between "directive leadership" and "supportive leadership" (an equally blurry concept) see House, R.J. and Mitchell, R.R. (1974), "Path–Goal Theory of Leadership," *Journal of Contemporary Business*, Vol. 7, No. 3, pp. 81–97.

6 This label was first used in Schwarz, R. (2002), *The Skilled Facilitator: A Comprehensive Resource for Consultants, Facilitators, Managers, Trainers, and Coaches*, San Francisco: Jossey-Bass. We prefer this term over the more commonly used name "supportive leadership" because the leader literally facilitates people to self-steer. Just like "directive," "supportive" is a muddled concept, throwing together a number of feel-good qualities such as friendly, helpful, respectful and just darn nice. As such, it is not the opposite of directive (or supervisory for that matter), as leaders can easily be supportive in combination with any leadership style. Implicitly what the term "supportive leadership" suggests is that directive/supervisory leaders don't support, but are unfriendly, unhelpful and disrespectful, which is an unfair and counterproductive characterization. This distinction between directive leadership and supportive leadership is a classic "bad style–good style" false dichotomy that neither helps our understanding nor encourages leadership style agility.

7 This argument is made by many authors, e.g. Kanter, R.M. (1989), *When Giants Learn to Dance: Mastering the Challenge of Strategy, Management, and Careers in the 1990s*, New York: Simon & Schuster.

8 Some supervisory leaders will argue that there are people who are not intrinsically motivated to work towards the organization's objectives. Whether due to "nature or nurture" these people are impossible to engage and will minimize their work-related effort if not adequately supervised. Without direct control performance will immediately suffer, making the supervisory leadership style the most effective. This view of people's motivation is widely known as *Theory X*, based on the publications of Douglas McGregor. See McGregor, D. (1960), *The Human Side of Enterprise*, New York: McGraw-Hill Education.

9 A classic article on the overworked supervisory leader is Oncken, W. and Waas, D. (1974) "Management Time: Who's Got the Monkey?," *Harvard Business Review*, Vol. 52, No. 6, November–December, pp. 27–36.

10 To a certain extent, the leader–follower relationship can be seen as a "principle–agent" relationship. Leaders as principles want to achieve certain aims and recruit agents to work on their behalf. In agency theory, the challenge of getting agents to do what principles want is described. But the relationship can be problematic in both directions; not only can agents act against the interests of principles, but principles can also neglect the interests of the agents; see Eisenhardt, K. (1989), "Agency Theory: An Assessment and Review," *Academy of Management Review*, Vol. 14, No. 1, pp. 57–74.

11 See Muczyk, J.P. and Reimann, B.C. (1987), "The Case for Directive Leadership," *The Academy of Management Executive*, Vol. 1, No. 4, pp. 301–311.

12 In an interesting twist, Chris Argyris has argued that there is another pitfall, namely fake empowerment. He states that many leaders send mix messages, along the lines of "do your own thing – but do it the way we tell you." This half-hearted facilitative leadership actually leads to disempowerment and cynicism. See Argyris, C. (1998), "Empowerment: The Emperor's New Clothes," *Harvard Business Review*, Vol. 76, No. 3, pp. 98–105.

13 Moral hazard is a common term in economics where people (often referred to as "agents") are tempted to behave in a risky and/or self-serving manner, as their bosses (often called "principles") have insufficient information about what they are doing. Paul Krugman describes it as "any situation in which one person makes the decision about how much risk to take, while someone else bears the cost if things go badly." See Krugman, Paul (2009), *The Return of Depression Economics and the Crisis of 2008*, New York: W.W. Norton Company Limited.

4 Interpersonal feedback
The paradox of challenge and appreciation

The dreary London rain made it even worse. This was the seventh large government bid in a row to be lost and Andrew was somber. As Managing Director of a consultancy firm working for companies and governments throughout Europe, he was used to regular rejections. Losing a government tender was all part of the game, but for his Public Sector team to be thrashed seven times in a row was worrying. Andrew's firm had put a lot of effort into building up its bidding capability and generally they had been able to win every second or third project they had gone after. Getting a good "hit rate" was very important, as much time and energy went into each bid and needed to be earned back on the projects secured. A low hit rate meant more and more costs that needed to be recovered over a narrower base of paid work.

Luckily the firm's other five teams were doing well. The Financial Services team was the absolute top performer, but the others – Industry, Media, Service Sector and Natural Resources – all made a healthy contribution to the firm, so Andrew was not worried about the firm's overall viability. What concerned him was that the Public Sector team, which in the past had been quite successful, now had little chance to meet their annual target. Strictly speaking that meant no bonuses at the end of the year and therefore a lot of disappointed employees.

As he got ready to sit down with Laura, head of the Public Sector team, Andrew reflected on what to say to her. Of course, they would do another "post mortem," to try to understand why the latest project had been lost, followed by discussion on some improvement ideas. But Andrew was still contemplating what the tone of his feedback was going to be. On the one hand, he felt it was now time to be more demanding. Almost a caricature of British politeness, Andrew had always taken a friendly and factual approach to his review meetings, but maybe now was the right moment to be more challenging, even confrontational. Laura and her team were not living up to expectations and maybe putting pressure on them to step up would trigger the desired performance. During previous review meetings, various improvement ideas had surfaced, but few had been implemented, so perhaps Andrew needed to confront Laura with these gaps and push her to act on them. Maybe he should also bring up the consequences of missing the team's annual targets. Not only would her team forfeit their bonus, but even the company-wide year-end payout would be lower, affecting everybody.

Yet, to Andrew it felt a bit harsh to "kick somebody already on the ground." He was quite sure that Laura was even more disappointed and worried than he was. Laura had been recruited into the firm six years earlier, in an unusual move to strengthen their public sector expertise and network. Normally the firm preferred to grow its own talent, but hiring a relatively senior consultant like Laura was seen as a quick way to build a position in this attractive market. From the very start, Laura had been a star performer. Moreover, being intelligent, confident and charming, she had rapidly won hearts and minds throughout the firm, leading to her promotion to department head last year. And now seven misses in a row.

Andrew had caught her gaze in the hallway earlier in the morning and she didn't look her confident self. Later, at the espresso machine, he overheard two senior colleagues from the Financial Services unit gossiping about the sad state of affairs in the Public Sector team and how they needed to get their act together – he assumed that these weren't the only voices Laura could hear behind her back. Maybe Laura was in more need of support than in need of reprimand. Yes, some things had gone wrong, but many more things had gone right. Andrew was certain that Laura was the right person for the job, so maybe that was what she needed to hear. Encouraging her to keep at it and not give up just might be more useful than demanding that she do better.

But wouldn't he be letting her off too lightly? Wouldn't he be sending a signal that poor performance had no consequences? As Laura entered his office, he stood up to greet her, still asking himself what type of feedback he should give – mostly comments or compliments?

The task of interpersonal feedback

> *I find the pain of little censure* (disapproval), *even when it is unfounded, is more acute than the pleasure of much praise.*
>
> Thomas Jefferson (1743–1826)
> American president and philosopher

Do you recognize Andrew's predicament? On the one hand, he clearly empathizes with Laura – he can feel her pain and doesn't relish the thought of rubbing salt in her wounds. As a colleague, he wants to be supportive, not vindictive, searching for a way to improve the situation, not to assign blame. He is also acutely aware that Laura's self-confidence has taken a beating. So, from this perspective, he is inclined to downplay the seriousness of the problem and to express his confidence in Laura's ability to turn the situation around. On the other hand, he feels it is time to "confront the brutal facts."[1] Instead of tiptoeing around the painful reality, while in the hallways Laura's reputation is being called into question, it might be better to get all doubts and frustrations out in the open. By having an in-depth discussion on where things have gone wrong, maybe he can help her to get them right next time.

While the previous chapter revolved around the choice of direct or indirect steering to impact other individuals, here Andrew is struggling whether to use more "positive" or more "confrontational" feedback in his steering. For Andrew, it is clear that to say nothing is not an option – that would be deserting, not leading. He knows the direction in which Laura should move but he doesn't know which "tone of voice" he needs to employ to trigger the right mindset and get Laura back on track.

Before delving more deeply into the different types of feedback that leaders can use, it is good to start with a better understanding of what feedback really is and why it is so important. The easiest way to explain feedback is to go back to the basic control system outlined in Chapter 3 (reproduced in Figure 4.1). Note that the arrow at the bottom pointing back at the leader is the feedback arrow. We speak of *feedback* when the effect of a controller's action is sent back to the controller to modify the next action. In other words, it is the behavior of the controlled system (the follower) that is the feedback for the controller (the leader). Put in plain English, for steering to work, it is the leader who needs to get feedback from the follower, not the other way around. To be good at steering, leaders need to be good observers and listeners, understanding how their actions have impacted followers, so that they can modify their next actions accordingly. Leaders who can only broadcast (feedforward) and have little sensitivity for the reactions of their followers – either verbal or nonverbal – will be steering blindly, which almost always ends in tears. It is for this reason that it is often quipped that leading starts with listening.[2]

Yet, this is not the feedback that is central to this chapter. We want to focus on the feedback leaders give, not the feedback they seek or receive. So, why do leaders give feedback while they are the ones doing the steering? Indeed, to allow followers to self-steer. Leaders return to the followers the necessary information on the basis of which followers can self-correct. In Figure 4.2, this means that the follower is both controller and controlled system, while it is the

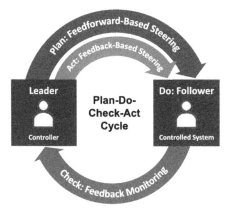

Figure 4.1 A simple control system

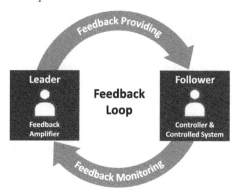

Figure 4.2 Providing a feedback loop

task of the leader to funnel relevant information back to the follower so that adaptive action can be taken. This is the *task of interpersonal feedback* – helping the follower to receive and interpret a constant stream of impact information, either directly from the leader or from others. Only in feedback-rich environments will followers be able to quickly learn and adjust their behavior, solve problems and develop themselves along the way. But as most environments are feedback-poor, leaders can have significant influence by providing specific types of feedback (and repressing others) and by helping people to make sense of the feedback they get and to draw conclusions about the follow-up actions that are required.

Leaders can have two objectives for giving feedback. The first reason is to help others to resolve an issue that they seem unable to crack themselves. The "intervention" is intended to assist in solving the problem at hand. You could say that the feedback is meant to help followers to *improve the situation* (problem-solving). The second reason to give feedback is to help others to *improve themselves* (personal development). The intervention is intended to develop the capabilities, knowledge and/or attitude of followers, making them better prepared for future issues. In both cases, the feedback is given so followers can learn more quickly and can adapt their behavior to be more effective.[3] In other words, feedback is communication directed back at followers to help them to do things better. It is only feedback if the leader has the intention to steer towards improvement – feedback is an instrument of influence, tailored to prompt a certain adaptive response. All other communication between people that is not intended to get followers to change their behavior is not feedback.

So, "getting things off your chest" doesn't qualify as feedback, nor does whining, pouting or being cynical. These are all forms of communication that are only concerned with broadcasting the sender's state of mind, with little to no regard for the impact on the receiver. Unfortunately, the word "feedback" has passed into popular vocabulary and is regularly employed to make negative forms of communication seem well-intended. Plenty of people will take their frustration, moaning and scolding, and dress them up like feedback ("Let me give you some feedback about what I think of you!"), in an attempt to make their complaining seem more acceptable, while in reality there is no intention to provide the other with information that could assist in adapting behavior. Criticism or ill feelings only become feedback when the sender packages the information with the intention of influencing the receiver to behave differently. In the same way, finding fault in other people's actions and assigning blame are commonly paraded as feedback, while in reality their true intention is to make the sender feel better and/or look good.

So, feedback is inherently "constructive," as it is intended to motivate the other to adapt. But constructive doesn't necessarily mean positive, which brings us back to Andrew. He wants to help Laura, which is the constructive part, but he vacillates between being more confrontational and taking a more positive stance. Andrew's struggle is not that surprising, as there is something to be said for both, which points to an underlying tension at the heart of feedback – the paradox of challenge and appreciation.

The paradox of challenge and appreciation

> *I have yet to find the man, however exalted his station, who did not do better work and put forth greater effort under a spirit of approval than under a spirit of criticism.*
> Charles M. Schwab (1862–1939)
> American steel magnate

To better understand what makes interpersonal feedback so tricky, it might be useful to start with a simple analogy. Say you had hired a professional portrait artist to make an oil painting of your family and on first viewing of the almost finished work you noticed that this modern-day Rembrandt had rendered your nose three sizes too large. After your initial shock – and a quick peek in the mirror – you probably would point out the flaw, wouldn't you? You would clarify what the true size of your nose is and then would contrast it with the Cyrano de Bergerac snout the artist had painted. Having identified the *gap* between what "should be" and "what is," you would finally request that the artist improve the "masterpiece-to-be" until it lived up to your expectations. The artist, being of a sensitive persuasion, might be a bit disappointed, maybe even a bit insulted, but would leave with a clear *challenge* that would need to be met.

Now say the six-year-old girl next door saw all this happening and came to you with her own portrait of your family, which she offered to you as a free alternative. In this work of art, you are drawn as a stickman and don't even have a nose. Would you again point out the gap and challenge her to do a better job? Or would you praise her beautiful use of color and perspective ("Almost like Van Gogh!") and compliment her on almost staying on the paper? Would you show *appreciation* for what she *did* achieve, instead of focusing on what she *didn't* get right?

These are two very different forms of feedback. The first type of feedback, *challenge*, focuses on what is *wrong* and needs to be done *better*. This type of feedback is based on identifying the gap between the expected output ("what should be") and the actual output ("what is"), with the intention of triggering corrective measures to close the gap. Challenge is all about saying: "This isn't good enough, it needs to be better." As such, challenge emphasizes what is *missing* and where expectations are not being met, putting pressure on feedback receivers to step up and meet the norm. Whether the gap is due to poor performance, or caused by rising expectations, feedback receivers are provoked to increase their efforts and achieve a more satisfactory result.

Appreciation, on the other hand, focuses on what is *right* and can be built on.[4] This type of feedback is based on identifying strong points and productive behaviors, with the intention of picking out these rough diamonds and polishing them further. Appreciation is all about saying: "These are some things you are good at, now build on these strengths." As such, appreciation emphasizes what is *successful* and could be leveraged, giving feedback receivers a sense of confidence in their ability to extend their achievements. Appreciation is a powerful way of showing respect for people's strengths and accomplishments, while at the same time creating a positive vibe by "thinking in possibilities" instead of "thinking in problems."

While these two types of feedback are not entirely mutually exclusive, they are highly at odds with one another. Emphasizing what is wrong doesn't blend very well with a focus on what is right. Both feedback types are based on fundamentally different assumptions of human motivation and learning – call them error-correction versus success-leveraging. Pointing to what can be improved taps into a different type of motivation than reinforcing what is already going well. At the same time, each form of feedback requires a different posture by the feedback giver. Being challenging requires one to be critical, constructively dissatisfied and even confrontational, pushing the other to perform better. Being appreciative requires the opposite stance, being positive, accepting and even admiring, supporting the other to keep on growing. It is for this reason that we speak of the *paradox of challenge and appreciation* – as Andrew already felt, a focus on challenging comments seriously conflicts with a focus on appreciative compliments. Therefore, leaders usually tend to favor one side over the other, giving rise to two opposite interpersonal feedback styles. As we will see, leaders often feel much more comfortable with the one than with the other.

The demanding leadership style

> *My job is not to be easy on people. My job is to take these great people we have and to push them and make them even better.*
>
> Steve Jobs (1955–2011)
> American businessman

Where leaders are inclined to place more emphasis on challenging feedback than on appreciation, it is said that they have a *demanding leadership style*. As the above quote by Steve Jobs nicely illustrates, a demanding leadership style is about pushing people to greater heights. These leaders have clear, often high, expectations and are willing to press others to live up to these standards. They are constructively dissatisfied, always seeing potential to do better.

The source of the gap between "what should be" and "what is" can come from both sides of the equation. On the "what should be" side, the gap is often enlarged by the high expectations held by demanding leaders. These leaders are often ambitious, seeing great potential to grow, improve and succeed. They set the bar high because they believe that great feats can be achieved with hard work and persistence. Sometimes this ambition comes from an inner drive to prove themselves and win, but sometimes also from an inner norm that nothing less than perfection is acceptable. Yet, the high expectations of "what should be" often also come from outside pressures, not only personal ambitions. Many demanding leaders will argue that they are not inherently demanding, but that the circumstances are – competition is fierce, customers have high standards, regulators set strict guidelines and higher management require better performance. All of these external pressures to perform are a reality that demanding leaders openly share with the people around them. Instead of sheltering followers from the cold wind of outside forces, demanding leaders stimulate people to step up and meet the challenges head on.

At the same time, looking at the "what is" side of the gap, demanding leaders feel that most people are insufficiently ambitious, focused and persistent, and therefore need to be goaded. When it comes to ambition, demanding leaders sense that most people are hesitant to leave their comfort zone if not pushed. People might talk about ambitions, but in reality, they set their sights (and targets) relatively low and are quickly satisfied when achieving them. Stretching themselves by taking on new tasks, developing new skills and committing to higher levels of performance is generally avoided, so it is up to the leader to challenge them to rise above themselves. By highlighting people's upside potential and refusing to accept that the current performance is the maximum achievable, the demanding leader can spur people to "jump higher" than they ever thought possible.

Besides limited ambition, people can also be hobbled by a lack of focus, spending their time and energy on activities other than those necessary to achieve "what should be." Instead of directing their efforts towards the required work and performance, they drift off into other activities that are not important to the organization. If left to their own devices, people easily get side-tracked into all types of unimportant work, wasting their time and energy on tasks that hardly contribute to the intended performance. This is obviously not good enough and it is up to demanding leaders to challenge people to stay on track and focus on "what should be." As such, demanding leaders discipline people to concentrate themselves on closing the gap between the current and expected performance.

Even where people are ambitious and focused, demanding leaders know that they won't be consistently so. Over time, people lose steam, slowly settling into the way it is. Routine sets in, ambitions get watered down, momentum slows and focus gets dissipated. It is hard for people to be persistent in their drive to achieve outstanding performance over an extended period of time. Demanding leaders know that even the best people require a regular external stimulus to keep their aims high and their activities on track. Therefore, demanding leaders know they must be unrelenting in their stretching and disciplining of people to get continuous excellence.

All this means that demanding leaders must push. They must be willing to let people feel uncomfortable, as they push them out of their comfort zone. They must be willing to stretch – to the edge of stress – looking for people's upside potential. They must be willing to challenge – to the edge of confrontation – not taking "no" for an answer. Yet, in all this pressuring, demanding leaders know not to go over the edge, as seemingly unreasonable demands will only backfire. Where people perceive a demanding objective to be just attainable, it will be seen as a challenge, but where a bold goal is perceived as a bridge too far, it will be seen as a demotivating delusion.

The encouraging leadership style

> *Treat people as if they were what they ought to be and you help them to become what they are capable of being.*
>
> Johann Wolfgang von Goethe (1749–1832)
> German writer, scientist and statesman

Leaders who place emphasis on showing appreciation, rather than on being challenging, are said to have an *encouraging leadership style*. Instead of focusing on what is going wrong, encouraging leaders focus their feedback on what is going right. They highlight the positive, identifying people's strengths and recognizing their achievements, while expressing confidence in people's ability and willingness to do a good job in future. Instead of saying what is deficient and needs to be improved, encouraging leaders praise what has gone well and support people to build on this success.

Encouraging leaders know that giving feedback showing approval and confidence is a much more powerful way to motivate and steer people than by trying to correct them. To start with, receiving compliments provides people with reinforcement that they are doing well. Hearing that they are on the right track and that they have certain strengths helps to build people's self-confidence. This belief in their own abilities in turn encourages people to try things out and learn, leading to a virtuous personal development cycle. At the same time, receiving compliments not only gives people self-confidence but also energy. In general, taking a positive approach in conversations, focusing on the drivers of success, identifying possibilities and celebrating achievements all invigorate people and make them more motivated to do their best.

At the relational level, receiving appreciative feedback strengthens people's sense of acceptance and trust – the meta-message is basically: "You are ok, I respect you." This sense of inclusion, support and security allows people to relax and perform without the fear of criticism, blame and rejection. Feeling secure also makes it easier for people to leave their comfort zone, learn by trial and error, and admit mistakes, again making it possible to develop more quickly. If what is done wrong is not emphasized, but what is done right receives public praise, people will be more willing to stick out their necks and take on more responsibilities. As is known with entrepreneurship, if you want more start-ups, failing must be no problem, or even a badge of honor. Actually, making mistakes shouldn't be seen as failure at all, but as valuable experience and an encouragement to keep on trying.

As Goethe points out in the above quote, maybe the ultimate form of encouragement is to treat people as if they already are the person they want to become. By treating someone as a success, they start behaving like one and then gradually become one. With a wink to George Bernard Shaw's classic novel about the flower-selling girl who becomes a lady, this psychological phenomenon is referred to as the *Pygmalion Effect*[5] – by dealing with Eliza Doolittle respectfully as a lady, she actually becomes one. This is a form of self-fulfilling prophecy, whereby treating people as their future better self triggers them to grow and fit this role. For this reason, encouraging leaders often behave towards people as if they are already competent, responsible and trust-worthy, knowing that showing this confidence is the most powerful way to get people to "become what they can be." It is much more than giving people the *benefit of the doubt* ("I assume you're good, but don't disappoint me") – it is giving people the *benefit of conviction* ("I know you're good, mistakes won't disappoint me").

All this means that encouraging leaders avoid the word "but." If you hear the word "but" being uttered, you almost know for sure that the speaker will pro-ceed to contradict, correct or call in to question. After "but" comes a comment, a criticism or a complaint, hardly ever a compliment or show of approval. A sentence with "but" is in essence negative, yet dressed up to sound considerate. "But" says you are wrong. "But" saps, while a compliment zaps – giving energy and instilling confidence. Therefore, "but" stands as a symbol of how not to give feedback. Encouraging leaders remain resolutely positive. They determinedly focus on strengths and potential, giving praise and expressing confidence, even when others see weaknesses and deficiencies. They doggedly think in possibi-lities, picking out the things going well and valuing them as the building blocks of future success, even when others only see problems. They actively support people to improve themselves, exhibiting belief in their ability to become their future selves, even when others would prefer to tell them what to improve. In short, encouraging leaders literally appreciate – "recognize and value the qualities in people" – and make sure to show it in their feedback.

Qualities and pitfalls of the demanding leadership style

> *It's not enough that we do our best; sometimes we have to do what's required.*
> Winston Churchill (1874–1965)
> British Prime Minister

Table 4.1 Differences between the demanding and encouraging leadership styles

	Demanding Leadership Style	Encouraging Leadership Style
Emphasis on	Challenge over appreciation	Appreciation over challenge
Motivating people by	Pointing to potential improvements	Praising current capabilities
Influencing by	Being critical and dissatisfied	Being positive and satisfied
Orientation towards	Building aspiration	Building confidence
Basic attitude	People will grow if challenged	People will grow if appreciated
Core quality	Pushing people out of comfort zone	Showing acceptance and trust
Intended impact	Inspiring the urge to do better	Inspiring the conviction you'll do well
Underlying conviction	People are easily self-satisfied	People need positive feedback
Guiding principle/motto	You can do better!	You are doing great!
Preferred tools	Comments ("the stick")	Compliments ("the carrot")

As was argued in the previous chapter, neither of these opposite leadership styles is inherently superior. Both poles have their own distinctive strengths, but also their own potential drawbacks. The qualities of each leadership style will appeal to different people in different situations, while both also have their own looming pitfalls that the overly enthusiastic leader can easily tumble into. This "dark side" of each style is typically due to the danger of overdoing a good thing (*the threat of exaggeration*), but can also be due to using a style at the wrong time and place (*threat of misfit*) or in the wrong way (*threat of misapplication*).

So, what are the qualities of the demanding leadership style that Andrew could have tapped into while giving feedback to Laura? First and foremost, the demanding leadership style is about asking more than people ask of themselves. By refusing to accept that the current performance is the best possible, demanding leaders raise the bar higher than people would do of their own accord. These leaders confront people with a challenge that stretches them beyond what they believe they can achieve, pushing them far out of their comfort zone. Although it feels scary and out on a limb, it is such a challenge that often brings out the best in people. Even when people do not succeed in reaching a stretching goal, taking on the challenge can be invigorating and enriching – as the founding father of the Olympic Games, Pierre de Coubertin, famously said: "The important thing in the Olympic Games is not to win, but to take part; the important thing in life is not triumph, but the struggle." It is the very process of struggling to improve, and often failing, that strengthens people's resolve, building character and resilience.

Besides this inspirational quality, the demanding style is also about getting people to live up to expectations. Even where demanding leaders have not set the bar very high, they do demand that people jump over it. If people don't achieve the performance level expected, this is a clear problem that needs to be corrected. Demanding leaders don't beat around the bush, but confront the brutal facts, identifying the gap and pinpointing the weaknesses and deficiencies that caused the gap to arise. They don't shy away from talking about the problem, analyzing what went wrong and spotting who made which mistakes. Demanding leaders are willing to be critical, if this leads to better insight and adapted behavior. By getting the problem out in the open, learning and improvement can take place.

It should be noted that while demanding leaders sometimes set the bar high to inspire, more often it is set high because that is what the circumstances require. Demanding leaders are the ones who translate external demands into internal ones, bringing in the reality of what is necessary to survive and succeed. They are demanding because the situation is demanding. Or as in Churchill's quote above: "It's not enough that we do our best; sometimes we have to do what's required." Demanding leaders might not always be directly prized for being the bearers of a tough message, but it can be extremely important that they challenge people to step up before an organization gets into more severe difficulties.

Yet, before they know it, demanding can become commanding. Once a performance level has been determined, there is a strong inclination to set it in stone, prompting the demanding leader to insist that people live up to expectations even when circumstances change. Especially if these expectations have been translated into key performance indicators (KPIs), there will be little wiggle room to deviate from the level set. The situation might change, making the stretch objectives a pie in the sky, but demanding leaders will often persist in challenging people to realize the unattainable anyway.

Often the stretch objectives that demanding leaders set are pipe dreams from the outset, even before circumstances change. These leaders formulate overly ambitious targets, not because this will push people to greater heights, but because it will push these leaders' own careers to a higher level. Or they set overly zealous expectations because of their own unrealistic dreams, perfectionist norms or lack of patience. The common denominator in all these cases is that these demanding leaders are led by their interpretation of "what should be," not "what could be" – they demand high performance with limited regard for the capabilities of the people who need to carry out the work. They insist on tough targets, without considering whether people are actually able to deliver such exceptional performance. They set the bar without looking at the length of the legs of the people jumping. Such expectations don't *stretch*, they *stress*.[6] And the feedback "it's not good enough, jump higher" will not be inspiring, but exasperating. Few things in organizational life are more frustrating than receiving critical feedback for not achieving impossible objectives.

The response to unreasonable demands can vary. Some people give up trying and disengage, while others try to "game the system," negotiating expectations down and massaging their results up, in an attempt to minimize the gap. Yet others pass the buck, pushing high demands on to others, in order to save their own skins. In almost all cases, the unreasonably high demands will be seen as unjust, undermining respect and confidence in the leader.

Besides this pitfall of being excessively demanding, there is also a clear danger of being excessively negative. In their drive to close the gap between "what is" and "what should be," demanding leaders can easily overemphasize what is wrong and what is lacking. They quickly zero in on mistakes made and dwell on actions that should have been taken. From here it is a slippery slope into expressing disappointment, then complaining, then condemning and eventually ending up blaming people for their missteps. Even where 95% of the work went right, some demanding leaders skip directly to the last 5% that "sadly went wrong," hammering on about the problems that desperately need to be improved.

Again, people can respond differently to such "unconstructive dissatisfaction." Of course, few people enjoy having their weaknesses and failures rubbed in, especially if their strengths and successes are taken for granted. Disappointment, defensiveness and frustration at the exaggerated attention paid to their deficiencies is a frequent reaction, but shame and a sense of inadequacy are also not an uncommon response. Yet when identifying shortcomings or mistakes starts to feel like a signal of disapproval, this is when people really become weary, sensing that fault and blame will not be far behind. This can lead to even more intense frustration and fear, resulting in all types of dysfunctional behavior such as engaging in defensive routines and avoiding responsibility. As people start playing the blame game – trying to keep their own slate clean by ensuring that others get blamed for mistakes – insecurity spreads, cooperation unravels and teams fall apart. In such situations, confidence in the judgmental leader will be low, while people's self-confidence will shrivel.

Qualities and pitfalls of the encouraging leadership style

We judge ourselves by what we feel capable of doing while others judge us by what we have already done.

Henry Wadsworth Longfellow (1807–1882)
American poet and educator

The encouraging leadership style, on the other hand, is all about building people's self-confidence. The very word "encourage" means "to fill others with courage" – to raise other people's confidence to dare to take on difficult tasks. Encouraging leaders know that even the most competent people will feel a bit of apprehension as they move out of their comfort zone to try new things and take on new responsibilities. People often feel uneasy not knowing what will happen and how to respond, and they will feel a little anxious as they make mistakes and learn by doing. Showing confidence in them is one of the most powerful ways of triggering confidence in themselves. By explicitly expressing their belief in people's ability to succeed, encouraging leaders strengthen people's resolve and help them to "just do it."

Encouraging leaders further enhance people's self-confidence along the way, by emphasizing what is going right, as opposed to what is going wrong. Of course, mistakes need to be acknowledged and lessons need to be drawn, but encouraging leaders make sure that problems don't occupy front stage all the time. They make an effort to celebrate successes and highlight issues that have been solved, to build a sense of momentum and a conviction that new problems can also be overcome. By underlining the positive, encouraging leaders avoid energy-sucking "thinking in problems" in favor of energy-generating "thinking in possibilities." By the way, looking for the positive not only boosts self-confidence, but also helps to find promising ideas and the seeds of success that otherwise get smothered under a layer of problems and mistakes. One can only find nuggets of gold between pebbles if one focuses on the gold and ignores all else.

Self-confidence can be further bolstered by emphasizing a person's strengths over their weaknesses. In the same way as highlighting successes over failures, it is much more motivating to recognize people's talents and potential, instead of dwelling on their limitations and missing capabilities. Of course, it is essential to know people's flaws and get them to work on improving their abilities, but encouraging leaders make sure that feedback doesn't revolve around addressing weaknesses. On the contrary, they go out of their way to acknowledge people's strengths and indicate how people have the potential to contribute to the organization.

All this support, acknowledgement and respect not only builds people's self-confidence, but also builds their confidence in the encouraging leader. Feeling valued and appreciated by the leader strengthens their bond of trust and sense of security. This in turn allows them to be more vulnerable, taking risks, making mistakes and sharing learnings. In this way, encouraging leaders are able to build high-performing teams, where mutual trust and respect are at the basis.

Yet some nasty pitfalls lie in wait for the overly enthusiastic encouraging leader. It starts with an excessive focus on being positive, even when the situation demands corrective feedback. Where leaders have a deep-seated belief that strengthening self-confidence is much more important than achieving short-term performance improvements, they will easily tip over into staying upbeat, regardless of the situation. So, they will readily justify lousy performance as "a phase in the learning process" ("I'm sure you'll do better next time!"). Where significant mistakes are made, they will shy away from discussing these, as they "don't want to generate negative energy" ("Let's look to the future!"). Where people's behavior can lead to a dangerous situation, they will avoid criticism, as this would discourage people from taking the initiative ("Just give it your best shot!"). Where serious problems arise, they will downplay these as "details that need to be ironed out," after which the encouraging leader will revert into cheerleading mode, to get the whole team back into a

Qualities of Demanding Leadership Style	Qualities of Encouraging Leadership Style
1. Sets challenging performance expectations	1. Shows appreciation for current performance
2. Focuses on the gap (what is missing)	2. Focuses on the great (what is working)
3. Emphasizes what is necessary	3. Emphasizes what is possible
4. Aspires to improve weaknesses & deficiencies	4. Aspires to build on strengths & successes
5. Instills hunger to do better	5. Instills confidence to do well
6. Inspires people to rise above themselves	6. Inspires people to trust themselves
7. Generates energy through stretching goals	7. Generates energy through positive reinforcement
8. Pushes people out of comfort zone	8. Supports people to explore possibility zone
9. Disciplines people to stay on track	9. Recognizes people for what they can be
10. Strengthens modesty & resilience	10. Strengthens mutual respect & acceptance

Pitfalls of Demanding Leadership Style	Pitfalls of Encouraging Leadership Style
1. Setting unrealistic performance expectations	1. Accepting lousy current performance
2. Limited focus on people's capabilities	2. Limited focus on external demands
3. Negatively emphasizing what is wrong	3. Turning a blind eye to what is wrong
4. Excessive complaining about mistakes	4. Excessive cheerleading about successes
5. Unreasonable expectations erodes respect	5. Lack of critical feedback erodes authority
6. Constant dissatisfaction wears people down	6. Constant satisfaction makes people complacent
7. Triggering performance stress	7. Triggering performance apathy
8. Creating fear of failure	8. Creating excessive self-confidence
9. Lack of confidence to overcome challenges	9. Lack of drive to search out challenges
10. Focus on own performance & avoiding blame	10. Disregard for problems & fatal flaws

Figure 4.3 Qualities and pitfalls of the demanding and encouraging leadership styles

"winning mood." If this sounds like the antics of a positive thinking guru, avoiding "negative thinking" at all costs, that is indeed the pitfall that many encouraging leaders willingly jump into.

Besides being excessively positive about the situation, encouraging leaders can also be excessively positive about people. By focusing on people's strengths,[7] encouraging leaders are often blind to weaknesses that need to be improved to become successful. They don't see the limitations that can be fatal flaws in certain circumstances. Yet, even when they do see people's weaknesses, they are frequently too optimistic about the ease with which people will quickly learn and self-correct along the way.

Not only are people's strengths overemphasized, but so are their beneficial contributions. By focusing on the positive aspects of people's performance, encouraging leaders often fail to recognize the negative impact that people have also had. They'll praise a person for the implementation project that went well, while not mentioning the five burning heaps of rubble also left behind for frustrated colleagues to clean up. They'll applaud the 6% rise in sales a person has achieved, while ignoring the damaged customer relations, the overworked delivery team and the investigation started by the external regulator. Generally, people will expect leaders to intervene in such cases, to correct ineffective actions and to condemn inappropriate behavior. Only giving praise and acknowledging the wrongdoer's positive contribution will do little to shore up people's confidence in the leader.

Yet it is not only the authority of the "spineless" leader that suffers. As people sense that encouraging leaders are excessively positive in their feedback and fail to confront and correct people where things go wrong, soon an atmosphere of "anything goes" can emerge – it doesn't matter what you do, because it won't be criticized anyway. To get some guidance, many people will seek out alternative corrective feedback from colleagues or customers, but others will do whatever they want, as the leader will "let you get away with murder." To many this lack of basic discipline will feel like anarchy, which some will love, but many feel will lead to dysfunctional chaos.

The reaction of "anything goes" is often reinforced by the excessive self-confidence that some people build by only getting positive feedback. As people grow accustomed to constant praise for even minimal effort, their self-perception as being highly gifted is further enhanced and their expectation of needing to work hard and endure setbacks gradually withers. Slowly but surely, exaggerated appreciation leads to complacency – a level of self-satisfaction at which openness to any form of challenging feedback is absent. People feel entitled to a steady stream of recognition and praise, while reacting as stung by a bee at the tiniest of critical feedback. In this way, encouraging leaders create prima donnas, complacent, yet touchy, and craving constant acknowledgement, even for just showing up to work.

Maybe the most fundamental danger is that leaders get trapped in the encouraging style not by choice, but by default. Many encouraging leaders are stuck in a positive mode of feedback, not because people's self-confidence requires it, but because these leaders find it just too uncomfortable to be critical. They find it much easier to be nice than to be confrontational. They feel anxious in expressing disagreement and challenging others to step up, preferring to keep the atmosphere pleasant.[8] Such avoidance of criticism can be further strengthened by cultural norms of politeness, honor and saving face.[9] So, while the encouraging style is all about instilling courage in others, it is these leaders' own courage to confront that fails them.

Profiling your leadership style

> *It is easier to discover a deficiency in individuals, in states and in Providence, than to see their real import and value.*
>
> Georg Wilhelm Hegel (1770–1831)
> German philosopher

Have you already identified your own preferred style? In Figure 4.4 there is a short leadership style profiler that can help you to plot yourself along the continuum between the two extreme poles described in this chapter.

As was argued in the previous chapter, it would be surprising if your "default style" is purely black or white, demanding or encouraging. You probably have your own preferred mix of challenge and appreciation that has served you well in the past, and you can probably tip the balance over to a bit more challenge or a little more appreciation under specific circumstances. The question for you

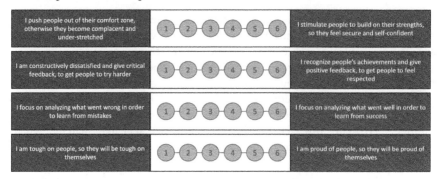

Figure 4.4 Profiling your leadership style: Interpersonal feedback

in terms of leadership development is whether you truly master the full range of interpersonal feedback styles at the highest possible level, or whether you see growth potential in one or a few areas. Maybe you recognized a number of qualities you have not yet achieved or a few pitfalls that you keep falling into. Hold on to your insights (or capture them using the accompanying Leadership LEAP App) for the last two chapters of this book, as we will then shift from identifying styles to developing your own.

As for Andrew, struggling to determine the type of feedback that he wants to give to Laura, if you want to know how other people would approach this situation, you can go to www.leadership-agility.com for the reactions of our invited panel and other readers.

Notes

1 Collins, J. (2001), *Good to Great: Why Some Companies Make the Leap…and Others Don't*, New York: HarperCollins.
2 The difficulty for leaders to truly listen is nicely described in Schein, E. (2013), *Humble Inquiry: The Gentle Art of Asking Instead of Telling*, San Francisco: Berrett-Koehler.
3 You might recognize that these two objectives are a bit similar to the two "loops" in *double loop learning*. Problem-solving is close to single loop learning, whereby the learning is specific to the problem and does not call the person/organization into question. Personal development is closer to double loop learning, whereby the follower is part of the problem and also needs to change. See Argyris, C. and Schön, D. (1978), *Organizational Learning: A Theory of Action Perspective*, Reading: Addison Wesley.
4 The importance of appreciation is extensively described in the Appreciative Inquiry approach. See: Cooperrider, D.L., Whitney, D. and Stavros, J.M. (2008), *Appreciative Inquiry Handbook* (2nd ed.), Brunswick: Crown Custom Publishing.
5 The original description of the Pygmalion Effect was by Robert Rosenthal and Leonore Jacobsen, see Rosenthal, R. and Jacobson, L. (1968), *Pygmalion in the Classroom*, New York: Holt, Rinehart & Winston. A recent discussion of this effect in the domain of leadership can be found in Whiteley, P., Sy, T. and Johnson, S. (2012), "Leaders' Conceptions of Followers: Implications for Naturally Occurring Pygmalion Effects", *The Leadership Quarterly*, Vol. 23, No. 5, pp. 822–834.
6 The concept of over- or understretching has been around for quite a while, going back to the work of Robert Yerkes and John Dodsen more than a century ago. See

Yerkes, R. and J. Dodson (1908), "The Relationship of Stimulus to Rapidity of Habit Formation," *Journal of Comparative Neurology and Psychology*, Vol. 18, pp. 459–482. The Yerkes-Dodsen bell curve is often used to illustrate an optimum level of "arousal" (challenge). Lower levels of challenge leave people understretched, in their comfort zone, while higher levels of challenge create overstretch, sometimes also called the panic zone. This notion of balancing between "boredom and anxiety" was further developed and popularized by Mihaly Csikszentmihaly. He argues that the optimal level of stretch, where challenges match a person's capabilities, leads to *flow* – the mental state of being fully focused on carrying out a specific activity. See Csikszentmihaly, M. (1975), *Beyond Boredom and Anxiety*, San Francisco: Jossey-Bass.

7 Kaplan, B. and Kaiser, R. (2006), *The Versatile Leader: Make the Most of Your Strengths Without Overdoing It*, San Francisco: Pfeiffer.

8 There is a significant body of literature around conflict avoidance. A good introduction is provided in Lencioni, P. (2002), *The Five Dysfunctions of a Team*, San Francisco: Jossey-Bass.

9 In the cross-cultural management literature, much attention is paid to the concept of *respect* – showing admiration or deference to other people because of their status/standing. In each culture status is attained in different ways. Trompenaars and Hampden-Turner (1997) make a distinction between *achieved* status (based on people's performance) and *ascribed* status (based on people's background). For leaders to successfully influence others they must show status-appropriate forms of respect, which will vary for different people in different cultures. Such expression of respect requires various forms of politeness. Disrespectful behavior will tarnish the honor of the other (making them "lose face"), leading to reactions to regain their honor (to "save face"). This is true of every culture, only what is seen as disrespectful varies widely and in some cultures the threshold can be quite low. This makes encouragement much "safer" than even "respectful confrontation" in most cultures and all the more so in a multicultural environment, where the leader is not familiar with the complexities of each person's expectations of respect. See: Trompenaars, A. and Hampden-Turner, C. (1997), *Riding the Waves of Culture: Understanding Diversity in Global Business*, New York: McGraw-Hill; and Huijser, M. (2006), *Cultural Advantage: The New Model for Succeeding with Global Teams*, London: Nicolas Brealey.

Part III
Organizational leadership

5 Organizational composition
The paradox of unity and diversity

"We might be slow getting started," the CEO, Francesca, told the journalist, "But remember that the tortoise eventually won from the hare! Just wait, in the coming years you will be surprised by our progress in e-commerce. We expect that within five years more than 25% of our sales will be online, while the growth in the number of our physical stores will continue at the current pace." As the satisfied journalist left her office, Francesca turned to Paolo, her newly appointed e-commerce director, who had also joined in the interview. She was pleased that they had gotten the message across that shoppers should now also flock to them online. As a leading women's clothing retailer with hundreds of fashionable outlets throughout the continent, they had indeed been painfully slow at getting their online strategy figured out. For years, their website had been merely a marketing tool, to entice women to come to their shops. But now they had decided to develop the website as a full-blown distribution channel in its own right and Paolo had been hired from a successful internet retailer a few months earlier to make the new strategy a success.

As their conversation continued, discussing the menacing steps of online giants like Amazon and the surprisingly slow response of even the biggest bricks-and-mortar retailers like Walmart, Francesca cautiously asked Paolo how he thought their digital transformation was progressing. He explained how challenging it was to figure out which women to target, how to reach them digitally and how to structure the website to serve them best, but that these were all things that would need to be learned along the way. He also shared how difficult it had been to organize the entire fulfillment process, from order-taking to home delivery, particularly because he was counting on 25% to 50% of the goods to be returned.

Yet, the biggest frustration, he had to admit, was getting people in the organization to help him out and to adapt their processes to accommodate the new e-commerce activities. Colleagues had been unresponsive at best, but more often downright hostile, almost sabotaging his efforts. The IT department had not given priority to his needs, finance had ignored his requests to streamline the payment process and the logistics people only saw difficulties in changing how processes had been organized. "And don't get me started about the pigheadedness of the marketing director, she obviously feels threatened by the new digital world she doesn't understand," Paolo groaned.

To Francesca's question how he was dealing with this resistance, Paolo confidently answered that he had decided to go around the conservative forces instead of trying to get them on board. He had recruited a small band of relatively young people from inside and outside the organization to quickly get the webshop up and running. This team of digital natives all strongly believed in Paolo's online strategy and were not held back by old-fashioned physical-world thinking. Some people had already started calling them the digital guerillas – a nom de guerre which they had gladly embraced, even printing black T-shirts with the name against a background of zeros and ones.

Yes, this was the development that Francesca wanted to discuss. Quite a few managers had been at her desk, loudly complaining about how Paolo had been circumventing them. Instead of listening to their advice and engaging in discussion, they claimed Paolo had branded them as obsolete and had started to build a parallel structure inside the company. Even Giovanni, the young head of IT, had complained to Francesca that Paolo's team wasn't really open to finding common ground and was now about to establish an incompatible IT architecture under his very nose.

Actually, it surprised Paolo that "the bomb hadn't burst earlier," but now that the issue was out in the open, he stated that it was his conviction that the only way to reach 25% online sales in five years would be to create a separate digital unit, not restrained by outdated systems and old thinking. Only a focused and unified digital team could realize the envisioned online growth.

Yet Francesca wasn't yet convinced. The potential synergies between the physical and online channels were too enticing to give up that easily. She questioned whether Paolo had truly been open to learn from people with different views and tons of retailing experience. Had Paolo really tried to build bridges between departments and bring everyone into a cross-functional coalition? "Let's discuss it again tomorrow," Francesca concluded. "But Paolo, please consider open-mindedly what would be in our long-term interest – you leading a separate tightly knit team of like-minded people, or you leading the whole group of directors into the digital world, differences and all."

The task of organizational composition

> *Organizing is what you do before you do something, so that when you do it, it is not mixed up.*
>
> A.A. Milne (1882–1956)
> British author

In this case, Paolo is faced with the task of organizing the successful implementation of the company's e-commerce strategy. He must determine who will do which activities and how they will work together to achieve a shared objective. This is the very essence of *organizing* – dividing the necessary work among people and then getting them to cooperate to reach a joint result. It is about the division of labor, which allows people to specialize in particular types of activities, and about achieving collaboration, which allows people to align their activities to accomplish a shared goal. In their classic 1967 work, *Organization and Environment*,[1] Paul Lawrence and Jay Lorsch call this *differentiation* and *integration* – deciding how to distinguish and split up activities, and determining where and how to reconnect them into a common whole.

So, Paolo must start by determining whether e-commerce activities should be differentiated from bricks-and-mortar activities and assigned to different people, or kept together and done by the same people. To make this choice, he must consider whether the e-commerce activities require significantly different skills and ways of thinking, in which case it would seem wise to split them off from the traditional retailing activities. At the same time, he must weigh the potential for cross-fertilization and economies of scale (in other words, synergy[2]) if the digital and physical retailing activities were kept together in the same hands.

Yet, Paolo must look beyond the need for differentiation to the question of integration – what is the best way to get the various activities that have been split between people aligned into an effective whole? If all e-commerce activities are integrated with the bricks-and-mortar activities on a function by function basis (i.e. integrated IT, integrated logistics, integrated marketing, etc.), to what extent might that frustrate the integration of e-commerce activities *across* the various functions? If each functional director is hesitant to collaborate and compromise, it might be impossible for Paolo to create an integrated webshop offering. Therefore, Paolo must consider whether he can convince the various functional departments to closely cooperate to make the webshop a success, or whether each department will behave as a separate silo, resisting attempts to achieve integration. If the existing functional directors all guard their own little kingdoms, fundamentally undermining collaboration towards a joint goal, Paolo might be better off integrating the various functions in a separate e-commerce unit.

As this example illustrates, the task of *organizational composition* – putting together teams, units and whole organizations in the optimal way to achieve success – can be highly challenging for leaders as there are many aspects to take into account. It begins with the fact that differentiation of activities can be done along many different dimensions. Paolo was focused on differentiation along business lines (i.e. splitting e-commerce activities from the physical stores) and along functional lines (i.e. separating IT activities from procurement, logistics, marketing and other activities). However, there are plenty of other ways to differentiate activities, such as along geographic lines (e.g. by city, region or country) and along customer lines (e.g. according to life style or distinguishing b2b and b2c segments). Within each set of differentiated activities further differentiation is possible. The IT function can be further split up into clusters of activities, which can also be split up, ad infinitum. Regional activities can be further divided into subregions, physical stores can be further segmented into big, medium and small, while the b2c activities can be further unraveled into separate consumer groups. Yet each act of differentiation raises the question how the separated parts can be persuaded to collaborate with each other to achieve a joint result – fragmenting the work is easy, putting it back together again is the big challenge.

Once activities have been differentiated and assigned to separate people, there are basically two integration mechanisms that can be used to achieve alignment between them. The first way is to give someone the formal authority to force people to work together. In Chapter 3 we called this *hard control* – having the official power to tell someone what to do. In organizations, this means creating formal positions endowed with carrots and sticks, and appointing managers to these positions who can oblige people to collaborate. In this approach, coordination between people is enforced by someone above them (therefore, we also call this *hard integration*). The second way to achieve integration is to get people to want to work together voluntarily. In Chapter 3 we called this *soft control* – being able to nudge people to do the right thing of their own free will. In organizations, this means creating conditions that will entice people to pull together to achieve a shared objective. In this approach, also called *soft integration*, coordination between people is realized by a mutual willingness to cooperate.

The challenge for leaders is to use differentiation and integration to develop organizations best suited to realizing the defined objectives. For the CEO, this task of organizational composition means developing the best possible company, but for everyone else this can mean taking on the responsibility for organizing at their own level. For each set of activities, leaders need to determine whether and how they should be differentiated and assigned to separate people, while also taking the lead in ensuring collaboration between people where necessary.

Some of the organizing taking place will be by differentiation into formal teams, units, departments and divisions, with integration taking place within each, and across each part. But much organizing also happens more fluidly along the way, as leaders initiate new activities and try to get other people in the organization to join in. Sometimes such ad hoc clusters of cooperating people are given a semiformal standing and called taskforce, project group or community, but more often they are informal networks of individuals brought together to get something done. Sometimes they are merely temporary coalitions, but in other cases they can become a more permanent part of the organizational fabric.

So, when it is said that leaders are organizers, their task encompasses much more than only contributing to the formal organizational design. Leaders mobilize and pull together people to get things done. They compose teams, groups and coalitions able to achieve joint results. Sometimes they only involve a few people, sometimes thousands. Sometimes they organize people within the company, sometimes they build alliances across formal organizational boundaries.

In Figure 5.1 a framework is given to clarify these various aspects of organizational composition.[3] At the top are the familiar formal aspects of any organization. The formal *structure* specifies how activities have been differentiated

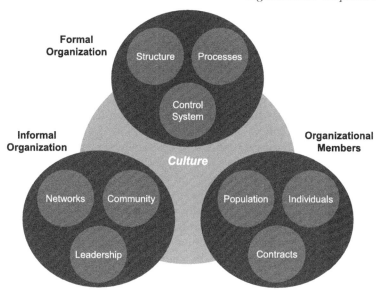

Figure 5.1 The organizational system[6]

and assigned to separate units and positions. The formal *processes* outline how goods and information are intended to flow within and between units. The *control system* encompasses the formal means by which the units and processes are steered. So, consistent with the distinction between management and leadership outlined in Chapter 1, management positions are part of this formal control system.

On the right are the people who inhabit the formal organization – the organizational members. Using the metaphor of a city, it could be said that a city is composed of a structure of housing blocks and buildings, connected by streets and controlled by traffic lights and police, but this is only the formal side. A city is also its people. Each city has a unique identity depending on its *population* – the specific blend of people living there. But it is not only the portfolio of residents that gives a city its character and competence, but also the actual *individuals* themselves. Each person has his or her own personality, beliefs, values, capabilities, relationships, ambitions and history, contributing to the functioning of the whole system. And as a city can have permanent residents, temporary workers and transient visitors, so too organizations have members with varying degrees of permanence and connectedness. It can be said that people's *contracts* differ – both in terms of legal arrangements (e.g. fixed versus temporary, full-time versus part-time) and in terms of psychological commitment (e.g. long term versus transient, exclusive versus open).

However, if you walk around a city for longer than a weekend, you start to look beyond the buildings and the individual people to see the informal fabric of the place. People know each other, there are extended families, groups of friends, neighborhood associations and maybe even street gangs. These are all informal *networks* – not designed together with the buildings and streets, but evolving along the way. There also may be a sense of *community*, whereby people feel emotionally connected to the larger whole. Sometimes this is also called team spirit – people experience a sense of belonging, shared identity and dedication to the larger group, triggering a willingness to contribute to the common good. And *leadership* emerges – community leaders step forward to mobilize people to achieve joint objectives. While managers are formally appointed, leaders step forward and are accepted, which makes leadership a part of the informal organization. Very real, but not formally designed.

These are all elements that leaders can try to influence. Paolo can try to create a formally separate unit, hire new people with the right attitude and use his leadership to build a tightly knit team with a strong sense of community. Or he can work within the existing formal structure and with the current people, using his leadership to change their attitudes and build a stronger internal network. Both are examples of the leader engaged in shaping the organizational composition. What is generally trickier to do is to change the organizational culture. This is why it is depicted in a different color, behind the three other elements. Put simply, an organizational culture determines "how we do things around here."[4] Culture has also been called "the unwritten rules of the game."[5] A culture sets certain behavioral norms that are rooted in shared values ("what is important") and beliefs ("what is true"). These values and beliefs are self-evident to everyone in a culture and therefore almost impossible to change directly through dialogue. It is only by changing the top three elements that the culture gradually shifts, while at the same time the existing culture influences everything that happens in the organization, including leadership.

So, in summary, leaders go about organizing by determining which people they want "on their team," either formally or informally, and finding ways to get these people to collaborate effectively to achieve a joint objective. Sometimes leaders can freely pick the team of their choice, but more often leaders need to mobilize the people already there – organizational composition is rarely started with a blank sheet of paper. Therefore, the challenge for leaders is how they should effectively pull together groups of people for different purposes within the reality of the existing organization.

The paradox of unity and diversity

> *We must, indeed, all hang together or, most assuredly, we shall all hang separately.*
> Benjamin Franklin (1706–1790)
> American writer, politician and scientist

Getting people to work together is hard. Once activities have been differentiated and assigned to individuals, people tend to "mind their own business," focusing on the tasks they have been allocated. Especially where people feel responsible – and are held accountable – for their individual performance, they will concentrate on getting their own work done first. Collaborating with others increases complexity and interdependence, requiring more effort and boosting the risk of underperforming on their individual tasks. Add into this mix the difficulty of understanding other people, the challenge of communication, the threat of conflict, the messiness of compromise and the danger of being blamed for other people's mistakes – it's a surprise that people are willing to collaborate at all.

So, to get people to *work together* leaders must get them to *pull together*. Leaders must unite. Leaders need to rally people around a shared cause and build joint commitment to achieve results together. Along the lines of "all for one and one for all," leaders need to entice people to buy in to the joint effort and to put the shared interest above the individual interest. To really unite, leaders need to inspire a strong team spirit and a willingness to support and fight for each other. To realize such integration, team members need to understand, appreciate and trust each other, and here too the leader can play an important role. By creating a common language and formulating common beliefs, team members will find it much easier to understand each other. By emphasizing shared values and shared norms, it will be less complicated to connect and have confidence in each other. Together such a shared team culture not only makes communication and trust much less problematic, but also provides team members with a feeling of belonging and even a sense of identity. If all this is backed up by common systems, common approaches, common tools and common procedures, then the common expectations will make it much simpler to work together as a highly integrated team.

Yet, while stimulating unity, leaders must also accommodate diversity. With the diversity of competences needed in a team, automatically comes a diversity of people – different backgrounds, different histories, different studies and different personalities. Not only will they look different, but they will speak differently, act differently and think differently. They will have different attitudes, different expectations, different priorities and different ambitions. Dealing with such diversity is hard, because it is difficult to build understanding, appreciation and trust between people who have so much differentiating them.[7]

However, diversity is not only complicated, it is also beneficial. Decision-making is often more robust if there is a diversity of views in a team and an organization. Diversity stimulates discussion, resulting in issues being analyzed from more angles and helping to highlight different opportunities and recognize different risks and threats. Diversity also stimulates creativity, as existing views are more readily challenged and new combinations of ideas can be made.[8]

Besides better decision-making, more diverse organizational units often find it easier to understand their diverse surroundings and to make a connection with all key stakeholders in the environment. Outsiders will see themselves reflected in the organization and have a higher level of trust that their voice will be heard. At the same time, it is much easier to draw in top talent from the environment if a unit is not only accommodating, but actually values the different perspective that a new person would bring in. In this sense, embracing diversity gives teams access to a much broader pool of talent, while also becoming more attractive for that talent to want to join.

The challenge for leaders is that unity and diversity pull in opposite directions.[9] It is for this reason that we speak of *the paradox of unity and diversity*. To get *unity* requires a certain measure of *uniformity* and that conflicts with the notion of diversity. No one disagrees that a diversity of skills is needed, but to get people to pull together as a tightly knit team requires them to have shared goals, shared beliefs and shared values, underpinned by a shared vocabulary and shared way of working. This can be summarized as uniformity of purpose, attitude and method. Yet, to get the best possible result often requires facilitating, or even welcoming, a diversity of people who bump up against one another in productive ways. It is because they represent different perspectives and engage in constructive conflict that diverse teams can often be effective.

As these two organizational composition principles – unity and diversity – pull in opposite directions, leaders often emphasize one principle over the other. Either by conviction or by disposition, leaders tend to lean over to one of the two poles and seldom flip between building highly unified teams and facilitating highly diverse ones. This results in two very opposite leadership styles – the *integrative* and *federative leadership styles*.

The integrative leadership style

> *Where there is unity there is always victory.*
>
> Publilius Syrus (1st century BC)
> Roman writer and mime player

Where leaders agree with Publilius Syrus and are inclined to emphasize unity over diversity when composing their teams and units, they exhibit an integrative leadership style. These leaders believe that victory comes to teams that are tightly knit and exhibit a strong sense of shared identity. Successful teams aren't loose collections of talented individuals, but cohesive squads that are willing to fight together and support each other in pursuit of a shared goal. They are teams first and individuals second. Team members are committed to putting the common good ahead of their own narrow self-interest, trusting that if the team wins, so will they.[10]

Integrative leaders drive such tight team integration. It starts with getting team members to identify with the team and experience a sense of belonging to something larger than themselves. Part of this bonding process is getting people to buy in to the purpose of the unit and to connect with the shared values and beliefs. Yet, integrative leaders know that to truly become a tightly knit team, members also need to bond with each other, not only with the abstract notion of the "team." Hence the concept of team building – getting to know each other personally, understanding each other's background and thinking, and connecting at the emotional level. Such team building can involve off-site activities like building rafts together, working on a common community project or doing a joint haka, but also on-site activities like building strategies together, working on a common IT project and experiencing a joint town hall meeting. Actually, some of the strongest team building happens on the job, where leaders help people to pull together to overcome a crisis or to remedy team dysfunctionalities.[11]

To fully understand how integrative leaders build a strong team identity, it can be illustrative to see how this happens at the national level. To encourage citizens to connect with the nation state they live in (and even risk their lives defending it) various mechanisms are brought into play.[12] Outward symbols such as flags, anthems, clothing, food and famous buildings are often used as shared insignia to distinguish oneself from other groups, while rituals such as greetings, meetings, holidays and ceremonies are used to draw sharp boundaries between the *in-group* and the *out-group*.[13] Especially important in this context are induction rituals that are used to signal that an individual has become part of the national "tribe.' Furthermore, shared institutions such as a royal family, a national sports team or a "mounted police department" can also strengthen a feeling of nationhood, while shared stories and myths about the joint national past and a sense of shared destiny complete the national identity package. Integrative leaders employ this same mix of symbols, rituals, institutions and myths to nurture a strong feeling of "we" over "I."

At the same time, integrative leaders often use a shared external challenge to mobilize people to pull together. This can be a common enemy, such as a competitor, a common threat, such as global warming, but also a common opportunity, such as winning a new contract. In all cases, it must be a compelling challenge, convincing team members to pull their weight, compromise for the common good and feel responsible to help struggling team mates.

What integrative leaders can't use are people who don't fit into the team and undermine the team spirit. If people don't buy in to the team's purpose, challenge and strategy, they will either constantly call into question what the team is doing or quietly disengage and "retire on the job." If people don't buy in to the team's values, beliefs, symbols and myths, they will constantly come into conflict with the expectations of their team mates and trust in them will drop. Therefore, for integrative leaders it is extremely important to select people who will fit in strategically and culturally – often referred to as "hire for attitude, train for skills."[14] They will also proactively weed out people who don't fit or turn out to be bad team players.

As strong advocates of tightly knit teams, integrative leaders are allergic to teams and units that need to serve multiple conflicting interests and/or must pursue diverse objectives at the same time. Nothing in organizational design is more deadly than poorly thought out team assignments. Without *unity of purpose* there can be no *unity of attitude* and therefore no unity. Hence, integrative leaders prefer clarity – either units should be split, so each team can again focus on its core purpose, or a unit is kept intact, but with a more focused assignment. Two tightly knit teams or one, but not one unfocused unit trying to do too many different things at the same time. "If you can't integrate a team, don't form it" is the integrative leader's approach to organizational composition.

The federative leadership style

The surest way to corrupt a young man is to teach him to esteem more highly those who think alike than those who think differently.

Friedrich Wilhelm Nietzsche (1844–1900)
German philosopher

Where leaders highlight the importance of diversity over unity they exhibit a federative leadership style. In their view, diversity is a fact of organizational life, while unity is the rare exception. It starts with a *diversity of individuals*, which is only increasing, not decreasing. In most countries and industries gender diversity is growing as more women enter jobs and positions previously dominated by men. These women are not only superficially different than the men that preceded them, but they often also bring in a different perspective. At the same time, cultural diversity is growing in many places, as more minorities and non-locals move into the workforce, again bringing in different beliefs, ideas and ways of thinking. Leaders also need to deal with generational diversity, as millennials start to complement the Generation Y, Generation X and baby boomer employees. Then there is life style diversity, as traditional living patterns start to wither, leaving individuals to find their own path in life. And don't forget career diversity, as increasing numbers of people switch employers, functions, industries, countries and career paths. Federative leaders embrace the diversity of people as a reality to be dealt with, and even a benefit to be leveraged.

Federative leaders also recognize that in most cases there has been growth in the *diversity of organizational activities*. Organizations have become more complex. Increased knowledge and technology have driven further task specialization in organizations, leading to a higher diversity of expert roles. Increased globalization and cultural learning have driven further task localization, leading to a higher international diversity of activities. Companies are also opening up more to cooperation with outside organizations, leading to a diversity of joint activities and relationships. And at the same time, companies are branching out into new businesses, innovating and incubating, again leading to more and more diversity in the organization. To federative leaders it is clear that this increasing diversity can't be simply dealt with by forming multiple small teams with separate assignments. Somehow all the parts need to be reconnected to one another, while respecting their differences. Someone needs to build bridges between the diverse activities, to get them to work together to achieve synergies. Federative leaders see themselves as the necessary catalyst, bringing together two or more different parts and finding ways of combining them to create a mutually beneficial situation.

So, whether it is the diversity of people or the diversity of activities, the approach of the federative leader is not to strive for uniformity, creating a *melting pot*. On the contrary, the federative leader respects the differences, while trying to bring people and units into connection with one another, creating a *meeting spot*. Federative leaders are similar to mediators, or discussion facilitators, in that they ensure that all parties are heard and can bring in their point of view, on the basis of which a shared solution can be found. This means that federative leaders must not only see and value each participant's perspective themselves, but must help others to see and value them as well. They must help to get unpopular positions heard and respected, while managing the emotions and potential conflict between parties with different interests or who don't understand each other. Building bridges sounds easy, but in practice federative leaders are constant go-betweens, listening, translating, reassuring, explaining, confronting and leading an ongoing dialogue. If all goes well, the dialogue will sharpen people's minds, spark new insights and lead to better understanding. Yet, there is always the threat of open conflict that federative leaders must keep in mind, and an even larger threat of "passive conflict" whereby people and units ignore or undermine each other. Federative leaders are keenly aware that diversity requires constant connecting and that if the bridges are burned, all that will remain will be the silos.

While starting with mutual appreciation, federative leaders will also want to achieve solutions that are accepted by all involved. They are coalition builders. This again means "negotiations," but preferably not to find a bland compromise that annoys all parties equally, but to find ways of combining strengths to create novel ways forward. Federative leaders want to avoid getting stuck in the middle between two perspectives, striving instead to get the best of both worlds. To achieve such a synthesis of ideas, federative leaders facilitate a constructive clash of perspectives, all the while guiding the team members to concrete actions that all can embrace.

Table 5.1 Differences between the integrative and federative leadership styles

	Integrative Leadership Style	Federative Leadership Style
Emphasis on	Unity over diversity	Diversity over unity
Orientation towards	Homogeneous, tightly-knit team	Varied, loosely-knit group
Leader needs to	Build cohesion and joint identity	Shape an open community
Motivating people by	Creating sense of belonging	Valuing differing qualities
Basic attitude	Shared worldview beneficial	Variety of worldviews beneficial
Core quality	Aligning people	Harnessing complementarities
Intended impact	Enhanced team cooperation	Enhanced adaptability and learning
Underlying conviction	Consensus determines success	Constructive conflict is vital
Guiding principle/motto	All for one, one for all	Let a thousand flowers blossom
Preferred tools	Induction programs	Diversity programs

Qualities and pitfalls of the integrative leadership style

If birds of a feather flock together, they don't learn enough.

Robert Half (1918–2001)
American businessman

As the two leadership styles differ so greatly in their approach to pulling together groups of people to achieve joint results, it should come as no surprise that they also have very different qualities and pitfalls. Let's first reflect on the integrative leadership style. Its key quality is that it focuses on creating true teams – cohesive squads of people working towards a shared purpose. Successful integrative leaders are capable of getting team members to place the common good above their own narrow self-interest. They build teams, not committees. One only has to look at sports teams to see how powerful it can be if players are willing to prioritize the collective interest over their potential individual gains. If a coach can get players to pass instead of trying to score themselves, the whole team benefits. If a forward player is willing to work harder and help in the defense, again the whole team benefits. Successful integrative leaders get people to buy in to the team, building up their trust that by serving the team their own interests will be better served.

Besides, by creating this *team purpose*, performance is also enhanced by creating *team spirit*. Successful integrative leaders are able to foster an atmosphere of mutual respect, trust and support, leading to strong commitment to the team and a higher level of engagement. This team spirit in turn strengthens people's emotional bonds with each other and their feelings of connection towards the team as a whole. People experience pride in belonging to the team and even gain a sense of identity from being a team member. All these elements further reinforce social cohesion and engagement, adding to team performance. With a wink, it could be said that a key quality of integrative leaders is that they are good at creating a tribe.

The integrative leadership style also allows leaders to shape a very distinct *team profile*. By selecting new team members on the basis of a strict set of attitude criteria and promoting a particular team culture, integrative leaders can develop a team or a unit with a unique identity, which could underpin the competitive advantage that the leader is trying to achieve. After all, strategy is not only about creating a distinctive business profile, but also a distinct organizational profile to match. The more special that the organizational capabilities and culture need to be, the more an integrative leader will need to selectively tailor the organizational composition to get the exact fit.[15]

Last but not least, it should be noted that the integrative leadership style also supports *team efficiency*. By working with people that share the same core values and have a similar worldview, communication and cooperation are much easier and error-free than in more diverse environments. Having a unity of attitude makes it easier to quickly understand each other and rapidly arrive at joint conclusions. Efficiency can be further boosted by having a unity of methods – a shared vocabulary, tools, processes and systems – all making internal collaboration more friction-free.

However, there are some nasty pitfalls that integrative leaders effortlessly topple into. It starts with the danger of *groupthink*.[16] As Robert Half remarks in the above quote: "If birds of a feather flock together, they don't learn enough." But not only do they fail to adequately learn, their world actually becomes smaller and smaller, as they only speak to others who share the same opinions. The more that people talk to team members with similar worldviews, the more they become convinced of their own correctness. Integrative leaders can accidently stimulate this intellectual inbreeding, or even worse, promote it as a form of "team building."

Groupthink in turn feeds into group chauvinism. As team members become increasingly convinced of their own superior worldview, they grow more and more disdainful of alternative perspectives. Their views turn into convictions and their pride turns into chauvinism, looking down on other people, units and organizations that are less enlightened. Again, integrative leaders can inadvertently trigger such a superiority complex by overdoing their emphasis on team uniqueness, but sometimes these leaders fall victim to their own propaganda and truly believe their team is better.

Group chauvinism can then deteriorate into group implosion, whereby the "we" against the "they" starts to lead to further inward-looking behavior, intolerance towards out-group members and taking a distance from other teams and units. In the worst case, such isolationism can lead to a siege mentality, whereby the team feels threatened by the outside world and pulls together to resist. Again, the integrative leader can be unintentionally caught up in this dynamic or can be at the forefront, organizing the wagons into a circle to withstand the impending onslaught.

The common thread through groupthink, group chauvinism and group implosion is an intolerance of diversity. In a drive to shape a tightly knit team, differences are seen as a problem to be overcome, not a reality to be accepted. There is often a fear that differences will lead to diffusion, with the team losing its unique character. It is also common to fear that differences will lead to conflicts, camps and a loss of team spirit. And there is a fear that those who are different won't pull their weight, will want exceptions and will think of their own interests first. All these fears are not totally unrealistic, but need to be put into perspective. However, it is a common pitfall of integrative leaders that they underestimate latent intolerance towards diversity and let it get out of hand. This can easily result in people being pestered to leave the team because they are judged to be "different" and to dodgy hiring practices, whereby there is a strong implicit preference to select "people like us."[17]

Qualities and pitfalls of the federative leadership style

> *Flocking birds not of a feather,*
> *Dissent at length when thrust together;*
> *Which means that forced diversity*
> *Creates its own adversity*

> Art Buck (dates unknown)
> American writer

Switching to the federative leadership style, it can be said that its main quality is not building teams, but building coalitions – groups of people working together around certain interests that they share. Federative leaders recognize that groups of people seldom strive towards a *common good*, but often share some *common ground*. Diversity of purpose is a fact of organizational life, so it is up to the federative leader to see where the purposes overlap and interests can be aligned. Individuals have their own interests, as do units and organizations, so it is a matter of finding a way to bring these interests together to achieve a joint result. So, while teams are *exclusive*, only admitting members that buy in to the joint purpose, coalitions are *inclusive*, open to all people and units that are willing to come on board and contribute to a joint venture.

Besides recognizing coalitions as the primary way of pulling people together within – and across – organizations, a further quality of the federative leadership style is its emphasis on the process of coalition building. Instead of getting all people to march to the beat of the same drummer, federative leaders acknowledge the diversity of interests and show respect for the diversity of attitudes, competences and methods, attempting to build bridges between them. Federative leaders connect, mediate, negotiate and innovate, looking for ways to keep enough people on board to get things done. It is not about team spirit, but about coalition support.

However, to federative leaders, diversity is more than an organizational reality to be dealt with – it is an opportunity to be leveraged. Yes, the diversity of perspectives can often lead to confusing discussions, horrible misunderstandings and mounting conflicts, but also to rich dialogue, stunning insights and delightful innovations. A key quality of the federative leadership style is to employ the rich diversity of perspectives to constantly learn and improve. This rich internal diversity should preferably reflect the external diversity in the market, so the organization is constantly "fed" by its environment and remains aligned with it.

With regard to the environment, it should be noted that the federative leadership style not only builds bridges inside the organization, but also between the organization and the outside world, as the environment is another rich source of diversity. As federative leaders emphasize openness and inclusion, they are able to build coalitions with other organizations, to stimulate innovation (e.g. research alliances and open innovation platforms), cut cost (e.g. outsourcing partnerships and shared service centers) and create supportive ecologies (e.g. supply chains and knowledge communities). They are also able to fish in a bigger and richer pond of external talent, as they know it will be relatively easy to fit outsiders in.

The looming pitfall for federative leaders is summed up in the short poem above, which gracefully warns that too much diversity leads to its own adversity. Where federative leaders allow an excess of diversity, people are no longer pulled together, but the units or the organizations are pulled apart. There are two common trajectories followed in this process of self-destruction – *corrosion* and *explosion*. In the corrosion scenario, the differences within and between units become so large that the federative leader finds it next to impossible to find common ground and build the necessary bridges.

As the shared interests decline and it becomes more and more difficult to understand the other's perspective, commitment to the relationship recedes and all parties focus more on their own agendas. As in a marriage gone bad, the partners gradually drift apart, interactions become less frequent and the sense of shared identity weakens. Slowly but surely the social bonds dissolve and separate silos are formed. The federative leader can still call people together to discuss the few remaining common themes, but people will not see it as a coalition gathering, but as a committee meeting, where they will only go to safeguard their (unit's) interests. Trust will be low and no one will want to take responsibility for the whole. Unaware of the irony, unsuccessful federative leaders often still insist on calling this grouping of diverse individuals "the management team," hoping to mask the utter lack of team commitment. While such units or organizations have largely fallen apart into autonomous segments, they often do stay together in name, with the various parts finding ways to deal with each other at arm's length and occasionally finding ways to agree on half-hearted compromises.

The alternative to going out with a whimper is going out with a bang. In the explosion scenario, the excessive diversity of interests and perspectives leads to a build-up of tension, eventually resulting in conflict. This conflict can be between individuals who don't get along, or between units that define their interests differently, have a different culture or have a different view of the future. Furthermore, the conflict can remain simmering for a long period of time or can erupt into the open. In all cases, there is too much diversity for the federative leader to bridge, either because the leader inherited it, took on board too much diversity along the way or let it grow unchecked.

It is in itself a pitfall of federative leaders to underestimate the amount of diversity in units and organizations and overestimate their ability to bridge the differences. Leaders will often remark that "in the end we are all just people," ignoring the enormous differences in worldview that can come with different cultural backgrounds, different life experiences and different career paths. Many leaders are not even aware of their own cultural biases, industry-specific learnings, company upbringing, functional area experiences, educational programming and personality quirks, let alone what makes other people tick. Naive about all of the ways in which people can be different and all of the manners in which communication can go wrong, some federative leaders set themselves up for failure.

Maybe the most alluring pitfall for well-intentioned federative leaders is the attraction of taking on more diversity than they need or than they themselves can handle. Wanting to stimulate creativity and innovation, some federative leaders will go beyond diversity to unwieldy *divergence*, putting together groups of utterly incompatible people, who go on to fight and frustrate each other. Wanting to bring in different views, some federative leaders will go a bridge too far, hiring outsiders with such disparate standpoints that misunderstanding

Qualities of Integrative Leadership Style	Qualities of Federative Leadership Style
1. Pulls people together into strong teams	1. Pulls people together into strong coalitions
2. Rallies group around the common good	2. Rallies group around the common ground
3. Shapes a distinct team profile	3. Builds bridges to connect different people
4. Stresses exclusiveness , limiting who can join	4. Stresses inclusiveness, welcoming all to join
5. Uses melting pot to create shared identity	5. Uses meeting spot to create shared agenda
6. Minimizes differences to improve cohesion	6. Accommodates differences to achieve buy in
7. Stimulates engagement through team spirit	7. Stimulates engagement by realizing synergies
8. Uses similarity to ease mutual understanding	8. Uses diversity to cross-fertilize ideas
9. Encourages consensus to improve efficiency	9. Leverages conflict to improve decisions
10. Uses external challenge to unite team	10. Uses external connections to tap into inputs

Pitfalls of Integrative Leadership Style	Pitfalls of Federative Leadership Style
1. Pulls people together into intolerant clans	1. Pulls people, but they remain divided
2. Rallies group around narrow self interest	2. Rallies group, but individual interests prevail
3. Forced submission to the common good	3. Insufficient emphasis on the common ground
4. Oppressive consensus pushes dissenters to exit	4. Underestimating fundamental differences
5. Preference to hire "people like us"	5. Overestimating ability to bridge differences
6. Difficulty finding new people to fit in	6. Difficulty creating group cohesion & identity
7. Similarity of opinions degenerates into groupthink	7. Diversity of opinions spirals into discord
8. Group pride turns into chauvinism	8. Group conflict turns into factionalism
9. Increasing division: Us vs. Them	9. Increasing corrosion: Everyone for themselves
10. Implosion: Group unable to work with others	10. Explosion: Group unable to work together

Figure 5.2 Qualities and pitfalls of the integrative and federative leadership styles

and mistrust abound. Wanting to connect with the variety of stakeholder groups in the community, some federative leaders will accidentally import external divisions and rivalries, replicating broader social tensions internally. In all these situations, the federative leader overestimates the beneficial impact of more diversity, while underestimating the damage done to the fragile social cohesion in the organization.

Profiling your leadership style

> *I don't want to belong to any club that will accept people like me as a member.*
> Groucho Marx (1890–1977)
> American comedian and actor

So, with whom do you sympathize most? Are you more partial to the integrative leadership style, believing in the power of unity and the strength of tightly knit teams? Is your notion of the ideal organization that of "a team of teams?"[18] Or do you lean over more to the federative leadership style, believing in the power of diversity and the strength of "coalitions of the willing?" Is your notion of the ideal organization that of "a team of rivals?"[19]

To determine your default leadership style, it helps to get a sense of where your heart lies, but of course it is your behavior that impacts the people you try to lead. Therefore, the key question is whether your comfort zone is more on the integrative leadership side of the continuum or more towards the federative style pole. If you are still slightly in doubt, Figure 5.3 offers a few opposite

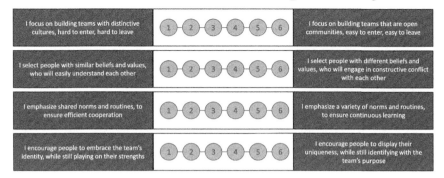

Figure 5.3 Profiling your leadership style: Organizational composition

statements that can help you to profile your preferred style. You might also want to ask yourself the tough question how good you think you are at this current style and whether it actually requires more developmental attention. Hold on to your conclusions, as we will get back to the topic of leadership development in Chapter 13.

Before moving on to the next set of opposite leadership styles, just a quick loop back to Francesca and Paolo. Have you already figured out what Paolo should do? Do you think he should go down the integrative leadership route, building a strong e-commerce team, accepting that this team will be more stand alone? Or do you believe he should go down the federative leadership path, building a coalition between the existing functional area heads to get them all connected to the e-commerce initiative? Or do you see a third way, making a combination of styles, getting the benefits of unity and diversity at the same time? Make sure you go to www.leadership-agility.com to share your approach and to read up on how others would deal with this situation.

Notes

1 Lawrence, P. and Lorsch, J. (1967), *Organization and Environment: Managing Differentiation and Integration*, Cambridge: Harvard University Press.
2 The differentiation–integration framework introduced by Lawrence and Lorsch was later expanded upon by C.K. Prahalad and Yves Doz in the context of multinationals, adding the emphasis that differentiation aided local responsiveness and integration was needed to realize global synergies. See Prahalad, C.K. and Doz, Y. (1987), *The Multinational Mission: Balancing Local Demands and Global Vision*, New York: Free Press.
3 See Meyer, R.J.H. (2014), "Strategy Development for Continuous Learning," in Rademakers, M. (ed.), *Corporate Universities: Drivers of the Learning Organization*, London: Routledge.
4 Schein, E. (1985), *Organizational Culture and Leadership*, San Francisco: Jossey-Bass.
5 Scott-Morgan, P. (1994), *The Unwritten Rules of the Game: Master Them, Shatter Them, and Break Through the Barriers to Organizational Change*, New York: McGraw-Hill.
6 See Meyer, R.J.H. (2014), op. cit.

7 See Williams, K.Y. and O'Reilly, C.A. (1998), "Demography and Diversity in Organizations: A Review of 40 Years of Research," *Research in Organizational Behavior*, Vol. 20, No. 1, pp. 77–140. In this article, Williams and O'Reilly review research showing how people struggle with diversity and generally prefer more homogeneous groups. Commitment and cohesion tend to be higher, with fewer conflicts and lower member turnover. This stream of research, which they call the social categorization perspective, has often found that work group diversity has a negative effect on performance.

8 In the same article cited before, Williams and O'Reilly review the stream of literature, that they call the information/decision-making perspective, that has often found that work group diversity has a positive effect on performance. This effect is attributed to the variety of information and perspectives that strengthen decision-making and stimulate innovative thinking.

9 These contrary forces are well described by Knippenberg, D. van, De Dreu, C.K.W. and Homan, A.C. (2004), "Work Group Diversity and Group Performance: An Integrative Model and Research Agenda," *Journal of Applied Psychology*, Vol. 89, No. 6, pp. 1008–1022.

10 This description of the importance of the team over the individual will be immediately recognized by those familiar with cross-cultural management literature. For example, Hofstede distinguishes between collectivist and individualistic cultures. The integrative leadership perspective aligns strongly with the values central to collectivist cultures. See Hofstede, G. (2001), *Culture's Consequence: Comparing Values, Institutions and Organizations Across Nations* (2nd ed.), Thousand Oaks: Sage.

11 See Lencioni, P. (2002), *The Five Dysfunctions of a Team*, San Francisco: Jossey-Bass. See also the classic about phases of team formation: Tuckman, B. (1965), "Developmental Sequence in Small Groups," *Psychological Bulletin*, Vol. 63, No. 6, pp. 384–399.

12 These aspects of culture are described as "the cultural web" in Johnson, G. and Scholes, K. (1988), *Exploring Corporate Strategy*, London: Prentice Hall.

13 The original article launching the concept of in-group versus out-group was Tajfel, H. (1970), "Experiments in Intergroup Discrimination," *Scientific American*, Vol. 223, No. 5, pp. 96–102.

14 See Taylor, B. (2011), "Hire for Attitude, Train for Skill," *Harvard Business Review* blog. Available at: https://hbr.org/2011/02/hire-for-attitude-train-for-sk

15 Note that various authors mention the importance of a distinct culture as a key competitive weapon. The most famous article making this point is Barney, J. (1986), "Organizational Culture: Can It Be a Source of Sustained Competitive Advantage?," *Academy of Management Review*, Vol. 11, No. 3, pp. 656–665. Some even argue that the distinct culture survives various strategy shifts and therefore makes a company "built to last." See Collins, J. and Porras, J. (1994), *Built to Last: Successful Habits of Visionary Companies*, New York: HarperBusiness. Collins and Porras even argue that building a "cult-like culture" is a key factor in determining the long-term success of many top companies. In their classic 1982 book, *In Search of Excellence*, Tom Peters and Robert Waterman also put organizational culture ("shared values" or "superordinate goals") at the center of their model.

16 The original work on groupthink was pioneered by Irving Janis. See Janis, I.L. (1972), *Victims of Groupthink: A Psychological Study of Foreign-Policy Decisions and Fiascoes*, Boston: Houghton Mifflin.

17 Burrell, L. (2016), "We Just Can't Handle Diversity: A Research Roundup," *Harvard Business Review*, Vol. 94, No. 4, July–August, pp. 3–6.

18 See McChrystal, S. (2015), *Team of Teams: New Rules of Engagement for a Complex World*, New York: Penguin. In this book, the retired American general argues that large organizations should be structured into smaller tightly knit teams to be more agile. Strictly speaking, this would make the whole organization more a "collection

of teams" than a "team of teams," but the label does have a certain ring to it and is fully in line with the integrative leadership style.

19 See Goodwin, D. (2005), *Team of Rivals: The Political Genius of Abraham Lincoln*, New York: Simon & Schuster. In this book, Doris Goodwin describes how Lincoln convinced many of the political rivals in his party to join his cabinet in 1861, in order to have the best people on board, keep his Republican party together and successfully conclude the Civil War. Goodwin vividly describes the challenges faced by Lincoln in keeping such diverse and conflicting personalities together in one cabinet, but also how this led to better decisions and broader support within the party.

6   Organizational decision-making
The paradox of direction and participation

"That's it...I'm announcing my decision tomorrow!" Adrian exclaimed, taking a first sip of his favorite *Affligem* beer. "My patience has been exhausted by this management team. How many times do we need to review the issues? They're driving me crazy! How many times do we need to go over the options and risks again? I've had it! From now on it's my way or the highway. I can't run a company like this!" Adrian slammed his fist down on the café table to emphasize his point, making Margaret smile even more. "Oh, calm down Adrian," Margaret laughed, picking up her glass of *Leffe Blond*. "Here's to patience!" she toasted, knocking the rim of her glass against his.

Just six months earlier, Adrian had been headhunted as new CEO of this European fast-moving consumer goods company, with the assignment to steer it away from impending bankruptcy and set it on a path to renewed profitability. The investors that had recently purchased the company were keen to get Adrian on board, as he had a strong track record in corporate turnarounds and a reputation for hard-nosed reorganizations. They knew that the company had been loss-making for years and that two previous owners and three previous CEOs had all failed to stem the bleeding, let alone chart a route to future health.

In his first 100 days, Adrian had taken the two key measures that had served him well before. First, he interviewed the top 20 managers to better understand the challenges faced by the company and to get a picture of the mindset of his senior people. Based on these interviews, he asked eight managers to leave, opening positions for additional outsiders to come in. He was particularly eager to make sure that his core "change team" were with him, so he asked his old colleagues Margaret, Josef and Andy to become HR director, CFO and head of business development respectively. Second, he hired one of the top tier strategy consulting firms to come in and do a full strategy review. After three months, they had delivered a thorough analysis of the company's ills and had outlined a number of strategic options open to the company to achieve renewed growth and profitability.

Much to his dismay, the consultants' report revealed that the company's situation was even worse than he had anticipated. Not only was the financial position shakier than he had been led to believe, but the company's business model was fast becoming obsolete, necessitating a major strategic overhaul. But what also surprised him was that this part of the fast-moving consumer goods industry worked totally differently than he was used to – customers behaved differently, distribution channels were different, competition played out differently, pricing was done differently. He was now running a business he didn't deeply understand and he needed to decide which strategic changes might work without having the industry experience on which to base his judgment.

At the same time, it became more and more clear to Adrian how thoroughly decentralized the company was. On paper, it seemed like the firm was run from its London headquarters, but in reality the corporate center was little more than a central bookkeeping department, with most decision-making power in the eight country units. These units were earlier acquisitions that had never been integrated into one firm and kept on doing things in their own way, while behaving highly defensively towards head office and towards each other.

It was apparent to Adrian that it would be difficult to impose any strategic renewal plan top-down. Not only did he not understand the business well enough to draw conclusions about all eight country units, but he needed to have the active buy-in of the eight "Regional Management Teams" to get real change to happen. Therefore, Adrian formed the European Management Team, consisting of the eight country unit managers, Margret, Josef, Andy and himself. It was with this management team that Adrian was intent on drawing up a joint strategic renewal plan in his second 100 days, after which he anticipated to quickly move to implementation, so the first results would be visible within his first year as CEO.

But the decision-making process had been agonizingly slow, with the country managers seeing problems and risks everywhere, and each wanting to go off in different directions. Now, at the end of the second 100 days, Adrian felt they had gotten nowhere, while precious time was ticking away and the investors were getting restless. Yet, in Margaret's view they had made enormous progress towards mutual understanding and shaping a shared vision for the future. "Are you sure, Margaret, that we should remain patient and build towards a consensus?" Adrian asked as he finished his beer. "Or is this the moment to break the gridlock and push through what must be done?"

The task of organizational decision-making

> *For every complex problem there is an answer that is clear, simple, and wrong.*
> H.L. Mencken (1880–1956)
> American journalist and social critic

Do you recognize Adrian's struggle? He's wondering who should be involved in the organizational decision-making process and which role each person should play. On the one hand, he believes the strategic renewal plan is his responsibility and that the circumstances require him to make a clear and quick decision. On the other hand, he realizes that the strategic renewal plan will highly impact the country unit managers and needs their commitment to be successfully implemented. Therefore, the country managers need to embrace a joint decision, which they will only do if they are involved in shaping it together.

This whole issue of organizational decision-making is central to the role of leaders. As leadership is about mobilizing people to move *in a certain direction*, it is very important that "a certain direction" is determined, in other words that choices are made. Therefore, it is a key task of leaders to ensure that organizational decisions are arrived at. However, this doesn't necessarily mean that leaders need to make these decisions themselves, they just need to make sure that organizational decision-making is successfully achieved. In other words, it is the task of leaders to safeguard an effective organizational decision-making process, whereby they themselves and/or others are involved and take decisions.

Before returning to Adrian's question of who should be involved in his specific organizational decision-making process, it is useful to start with an overview of what the process actually entails. In Figure 6.1 a simple overview is given of an organizational decision-making process. Whether an issue is strategic, tactical or operational, in each case the process can be roughly divided into two phases. In the first phase – *formulation* – a proposed plan of action is drawn up on which a decision is taken. This phase generally involves investigating the nature of the issue, considering various alternative solutions and evaluating the alternatives to arrive at a particular choice. In the second phase – *implementation* – the selected plan is put into action. This phase generally involves communicating the decision to all those involved, translating the choice into tangible actions and securing that the actions are in fact taken.

Note that there is quite a bit of confusion around the term decision-*making*. The word "making" should actually be taken quite literally to mean "creation" or "production," which implies that decision-making is about the overall

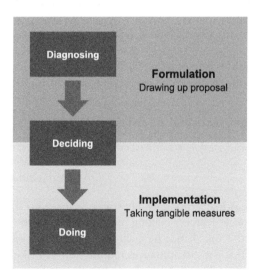

Figure 6.1 A two-phase framework of organizational decision-making

process of creating a tangible "certain direction." So, decision-making is much more than the specific activity of *deciding* – before you can take a decision a proposal first needs to be made. Therefore, it is useful to distinguish between the specific act of decision-*taking* (making a choice) and the overall process of decision-*making*, which encompasses all of the above activities.

There is also some confusion whether the decision-making process ends once *decisions* have been taken or once *actions* have been taken. In other words, does decision-making only encompass the formulation phase or also the implementation phase. Many would argue that a decision is only really made once tangible actions are taken, i.e., once implementation has been taken to hand (before that, it is merely an intention).[1] However, others argue more strictly that only the formulation phase should be seen as "decision-making," while the implementation phase should be seen as "decision-execution." Whichever definition you prefer, the key point for leaders is that without successful implementation, formulation is an irrelevant paper tiger. Therefore, leaders need to keep the entire process in mind when determining who needs to be involved at which moment.

To truly keep the entire process in mind, leaders actually need to recognize that there are two phases preceding formulation that are also crucial to successful decision-making (see Figure 6.2), although these phases are often given less attention. Before an issue can be diagnosed and a plan can be formulated, it must be clear that something is an important issue in the first place. This is the phase of *interpretation*, in which the issues that have been detected are screened, deciphered and prioritized, to determine which should be treated with a sense of urgency and need to be put on the decision-making agenda. In this phase, it is about making sense of what is going on,[2] whereby decision-makers often need to take a fresh look at issues, using different perspectives, to be able to

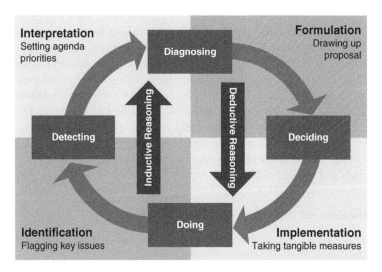

Figure 6.2 A four-phase framework of organizational decision-making

reframe old problems and to see new possibilities. They need to literally interpret the multitude of issues confronting the organization, to understand what
needs to get high up on the decision-making shortlist.

Yet, before this agenda-setting can be done, issues need to be detected in the
first place. This is the phase of *identification*, whereby certain current activities
are flagged as being an issue, either because they represent a (potential) problem
or opportunity. This is a very challenging phase in decision-making, as most
problems and opportunities don't immediately present themselves as clearly
defined issues and won't be spotted by those not looking for them. In this
phase, problems and opportunities don't jump out at you, but give off "weak
signals" that need to be detected and magnified to get other people's attention.
This is a phase in which issue-sensing, foresight, intuition and trend-watching
are important ways of picking up future possibilities and threats.

Together, identification and interpretation form the *inductive* half of the decision-making cycle, whereby decision-makers need to draw conclusions from what
is happening in practice. Induction is about reflecting on "the doing" and learning
about what seems to be working and which new challenges are presenting
themselves. It is a messy process, with few fixed methodologies. The *deductive*
half of the decision-making cycle is about drawing conclusions about what *should*
be done in practice. Deduction is about analyzing information and making
educated guesses to arrive at specific choices and tangible actions. In general,
there are more methodologies available to support these phases of the process.

Now, back to Adrian's question of who should be involved in the decision-
making process. We can now see that it is not merely a question of who should
decide, but more broadly who should participate in each of the four phases of the
decision-making cycle. On the one hand, Adrian believes that he knows the
direction in which the organization needs to go, having done the first three phases
himself (aided by the strategy consultants and Margaret, Josef and Andy). He
would feel comfortable making the decision himself, if he could count on the
country unit managers to wholeheartedly participate in the implementation phase.
Yet, on the other hand, he anticipates that if he doesn't take his country managers
through the first three phases with him, they will not truly understand and
embrace the necessary changes and will passively or actively resist implementation.

So, what should he do? Decide on a clear direction himself or get the entire
management team to participate in coming up with a decision they can all support? A tough call, as there are arguments supporting both sides, which points to
an underlying tension at the heart of organizational decision-making – the paradox
of direction and participation.

The paradox of direction and participation

> *In any moment of decision the best thing you can do is the right thing, the next best thing
> is the wrong thing and the worst thing you can do is nothing.*
>
> Theodore Roosevelt (1858–1919)
> American president and naturalist

To determine the best way of making organizational decisions, one must start with a clear understanding of what constitutes a good decision. After all, the best "production process" depends on what it is that we are trying to "produce." So, what does a "good quality" decision look like and which criteria does it need to meet?

First and foremost, a decision is "good" if it is "correct." If a decision offers a workable solution to the issue identified, it is "fit for purpose" and therefore qualifies as "good." Decisions that do not sufficiently answer the stated challenge or give an ineffective answer are clearly not good. It should come as no surprise that much of the discussion around organizational decision-making focuses on this aspect of good quality – everyone wants to ensure that the decisions made offer the best possible solution to the issues on the organization's agenda.

Yet, a good decision is more than the solution that is technically the most suitable. Many decisions are technically brilliant, but never get further than a PowerPoint presentation. If a decision is not acted on, it is not a "good decision." Besides being correct, a decision needs to trigger implementation, otherwise it is useless. In other words, besides the criterion of "suitability," decision quality is determined by "actionability" – will the decision get people to move and do things differently than they are currently doing? A "good decision" is a decision that has effect – it prompts people into action. It gets people to *want to* move along a particular path.

Two factors are key in determining whether people actually embrace a decision and take action to implement it. The first factor is *direction*. If a decision offers people a convincing route forward, there is a large chance they will buy in to the decision and commit themselves to implementing it. But for a decision to truly offer direction it must be clear, consistent and timely. *Clear* means that a decision must make real choices, also indicating what will not be done. *Consistent* means that a decision must not have missing and/or self-contradictory parts. To be clear and consistent usually means avoiding messy compromises that try to keep everyone happy. *Timely* means that a decision must be available at the right moment, which often means that it must be made efficiently and quickly. Yet maybe the most important element making a direction convincing is that leaders are willing to take ownership of a decision themselves. If leaders are willing to take responsibility for key choices and put their weight behind implementation, this signals to people in the organization that the decision will have consequences. The commitment of leaders to a decision gives a clear sense of direction, triggering others to jump on the bandwagon and also commit themselves to implementation.

All these elements that give people a strong sense of direction – clarity, consistency, timeliness and leadership commitment – all point to the need for leaders to step up and play a key part in organizational decision-making. In fact, these elements could be optimized if leaders took the responsibility for decision-making themselves. If leaders made key decisions on their own, it would be faster, clearer, more consistent and more convincing, while at the same time making very tangible who was accountable for making the decision and driving implementation.

Yet, there is a second factor determining whether people embrace a decision and show willingness to move to execution. This second factor is *participation*. Besides believing in the direction, most people also want to have a say in the decisions that are taken. They don't want decisions imposed on them from above, but want to be involved in the thinking, discussions and eventual decision-taking. They don't want to be told what has been decided higher up the organizational hierarchy, but want to co-create their own future. They don't want to be hired-hands, but want to share ownership of the key decisions impacting their organizational lives.

This means that the need for direction is at least partially at odds with the need for participation. Both organizational decision-making principles – direction and participation – are intended to get people to embrace decisions and commit to action, but they push leaders towards opposite types of behavior. While the need for clear direction encourages leaders to be the key decision-makers, the need for participation points the opposite way, to the people in the organization as joint decision-makers, with the leader more as process facilitator. To get a clear, consistent and timely direction for people to embrace, leaders need to take responsibility for making good decisions themselves. Yet, at the same time there is pressure to involve people in decision-making, sharing the responsibility with them to come up with decisions that all can embrace. It is for this reason that we speak of *the paradox of direction and participation*. Making clear decisions themselves and making supported decisions together are contradictory approaches that are difficult to do at the same time. This was already recognized back in the 1950s by Robert Tannenbaum and Richard Schmidt, who drew up their famous continuum of organizational decision-making approaches, showing different blends of "top-down" direction and "bottom-up" participation (see Figure 6.3).

With such opposite principles, it is not surprising to see that leaders generally lean over more to one side or the other. Either because of their beliefs,

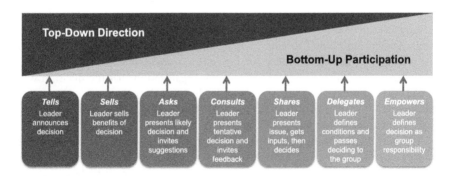

Figure 6.3 Approaches to organizational decision-making
Note: Adapted from Tannenbaum, R. and Schmidt, W.H. (1958), *How to Choose a Leadership Pattern*, Los Angeles: Institute of Industrial Relations.

experiences or personality, leaders tend to focus more on the importance of direction or of participation, giving rise to two very different leadership approaches to organizational decision-making – the *autocratic* and *democratic leadership styles*.

The autocratic leadership style

> *A ship, to run a straight course, can have but one pilot and one steering wheel. The same applies to the successful operation of a business. There cannot be a steering wheel at every seat of an organization.*

Jules Ormont (dates unknown)
American motivational speaker

Admittedly, "autocratic leadership" doesn't have the ring to it that would work well during a job interview – "Hi, I'm Ron, and I strongly prefer an autocratic leadership style." Nope, won't work. Nor do we expect many participants to sign up for a program on Autocratic Leadership. Clearly, the label isn't as aspirational as many of the other labels that we use in this book, and for many the term "autocratic leadership" even carries a bit of a dictatorial connotation. But this is an unfair characterization. Autocratic simply means "self-ruling" and implies that decisions are made by one person, as opposed to democratic, which means "rule by the people," implying that decisions are made by the citizens jointly. As these labels have a long history and are well-established in the leadership literature,[3] it seems only appropriate to keep them and change our prejudice towards the term autocratic instead.

Leaders with an autocratic style simply prefer to make key decisions themselves. They want to set a clear direction and believe that too much participation generally leads to endless discussions, infighting, bland compromises, rampant inconsistency, constant flip-flopping and ongoing stalemates. It starts with the fact that people all have different ideas and different worldviews, which makes it extremely difficult to get them to agree on a common understanding of an issue, let alone a shared view on what should be done. The bigger the organization, the more complex it gets, with each functional silo reasoning according to its own logic and each business unit or country office looking at an issue from its own local perspective (you might know the old saying that: "A camel is a race horse designed by committee"). This doesn't mean that autocratic leaders are unwilling to listen to this variety of viewpoints and let themselves be informed and inspired by the richness of different angles. It's just that autocratic leaders know that these people will never fully agree with one another, so that somebody needs to have the authority to cut through the disagreement and make a clear and consistent decision.

Not only do all these people have different perspectives, but each individual and each unit in the organization will also have different interests, which they will all try to defend and further strengthen. Although most people will try to dress up their self-interest as rational analysis, autocratic leaders know that "where people stand depends on where they sit." This means that any important decision will be opposed by one or more stakeholders, as few decisions will benefit all. And even if all stakeholders have something to gain, some will benefit more than others, upsetting power balances, which in turn might lead the lesser winners to undermine the proposed decision. To autocratic leaders it is clear that such political maneuvering is inherent in organizations and can only be overcome by having someone above the parties with the authority to push through decisions despite political resistance. Much like Plato's philosopher king, this should be someone chosen on the basis of merit, with the ability to decide wisely.

Even if there weren't all these differences to overcome, it would still be extremely inefficient and slow to have everybody involved in all four phases of the decision-making cycle for each and every decision. That is why autocratic leaders tend to be rather restrained in getting people involved in decision-making, preferring a "lean approach," whereby only people with key information are necessarily involved. This allows decisions to be made fast and efficiently, with much less danger of the message being explained differently by the various participants.

In the end, maybe the most important aspect of having an autocratic leadership style is showing willingness to take responsibility for the direction of the organization. Autocratic leaders know that decisions need to be made and that many of them are tough. Often the stakes are high, important information is lacking, the future is unpredictable, multiple risks are lurking, stakeholders are divided and the solutions are unproven – and these are just the easy issues. Besides such "tame problems," organizations often also encounter "wicked problems,"[4] in which it is unclear what the true nature of the problem is, unclear what the options are, unclear what the future will bring and yet action needs to be taken. Autocratic leaders are willing to step up and take this responsibility for making a decision and are willing to be held accountable for the results. For they know one thing very clearly – someone needs to accept the duty of taking the lead. Because "if everyone is responsible, no one is responsible."

The democratic leadership style

> *A genuine leader is not a searcher for consensus but a molder of consensus.*
>
> Martin Luther King, Jr. (1929–1968)
> American Baptist minister and civil rights activist

Just like "autocratic," the term "democratic" comes with quite a bit of baggage. To some it reminds them of a specific political party, while others will immediately think of leaders that are elected. Clearly, here we mean neither. Yet the most common misconception is that democratic leadership means that decisions are made on the basis of voting. This, too, is not what the democratic style is about.

Individuals using a democratic leadership style fundamentally oppose deciding *for* people, preferring to decide *with* them. They refuse to impose their will on others, preferring to shape a joint will. Democratic leadership is all about getting people to find a shared path forward to which they can jointly agree. It is about getting everybody on board, building a consensus. As this consensus generally does not exist at the outset, democratic leaders see it as their task to mold this consensus, exactly as stated by Martin Luther King in the above quote. This means facilitating a joint "will-forming" process, bringing people into dialogue with one another, exchanging information, arguments and perspectives. Democratic leaders are aware of the different ways of thinking and different interests, but instead of cutting through these, they make them transparent, in an attempt to find a solution that everyone can support.

Even where some people oppose a certain solution, democratic leaders will try to get them on board – agreeing to disagree – asking them to loyally support the group decision. Voting is actually a very crude way of forcing a decision, showing people they are in the minority and pressuring them to concede defeat and bow to the majority. Democratic leaders generally try to avoid such heavy-handed methods, instead exploring ways to win over the minority and reach a broad accord.

In practice, this means that democratic leaders don't wait until the moment of deciding to get people involved. At the very least, key stakeholders need to participate throughout the formulation phase, so they deeply understand the issues and the different points of view, and have gone through the tough process of interpreting the data, weighing the evidence, guesstimating the potential outcomes and making the difficult trade-offs. Only once stakeholders have gone through this process together, will they jointly embrace the outcome. However, democratic leaders generally also get people involved in the earlier phases of identification and interpretation as well, as it is extremely important that all stakeholders are willing to question the status quo and build a shared sense of urgency that particular issues need to be addressed.

For democratic leaders, all this involvement in organizational decision-making can be motivated from the practical perspective that participation leads to swifter and better implementation. Yet, for some democratic leaders broad participation is also important from a quality perspective, as they believe that the dialogue between different points of view generally leads to better decisions. By confronting and testing different ideas, creativity is enhanced, assumptions are surfaced and risks are better understood.

Some democratic leaders will also be motivated from an organizational development perspective. What often happens is that team members lean back and let the leader decide, so that they remain only half committed and retain the freedom to heckle from the sidelines. As it isn't their decision, they don't feel bound by it – there is no psychological contract. But if the democratic leader doesn't take the decision, but leaves the responsibility with the team, this will provoke team members to step up and take joint responsibility for decision-making.[5] Instead of allowing team members to act like kids – letting Mom/Dad decide and then complain – democratic leaders treat them like adults, stimulating them to take their responsibility together.[6]

Table 6.1 Differences between the autocratic and democratic leadership styles

	Autocratic Leadership Style	Democratic Leadership Style
Emphasis on	Direction over participation	Participation over direction
Motivating people by	Giving clarity	Offering involvement
Decision-making should	Be top-down	Be bottom-up
Orientation towards	Making decisions	Facilitating decision-making
Basic attitude	Leaders need to decide	Teams need to decide together
Core quality	Fast decision-making	Swift implementation
Intended impact	Maintain focus	Build commitment
Underlying conviction	Good decisions will be accepted	Acceptance requires involvement
Guiding principle/motto	The buck stops here!	What do you propose?
Preferred tools	One-on-one sparring	Team meetings

Qualities and pitfalls of the autocratic leadership style

> *Nearly all men can stand adversity, but if you want to test a man's character, give him power.*
> Abraham Lincoln (1809–1865)
> American politician and president

So, why should Adrian consider adopting an autocratic leadership style vis-à-vis his management team? First, because autocratic leaders are good at breaking through inertia and getting the organization moving. Autocratic leaders dare to make decisions. In far too many cases, organizations are incapable of arriving at decisions, either because the various camps are all dug into their trenches, or because there is a general lack of willpower to push through important decisions. These zombie organizations, not dead, but not alive either, lumber on without making any clear choices, postponing essential changes and spreading their resources across too many different activities. Usually everyone agrees that "something should be done," but then throw their hands up in the air and go back to what they were doing. Autocratic leaders don't accept such gridlock, but take the responsibility to impose a decision on the organization. The decision doesn't even have to be the best one, but is better than no decision at all.

Actually, often autocratic leaders do know best and this can be another reason why they should not hesitate to call the shots. Why trust the "wisdom of crowds"[7] when the "wisdom of the individual" is superior? Isn't it better to let the best qualified take the lead and then accept this person's expert judgment, instead of giving each amateur an equal say in what should be done? Moreover, it is not only that leaders often know better, but they are better placed to make unpopular and/or daring decisions. To build an organization that is not "vanilla," but that has a unique profile, means that many specific decisions need to be made that are tough, unconventional and controversial. To shape an organization with a distinct personality requires sharp choices, which can't be done "by committee." So, the more a leader like Adrian wants to grow an exceptional organization, the more he will need to personally shape it through the autocratic decisions he makes.

The clear direction set by autocratic leaders might not appeal to everyone in the organization, but that in itself is also a key quality – it stimulates self-selection. The people who embrace the direction and are eager to implement it will stay, while those who are less enamored will leave. So, instead of trying to build a consensus across groups with fundamentally different ideas about what should be done, imposing a clear choice creates its own consensus, as those who disagree exit the team or the organization. If you can't please everybody, why try? For Adrian, this would mean giving his senior people the choice to buy in or move out.[8]

Add to these qualities that the autocratic leadership style can be much faster at getting a decision and much more efficient, as fewer people need to be consulted and leaders only need to convince themselves of which decision to take. And with this decision ownership comes clear accountability – "It's your call, but it's also your neck on the line."

Yet, the negative connotations attached to the term "autocratic" didn't come out of nowhere. There are some nasty pitfalls that autocratic leaders can fall into, all well-known to us from the autocratic leaders of nation states. As autocratic leaders take it upon themselves to make key decisions, they in fact firmly take the reins of power into their own hands and as we know: "Power corrupts and absolute power corrupts absolutely."[9] Or as Lincoln's quote above puts it, giving someone power can be a true test of character, as power easily leads to arrogance, overconfidence and disdain for the less powerful. It is this corrupting influence of unchecked power that is central to most of the pitfalls of the autocratic leadership style.

The first danger is that autocratic leaders, who often know better, start to believe that they always know better. To be willing to take the lead usually means that a person has a certain measure of self-confidence and this is even more true for autocratic leaders, who are willing to take responsibility for calling the shots and who know that they will eventually be held accountable for the results. For such highly confident leaders, the pitfall of overconfidence is only one step away. They know they are smart, they've often had success in the past and they trust their own judgment, so why would they believe somebody with a different opinion? Every human has difficulty being open-minded to views, ideas and solutions that are at odds with their own mental maps,[10] but if someone experiences "being right" too often, this does not stimulate self-doubt and receptiveness to alternative points of view. Yet the successful autocratic leader is frequently right and even more frequently needs to have the patience to listen to the ill-informed and the not-straight-thinking, reinforcing a sense that it is better to trust their own judgment and to not take other opinions too seriously.

It also takes too much time and energy to listen to divergent opinions, so autocratic leaders will often try to avoid dissenting voices, instead enjoying the confirmation and compliments of people who are in agreement. This is even more true for the autocratic leaders who are less self-assured, as listening to people with different views threatens to undermine their frail self-confidence. It is much more appealing to only seek out voices that reaffirm and strengthen one's beliefs, so one can cling to the idea that one actually always knows better.

It is this unwillingness to openly interact with people with alternative views and truly value differences of opinion that puts the autocratic leader on the slippery slope towards authoritarian behavior. It starts with promoting people in the organization who are in agreement and only allowing "yes-men" (and "yes-women") into the inner circle. Soon, dissident voices are asked to leave, or sent to "organizational Siberia," signaling to all others that it's better not to disagree, but simply to comply. As autocratic leaders hear increasingly fewer opposing views, this further strengthens their belief that they are right and that "everyone supports them." Ironically, the less often autocratic leaders are contradicted, the more prickly they react to the odd challenging remark that someone dares to utter.

Even where autocratic leaders have not slid into dictatorship, but do use a commanding approach, the key weak spot is implementation. Autocratic leaders might be good at making quick decisions, but they are notoriously poor at getting quick results. Partially this is due to the lackluster support by people in the organization who don't feel ownership of the decision. But it is also due to a lack of understanding of the decision by people in the organization who have not been involved in the thinking, don't know the underlying assumptions and don't know how to interpret the decision in the light of their own situation. Implementation is not simply "doing," but starts with translating the decision into specific actions and clarifying who should carry out which action when and to which effect. But if people don't have a clear understanding of the "language of the decision," translations will be haphazard and plenty of misinterpretations made that only show up when things have gone awry. Therefore, autocratic leaders must beware of the "illusion of speed" – fast decisions are generally irrelevant; it is fast understanding, acceptance and action that bring tangible results.

Qualities and pitfalls of the democratic leadership style

> *One of the best ways to persuade others is with your ears – by listening to them.*
> Dean Rusk (1909–1994)
> American Secretary of State

Fast and successful implementation based on people's understanding and acceptance of a decision is in fact the key quality of the democratic leadership style. By taking all key stakeholders involved in implementation along through the phases of identification, interpretation and formulation, democratic leaders actually shorten the overall decision-making cycle – during implementation they win back all of the time "lost" in the first three phases. So, Adrian might not be losing time at all, but investing his time wisely in building a supported consensus. By the way, note that democratic leaders don't involve everybody in the organization on every decision that needs to be made. That would be truly inefficient. On the contrary, the rule of thumb is "they who implement the plan, must make the plan." This ensures that only stakeholders impacted by a decision and whose input is needed to formulate a good decision are asked to participate.

As these stakeholders have all participated in the analysis of the issues, generation of potential solutions and choice of the best option, they will have shaped a joint understanding of why a certain decision is required and which tough trade-offs were necessarily made. Such a shared understanding and conviction about what needs to be done supports effective implementation in many ways. It strengthens commitment and a sense of team spirit, encouraging people to work together to achieve the shared objective and helping people to accept sacrifices that are part of the solution. At the same time, each stakeholder will know how to translate the decision into actions within their own area. Even when things change a bit during implementation, due to shifting external circumstances or an incorrect assumption, the stakeholders will be able to change along much more easily, because they understand the thinking behind the decision and can reinterpret what needs to be done under the slightly different circumstances. And if implementation gets really difficult, people will be less inclined to give up, as they own the decision and know how important it is.

Besides stimulating people to be more committed, adaptable and resilient during implementation, the democratic leadership style also encourages people to be more responsible, open-minded and creative during formulation. The very fact that democratic leaders refuse to impose a decision, or allow one group of stakeholders to impose their will on the others, means that stakeholders must step up, participate in the decision-making process and take responsibility for the joint result. Successful democratic leaders don't allow particular stakeholders to distance themselves from the rest of the organization and withdraw into their silo – they get a say in the joint decision-making, but have to commit to implementing what is eventually agreed on. By facilitating real dialogue between all the stakeholders and valuing their different angles, ideas and suggestions, democratic leaders foster open-mindedness and a rich exchange of views, leading to faster organizational learning and a more robust understanding of the problems and possibilities facing the organization. Moreover, by pushing consensus, democratic leaders encourage all participants to creatively search for win-win decisions, instead of easier win-lose ones.

The real genius of the democratic leadership style is that it hardly looks like leadership, because the participants seem to be doing all the work. The stakeholders are shaping the decisions themselves. The "only thing" the leader is doing is a bit of process facilitation. Of course, in reality this molding task is hard work – bringing people into dialogue with one another, setting the rules of engagement, pressuring all to fully participate, stimulating mutual trust, bridging the misunderstandings, managing conflict, encouraging creative reframing of issues, pushing for consensus building and demanding commitment to the result. Yet, if all goes well, in the end the participants will predominantly have a sense of "we did it ourselves"[11] and feel that the decision is theirs.

Still, democratic leaders too have plenty of pitfalls lying in wait. Actually, the very roots of the term democratic already reveal the key peril of this leadership style – in ancient Greece democracy meant less "rule of the people" than "rule of the mob." To many Greeks, democracy was the frightening situation where the unsophisticated rabble of society determined which decisions were made. Instead of the wise having the power to make the choices, the uneducated masses would be in charge of determining what should be done next. To a certain extent, this is also the key risk of the democratic leadership style, namely that decisions will be the outcome of irrational interactions and/or destructive infighting between the stakeholders. Democratic leaders might want to guide a constructive consensus-molding process, but this assumes that the participants have the ability to listen to each other, discuss points of view, weigh arguments and formulate alternative approaches, all the while guided by rational reasoning and problem-solving thinking. But groups of people are notoriously irrational in many ways – they grow their own culture of do's and don'ts, hold grudges, are strongly biased and jump to conclusions, to name just a few. Researchers have found that group decisions are often worse than individual ones, and frequently more inconsistent.[12]

Moreover, if no one is in command of decision-taking, a power struggle will quickly emerge to determine who will really call the shots. In the power vacuum created by the democratic leader's unwillingness to take decisions, others will fight to impose their will on the organization. This can result in the rise of a new autocratic leader right under the nose of the ineffectual democratic leader, but it can also descend into a "failed state" form of factionalism, where ongoing turf wars and decision-making stalemates are commonplace.

Even without letting the organization slide into anarchy, democratic leaders can easily be ineffective at getting people to make decisions together. It is difficult to get people to really open-mindedly listen to each other and take responsibility for finding a win-win solution. A democratic leader can try to push and pull stakeholders to do so, but in the end many people will stick to their own views and try to get it their way. Actually, many people will figure out that being stubborn and unreasonable is a good negotiation tactic, despite all of the democratic leader's efforts to bridge differences. Moreover, winning the "political game" will involve forming alliances against opposing stakeholders and undermining their credibility, to name just two of the many ploys available to the scheming person. If democratic leaders are not strict on the process and put up with such unwanted behavior, soon others will see themselves forced to engage in the same type of maneuvering. It is not for nothing that the tongue-in-cheek definition of organizational culture is "the worst type of behavior that a leader is willing to tolerate."

Yet others will just be frustrated that "the organization is so political" and resolve to keep their distance, hoping that if they don't get involved they can avoid the

Qualities of Autocratic Leadership Style	Qualities of Democratic Leadership Style
1. Takes personal responsibility to decide	1. Shares joint responsibility to decide
2. Makes coherent decisions	2. Molds consensus decisions
3. Imposes own will on the group	3. Shapes common will with the group
4. Leverages leader's intelligence	4. Leverages collective intelligence
5. Cuts through disagreements	5. Bridges disagreements
6. Sets clear direction	6. Sets accepted direction
7. Gets fast decisions	7. Gets fast implementation
8. Establishes clear decision accountability	8. Provokes people to take decision ownership
9. Makes taking distinctive decisions easier	9. Builds organizational agility and resilience
10. Makes taking unpopular decisions easier	10. Focuses on making win-win decisions
Pitfalls of Autocratic Leadership Style	**Pitfalls of Democratic Leadership Style**
1. Authoritarianism: Rule of the tyrant	1. Anarchy: Rule of the mob
2. Unwillingness to listen to others	2. Inability to get people to listen to each other
3. Convinced of own opinion	3. Unconvincing in bridging different opinions
4. Too dictatorial: Obey my commands	4. Too diplomatic: Let's accept a weak compromise
5. Promotes yes-men	5. Incapable of stopping political infighting
6. Pushes out dissenters	6. Allows dissenters to sabotage decision-making
7. People become fearful and leave	7. People become frustrated and withdraw
8. Implementation half-hearted and slow	8. Formulation half-hearted and slow
9. People lack commitment: Say yes, but do no	9. People lack direction: No clear decisions taken
10. Makes taking incorrect decisions easier	10. Makes taking inconsistent decisions easier

Figure 6.4 Qualities and pitfalls of the autocratic and democratic leadership styles

consequences of any decisions made. So, with some stakeholders drifting off, others plotting to gain more power and no one really interested in shaping a consensus, democratic leaders can still attempt to bring the parties together, but the joint decision is more likely to be a weak compromise than a win-win solution. But often even this vague middle ground will be sabotaged by one of the stakeholders, leading to prolonged indecision and further drifting without a clear direction.

Over time the pattern of decisions that emerges out of this free-wrestling approach to decision-making will be inconsistent at best – the haphazard outcome of constantly changing coalitions and shifting power struggles. Sometimes the inept democratic leader overseeing this ongoing melee truly believes that this is the best process possible given "organizational realities," but more often than not such "leaders" are sadly aware that they simply miss the essential process facilitation skills to pull off such a difficult style of leadership.

Profiling your leadership style

> *Autocracies may survive for intermittent periods with populations of "yes men," but democracies need a perennially renewed supply of "know men."*
>
> Robert Gordon Sproul (1891–1975)
> American academic

Have you already figured out what Adrian should do? Should he continue going down the democratic leadership route, as Margaret is urging him to do?

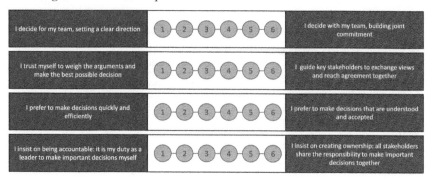

Figure 6.5 Profiling your leadership style: Organizational decision-making

Or do you suspect that he is falling into the pitfalls of the democratic style, with all stakeholders only defending their own political interests, with little motivation to build a consensus around a renewed business model? Should he in that case switch to the autocratic leadership style to force a decision on his management team, quickly, clearly and decisively? Or will that backfire by triggering foot-dragging and sabotage during implementation? And does Adrian even know what the best decision is? As in the previous chapters, there is obviously not one right answer, so you might want to read what other people think and maybe add your own insights to the discussion (again at www.lea dership-agility.com).

At the same time, you have probably recognized some of your own behavior and some of the pitfalls you have had the displeasure of seeing up close. Although almost everyone will use both styles occasionally, particularly for different types of situations, have you determined your default style? As before, in Figure 6.5 there is a short profiling tool to assist you in your assessment.

Do you sense that one or both of these two styles needs further development to be truly flexible? And do you think you can quickly switch between them and make new combinations? Hold on to your answer, as we will get back to boosting your leadership agility in Chapter 13 (or just flexibly jump there now).

Notes

1 In many publications, Henry Mintzberg has made the point that managers are overly focused on the formulation phase, as opposed to the implementation phase. Focusing on strategic decision-making he argues that people call the outcome of the formulation phase "strategy," while the outcome of the implementation phase is called "performance." He suggests calling the first "intended strategy" and the second "realized strategy," emphasizing that a large part of the actual decision-making happens along the way during the implementation phase. See Mintzberg, H. (1994), *The Rise and Fall of Strategic Planning*, Englewood Cliffs: Prentice Hall.

2 The term "sense-making" was first introduced by Karl Weick, see Weick, K.E. (1979), *The Social Psychology of Organizing*, New York: Random House.

3 The distinction between autocratic and democratic leadership styles was first intro-duced into the scientific literature in: Lewin, K., Lippitt, R. and White, R.K. (1939), "Patterns of Aggressive Behavior in Experimentally Created 'Social Climates,'" *The Journal of Social Psychology*, Vol. 10, No. 2, pp. 269–299. These terms have been commonly used since then, although the autocratic style has sometimes been labeled authoritarian and the democratic style has sometimes been called participative.

4 This distinction between tame and wicked problems was first introduced by Horst Rittel and Max Webber. See Rittel, H. and Webber. M. (1973), "Dilemmas in a General Theory of Planning," *Policy Sciences*, Vol. 4, No. 2, pp. 155–169.

5 If all team members step up and decide together, they will be leading and following each other, making them all democratic leaders. Some authors refer to this situation as shared leadership or collective leadership. See Pearce, C. and Conger, J. (eds.) (2003), *Shared Leadership: Reframing the Hows and Whys of Leadership*, Thousand Oaks: Sage.

6 This refers to the distinction between parent, adult and child behavior, as described in Transactional Analysis. For the original model see Berne, E. (1964), *Games People Play*, New York: Grove Press.

7 This is the title of a well-known book by James Surowiecki, in which he argues that large numbers of individual decision-makers are often better at making predictions and estimations than individual experts. See Surowiecki, J. (2004), *The Wisdom of Crowds: Why the Many Are Smarter Than the Few and How Collective Wisdom Shapes Business, Economies, Societies and Nations*, New York: Doubleday.

8 Note that we don't mention "stakeholder satisfaction" here as a quality of the autocratic leadership style, but neither do we mention it as a quality of the demo-cratic leadership style. The reason is that research has been rather inconclusive about which style people like best. In an insight overview of 50 years of research on the topic, Foel, Driskell, Mullen and Salas conclude that various research findings reach opposite conclusions, largely because the circumstances of each decision-making situation are different. Interestingly the authors of this article do find a strong bias towards the democratic leadership style in many psychology textbooks, leaving out research findings that indicate that autocratic leadership sometimes leads to higher satisfaction among group members. See Foels, R., Driskell, J.E., Mullen, B. and Salas, E. (2000), "The Effects of Democratic Leadership on Group Member Satis-faction and Integration," *Small Group Research*, Vol. 31, No. 6, pp. 676–701.

9 This famous quote is from Lord Acton (1834–1902), British politician and writer.

10 We speak of cognitive dissonance to describe the discomfort felt by people who hold two or more inconsistent ideas in their mind at the same time. A common situation is where a person hears new information that does not fit with their existing mental map ("cognitive structures"). Much research has been done into their reaction to this form of cognitive dissonance and it is found that people over-whelmingly tend to discard non-matching information instead of altering their mental maps. In a similar fashion, they tend to actively select information sources that confirm their existing mental map, rather than information that calls their beliefs into question. For a good overview see Cooper, J. (2007), *Cognitive Dissonance: Fifty Years of a Classic Theory*, London: Sage.

11 This is a wink to ancient Chinese philosopher Lao-Tsu, who famously wrote: "To lead people, walk beside them … As for the best leaders, the people do not notice their existence. The next best, the people honor and praise. The next, the people fear; and the next, the people hate … When the best leader's work is done the people say, 'We did it ourselves!'"

12 Two recent books reviewing the irrationality of group decision-making are: Shepsle, K.A. (2010), *Analyzing Politics: Rationality, Behavior and Institutions*, New York: W. W. Norton & Company; and Munger, M.C. and Munger, K.M. (2015), *Choosing in Groups: Analytical Politics Revisited*, New York: Cambridge University Press.

Part IV
Strategic leadership

7 Strategic goal-setting
The paradox of idealism and realism

The management team was gridlocked and precious time was ticking away. The annual Global Management Summit, where the management team was scheduled to unveil its new digital strategy, was going to be held in Vienna in less than a week, but the team members were still in disagreement on what to present. Worse, they were fundamentally at odds about the key message. Hans, the new head of Digital Media, had put together an awe-inspiring presentation on the future of the media industry that they were in. It identified how industry after industry had been hit by digitalization and how the new rules of the game were still unfolding. In the media industry, books had been slammed, newspapers were in a tail spin and TV felt the online world nipping at its heels. Yet the changes were just as much opportunity as threat, was the point Hans wanted to make. Now was the moment for the company to reinvent itself and grab the initiative. It was time for all business units to throw off their analogue shackles and venture into the digital realm. The strategy that Hans championed was to seek cross-media opportunities, leveraging existing content and brands towards the digital world. Even more importantly, it was his vision to sell advertising space across these different media channels as one package to advertisers.

Karin, in charge of the Magazines unit, and Gerard, head of Television, were in total agreement with Hans, emphasizing how this new direction would unleash enormous creativity in their units. However, Ben in Books and Carla in Newspapers sided with the outspoken CFO, Walter, who bluntly referred to Hans's presentation as "infotainment" and "daydreaming." In his view, Hans had failed to come up with a tangible digital strategy and there was little to present at the Global Management Summit besides "we don't really know." Instead of being inspired, Walter was concerned that the audience would be disoriented by the lack of clarity and disillusioned by so little explicit direction. Moreover, as CFO, he was worried that he had no idea where to allocate capital and how to track performance. Walter concluded that the management team should either put forward a specific and realistic plan, or should postpone presenting "the digital strategy" at all. Their credibility in the organization was at stake.

All this put Esther, the CEO, in a rather difficult position. She was obviously not going to get the consensus she always preferred to build. Her team was split down the middle. As she initiated a last round of discussion, she focused the team's attention on what seemed to be the key point of disagreement – how specific would the strategic goals need to be to mobilize people to move in that direction? Hans, Karin and Gerard reiterated that getting people to move forward required giving them an inspiring "dot on the horizon" and letting them find ways of getting there. Karin spoke of a "moon shot goal" that would energize the troops, while Gerard emphasized the importance of being honest about the fact that no one has a map of the digital *Terra Incognita*. Leading people into the big unknown, Gerard stressed, would require stirring up their desire to start on a great journey however unclear the path.

While these arguments strongly appealed to Esther, she shared Walter's concern that the broad vision outlined by Hans lacked tangible choices and was difficult to put into action. She wouldn't use Walter's words like "fluffy" and "the emperor has no clothes on," but she shared his sentiment that the digital strategy wasn't really a plan that could be implemented. She, too, was anxious that people would come away from the Global Management Summit more puzzled and unclear about what to do than before. Moreover, she was troubled by what the responses would be of other stakeholders, such as the press, financial analysts and of course shareholders.

To break the impasse, she decided to call her team together one more time, but now not in the boardroom, but over dinner in her favorite restaurant. As she parked her car and considered whether to take the fantastic saltimbocca again, her mind turned back to the two issues that she needed to resolve that evening. She needed to determine how the decision-making would take place and what the decision would be – to go with a more broad and aspiring strategic goal, or a more specific and implementable one.

The task of strategic goal-setting

> *To accomplish great things, we must not only act, but also dream, not only plan, but also believe.*
>
> Anatole France (1844–1924)
> French poet, journalist and novelist

"Where are we going?" is a question that concerns everyone in the organization. People want to know the direction in which to move. They want to understand where the organization is headed and how it will change to remain relevant. They want to have a sense of the organization's ambition to make an impact and the type of performance at which the organization wants to excel. Often they want to grasp how the organization will continue to create value, remain competitive against rivals and stay financially viable. With these strategic goals set, a course of action can be determined and the voyage can begin.

Yet, setting strategic goals is inherently challenging, as the media management team experienced, because environments and organizations are constantly in flux. As people look at the world surrounding their organization, they witness an environment that is rapidly changing in unpredictable ways, where it is difficult to see what influences what. They face a world that is VUCA – volatile, uncertain, complex and ambiguous.[1] Some trends sweep the globe, while other trends don't make it to another city. Breakthroughs often come from nowhere, while existing trends unexpectedly reverse. New behaviors evolve in seemingly erratic ways, while promising business model innovations turn out to be duds. In general, making long-term market forecasts is not more successful than doing the same for the weather.

Inside the organization the predictability of developments is not much higher. New people come in with different ideas, values, competences and experiences, changing the constellation of teams. Power shifts to different managers, while others are forced out, and new networks and coalitions are forged. Organizational crises, as well as successes, influence cooperation across units and the unfolding of the organizational culture. New business processes are unexpectedly adopted by local initiative, while other capabilities seem impossible to learn.

The inherent external and internal unpredictability is often aggravated by the strategic desire to be disruptive.[2] Strategists know that organizational success might require doing more than adapting to market developments – organizations might need to "break the rules," instead of playing by them. Organizations might want to "make the waves" instead of catching existing ones. To a certain extent, this means creating a new outside world and reshaping the organization into something that doesn't exist yet. This doesn't make the question "where are we going?" very much easier to answer.

In all of this uncertainty, people look to leaders for direction. Not that leaders need to come up with the strategic goals themselves, but they must make sure they are set. Suggestions for the strategic goals can come from employees, partners, consultants and the leaders themselves, and then decided upon autocratically or democratically, as discussed in the previous chapter. What strategic leadership is about is communicating the strategic goals in a way that gives people a sense of direction and entices them to move. Strategic leadership is about pointing the way forward and winning the hearts and minds of people to embrace the direction and embark on the journey.

It is not only a challenge for leaders to determine *what* the strategic goals should be, but also *how specific* they need to be to give people a sense of direction and get them engaged. This is the issue faced by Esther, who has half of her management team asking for a dot on the horizon, while the other half seems to be insisting on detailed GPS coordinates. Strategic goals can vary from extremely broad to particularly specific and leaders must decide what level of detail to focus on.

This continuum from broadly defined to specifically detailed strategies is illustrated in Figure 7.1, using Meyer's levels of strategy specificity.[3] At the highest level of abstraction, leaders can opt to only outline a *strategic vision*. This rough sketch of the desired future state of the organization sets a beacon people can use to orient themselves, yet leaves most of the particulars open to be filled in along the way. A strategic vision can be communicated using words – sometimes

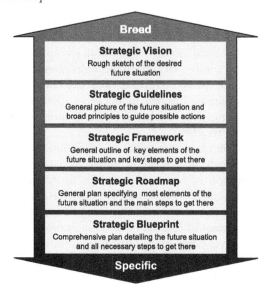

Figure 7.1 Levels of strategy specificity

many, often only a few – but also via pictures, symbols and metaphors. Always, a vision sets a *direction* without giving *directions*.

Leaders can make the vision a bit more tangible by identifying a few key principles that need to be adhered to in order to realize the vision ("leverage content and brands across media" and "go for cross-media advertising"). These *strategic guidelines* offer direction by setting boundaries around what is desirable, still without determining in detail what needs to be done. Guidelines are often communicated as "rules," "pillars," "fundamentals" or "thrusts," all providing general headings for the voyage, but not providing a map.

Leaders can go a step further in detailing the strategy by specifying the core objectives and deciding on the main initiatives that need to be taken to realize these objectives. Such a *strategic framework* provides the general outline of the strategy, to be further filled in along the way. If the strategic vision is the "story idea" and strategic guidelines are the "story line," then the strategic framework is the "story plot" – the whole narrative is there schematically, but it hasn't been written up into a full-blown book yet. Or if you prefer movies, a strategic framework can be compared to a film scenario, that can be pitched to the studios to get them engaged.

Yet studio executives might want to see a more detailed script if they are to be swayed. The same is true in organizations, where people might want to have tangible targets and know which roles to play and actions to take. Therefore, leaders can specify the strategy even further, drawing up a *strategic roadmap*, in which goals and activities are planned in more detail. Typical of strategic roadmaps is that actions and milestones are clearly defined and assigned to specific departments or teams. This was what Esther's CFO, Walter, was looking for: clear choices, investment plans, specified action plans and clear milestones with which to measure progress and performance.

At the most detailed level, leaders can take away almost all room for uncertainty about the direction in which to move by providing a comprehensive plan specifying all targets, activities and performance measures. Such a *strategic blueprint* gives clarity to everyone in the organization, all the way to the individual level. As with a building blueprint, such a meticulous plan need not be a straightjacket if it is interpreted and adapted along the way, as circumstances require. But if one part changes, the blueprint will make clear which other parts of the strategy will be impacted and might need to be adapted as well.

So, where along this continuum should leaders set their strategic goals? As before, there is a perplexing paradox at the heart of the matter, making the answer to this question even more challenging than it first seems.

The paradox of idealism and realism

> *He who wants to lead people must be a pragmatist and a realist. But he has to speak the language of the idealist and the visionary.*
>
> Eric Hoffer (1902–1983)
> American writer and philosopher

Setting strategically appropriate goals for an organization is difficult enough in itself, but leaders have the additional challenge that strategic goals serve two very different psychological needs of followers. These two needs, the desire for *idealism* and *realism*, are very different, to the extent of being conflicting opposites.

Idealism is about aspiring to something more, higher, better. It is about picturing the perfect and holding up this ideal as a guiding light. Idealism is not about what is, but what could be – what should be! It is about not accepting the messy present and striving to get closer and closer to the very best imaginable. Many people have an idealist bent, looking beyond the current situation to something wonderful that could be. They are inspired by being on a journey to achieve something fantastic, not something ordinary or easy. They get enthusiastic by the prospect of getting the organization to rise above what it currently is capable of doing, to reach a higher level.

To meet the desire for idealism, leaders need to set strategic goals that are ambitious and stretching, almost unimaginable. They need to offer a compelling vision of an attractive future that will meet people's need to embrace a dream. They need to offer a quest that will challenge people to rise to the occasion. By providing an idealistic goal, leaders can light a fire that mobilizes the entire organization to work hard over an extended period of time.

Realism, on the other hand, is about being sensible and practical. It is about seeing things as they truly are and setting targets that are achievable. Realism is not about what *should* be, but what *can* be. It is about facing the brutal facts and making a balanced estimation of what is reasonably possible. Many people have a desire for levelheaded realism, preferring to work towards attainable goals, instead of overreaching in a vain pursuit of some unsubstantiated dream. They are inspired by being on a journey that gets results, not by being on "mission impossible." They like to have the confidence that the organization will only engage in activities it is capable of doing and that the risks will be manageable. And they want to know that they personally will be able to live up to expectations.

To meet the desire for realism, leaders need to set strategic goals that are well-considered and doable. They need to offer a pragmatic plan of a feasible future that will meet people's need to know with reasonable certainty that the goals will be achieved. They need to propose rather detailed steps to show what needs to be done and that it can be done. By providing such a realistic plan, leaders can instill confidence in the organization that it is in control of its future, thereby mobilizing the entire organization to work hard over an extended period of time.

However, strategic goals that are ambitious and stretching will not score high on feasibility and practicality, and vice versa. Bullish objectives that stimulate people to rise above themselves don't fit well with the desire to have specific and attainable aims. This tension between inspirational and feasible strategic goals is the *paradox of idealism and realism*. Idealism and realism are conflicting psychological requirements of followers, making it complex to meet both demands simultaneously.

At the same time, the leadership competences and mindset needed to engage people on the basis of idealistic goals are very different than those needed to lead using realistic goals. Leaders capable of getting people to think big and stretch themselves often have different skills, routines, approaches and ways of thinking than leaders capable of getting people to be disciplined and results-oriented. For this reason, too, there is a tension between idealism and realism. The consequence is that leaders tend to emphasize one over the other, which strongly colors their strategic leadership style.

The visionary leadership style

> *Ideals are like stars: You will not succeed in touching them with your hands, but like the seafaring man on the desert of waters, you chose them as your guides, and following them, you reach your destiny.*
>
> Carl Schurz (1829–1906)
> German-American statesman and general

Leaders leaning over to the side of idealism have a *visionary leadership style*, as they outline an inspirational and challenging long-term vision, far beyond the organization's current capabilities. We like to speak of a BOLD vision – broad, optimistic, long term and daring. Such a strategic vision generally sketches a picture of a desirable future, but also places the organization's development in the broader context of fundamental trends in the market and society.

Having set a "big hairy audacious goal"[4] that encourages people to think big, visionary leaders tend to give plenty of leeway to followers to find innovative ways of making it happen. It is not the visionary leader's intention to provide a specific blueprint of the future, but rather to trigger other team members to co-create the next steps. As an ideal, a strategic vision is not meant to be marching orders, but a guiding light, offering a general direction, not a concrete plan. This allows for creative people to feel inspired to come up with various initiatives and potential solutions, instead of feeling forced into an implementation straightjacket. It also promotes followers to consider themselves co-owners of the organization's future, taking responsibility to contribute to shaping developments and actions.

John F. Kennedy is probably the most celebrated example of this leadership style, particularly with regard to his "man on the moon" vision. By setting the daring strategic goal of sending a mission to the moon before the end of the decade, he defined a shared quest for all people within NASA (and often beyond the organization's borders) and unleashed their creativity to come up with ways of making it happen. In the same vein, Martin Luther King's famous "I have a dream" speech projected a vision of an almost unimaginable future, with little tangibility about how his followers should go about realizing this dream. Yet the vision itself inspired a whole generation to think big and to take steps, large and small, to get closer and closer to King's ideal.

These legendary examples might give the impression that visionary leaders can only be found among the ranks of senior statesmen and CEOs. Yet ideals can be found everywhere and so can people leading on the basis of these ideals. School girl Malala Yousafzai didn't have a plan how she was going to improve education for females in her native Pakistan, but her vision has motivated many people to take initiatives to improve learning opportunities for women across the region. Visionary leaders can be found in every type of organization and at every level – the business unit manager whose vision is to expand globally, the quality manager whose vision is to do away with the quality department, and digital chief Hans whose vision is to build cross-media capabilities. They might not be as well-known as Kennedy and King, but their style of setting a stretching vision and inviting others to help co-create the future is the same. And how about start-ups, which often don't have realistic business plans, but rather wild aspirations to disrupt the industry they are in. They get people to sign up for a job or to finance their ideas, not because the venture is predictable and controlled, but because it is challenging and a potential breakthrough.

It should be noted that being a visionary leader is quite different than being a visionary. Many visionaries have no intention to lead. They have beliefs about the long-term future, with regard to society, technology, the economy or the environment, and they wish to share these views or even convince others that they are right. However, being a visionary leader is not about winning the argument in itself, but about inspiring others to act. A visionary *sees*, but to be a visionary leader one needs to *mobilize* using this vision.

The pragmatic leadership style

> *An idealist believes the short run doesn't count. A cynic believes the long run doesn't matter.*
> *A realist believes that what is done or left undone in the short run determines the long run.*
> Sydney J. Harris (1917–1986)
> American journalist

Leaders emphasizing realism over idealism have a *pragmatic leadership style*, as they make clear to others what can be, and needs to be, done. They set targets that are practical and implementable. Their goals are SMART – specific, measurable, achievable, realistic and time-bound – focusing on the period for which they can plan. Having determined such tangible objectives, they tend to work with their teams to detail actions, specify the required resources and set key performance indicators to monitor implementation progress.

Being realists, pragmatic leaders prefer to avoid sweeping generalities and vague sketches of future bliss. Instead, they favor setting down-to-earth strategic goals that give people solid and feasible aims to focus on. They take the responsibility of working out their strategy into a tangible strategic roadmap or blueprint, giving people clarity on what the organization needs to do and what is expected of each individual. By detailing their strategy, pragmatic leaders accept the challenge of thinking through the logic and implementability of their plans. At the same time, such realistic plans make it easier to coordinate activities and ensure consistency across people and units. And with clear targets and actions, it becomes easier to measure progress over time and track performance.

Let it be clear that pragmatic leaders can also have a vision. It is not as if they are shortsighted and incapable of looking further into the future. They, too, can have a big picture view of the general direction in which they want to head. However, they subsequently translate their broad strategic vision into a more specific strategic plan and use this to give people tangible direction and to mobilize them to achieve results.

While visionary leaders tend to grab the headlines with their lofty words about the brave new world they envision, pragmatic leaders tend to be more low key. They don't set surprisingly overambitious goals that get people talking. Understanding their strategic plans requires a bit more effort than listening to catchy vision statements. And they often speak more to the head than the heart – their presentations are more like lectures than sermons.[5] So, it shouldn't be surprising that there are more famous visionary leaders than well-known pragmatic ones. But don't let appearances fool you, pragmatic leaders are everywhere.

More worrying is that some people don't see pragmatic leaders as actual leaders, but "merely as managers." The implicit assumption is that leaders are always idealistic visionaries, somewhat above simple mortals. As soon as someone is a more down-to-earth realist, somewhat like a normal person, they no longer deserve the honorary title "leader." This misconception goes back to the stereotype of the strategic leader as prophet (see Chapter 2). Indeed, visionary leaders are closer to this stereotype than pragmatic ones, letting them seemingly qualify more readily as "true leaders." But labeling pragmatic leaders as "managers" is not only incorrect, but also counterproductive, as it suggests that the pragmatic leadership style is second rate. It implies that the visionary leadership style is superior – and therefore more desirable – while the pragmatic style is employed by those who are incapable of moving up to the visionary style. Of course, this is an unfair bias. The two styles are very different (see Table 7.1),

Table 7.1 Differences between the visionary and pragmatic leadership styles

	Visionary Leadership Style	*Pragmatic Leadership Style*
Emphasis on	Idealism over realism	Realism over idealism
Motivating people by	Outlining inspiring vision	Setting specific targets
Goals should be	Broadly defined and stretching	Narrowly defined and feasible
Orientation towards	Unlocking potential	Doing the possible
Basic attitude	Think big	Get it done
Core quality	Creating a desire	Creating certainty
Intended impact	Accomplishing the impossible	Achieving predictable results
Underlying conviction	Stretch brings out the best	Feasibility brings out the best
Guiding principle/motto	I have a dream!	Keep your feet on the ground
Preferred tools	Presenting a BOLD vision	Using SMART targets

but equal. That is, they both have their qualities and pitfalls, as will be explored in the next section.

Qualities and pitfalls of the visionary leadership style

> *Idealism increases in direct proportion to one's distance from the problem.*
>
> John Galsworthy (1867–1933)
> English author

When it comes to the qualities of the visionary leadership style, they more or less line up with the BOLD abbreviation. The first letter stands for *broad* and indeed this style is excellent at giving people an overview of the bigger picture and indicating how their actions will contribute to the overall direction. Instead of getting bogged down in detail and diluting the inspirational message with distractive clutter, the visionary leadership style focuses on presenting a helicopter view of the landscape and the broad strokes of the route forward. By zooming out and sticking to the key "dot on the horizon" message, visionary leaders can often be much clearer than leaders who dwell on details.

The second letter stands for *optimistic* and indeed this style is well-suited to get people to think in possibilities instead of them thinking in probabilities. Leaders using the visionary leadership style tend to paint a positive picture of the future, sketching an attractive ideal for people to buy into. They entice people to look forward to what will come, instilling them with confidence that it will all be worthwhile. At the same time, visionary leaders generally gloss over some of the challenges and risks, preferring to focus on the upside potential, to avoid people getting cold feet. An additional advantage of this optimistic dreaming about a shared future is that it also strengthens a group's sense of mission, while helping to build team spirit and a strong will to succeed together. Joint dreaming is often more powerful than formulating individual ambitions.

The third letter stands for *long term* and indeed this style gets people to think further ahead, to see the direction in which it is all going. Instead of getting caught up in detailed analyses of the near future, visionary leaders skip over the nitty-gritty to look deeper into the future, helping to give people a reassuring view that there is a viable long-term outlook. At the same time, this peek into what's in store can also trigger people's imagination and stimulate them to think ahead and start to make changes early.

Last but not least, the fourth letter stands for *daring* and indeed this style is good at provoking courageous stretch objectives and arousing a sense of adventure. It is great at stimulating people by the very challenge of pursuing something big – aspiration triggers inspiration. Setting an ambition beyond the current capabilities of the organization can create a positive type of stress, leading to a "runner's high." Being pushed out of one's comfort zone can be motivating and spark creativity to come up with novel solutions. This can be especially important in situations where the leader doesn't have all the answers – can't have all the answers – and needs people in the organization to be innovative and co-create the future. For relatively capable and confident people, this type of involvement in shaping the organizational direction and this level of stretch is more than acceptable, it is desirable.

Yet the visionary leader can easily mess up. Formulating a crisp and appealing vision is much more difficult than outlining a fuzzy and dull one. A vague vision can leave people confused or with different perceptions of what is intended, leading to a standstill or people going off in different directions. A boring vision can leave people apathetic or even sap their energy. The visionary leader can also totally overshoot, with a vision that is literally unbelievable – a pie in the sky – leaving people disoriented and dismayed, clueless on how to proceed. Or the vision can be megalomaniacal, encouraging people to pursue far-fetched objectives, take high-risk actions and make dangerous investments.

Even when the vision is spot on and rallies the troops, events can go entirely amiss if the visionary leader doesn't ensure follow-up. If people are excited and anticipate great leaps forward, but are unsure of what to do, they might hang back and wait for more concrete actions to be announced. They might freeze at the daunting enormity of the challenge presented, not knowing how to continue. Where people do take steps, it might be difficult to verify whether these actions really contribute to realizing the vision. Before you know it, with a little bit of cosmetics, any action can be made to fit with the vision, letting people go off to do their own thing.

Qualities and pitfalls of the pragmatic leadership style

> *Action is the last resource of those who know not how to dream.*
> Oscar Wilde (1854–1900)
> Irish playwright, writer and poet

While the qualities of the visionary leadership style are aligned with the abbreviation BOLD, in the same manner the qualities of the pragmatic leadership style fit tightly with the abbreviation SMART. The first letter stands for *specific* and indeed this style is excellent at providing people with clarity around the detailed goals being pursued and the necessary actions to be taken. Pragmatic leaders help people to know what to do. By making strategy concrete and actionable, pragmatic leaders help people to get moving and achieve results. At the same time, concrete plans also make it easier to align individuals and units around shared objectives and activities.

The second letter stands for *measurable* and indeed this style is good at translating the tangible strategic activities into assessable actions and intended results. As a highly specified strategy can be made measurable, this makes it possible to follow progress and performance, which in turn aids course corrections and ongoing improvements. Tracking implementation also supports people's discipline to achieve their targets, while enabling the leader to hold people accountable for their efforts and results.

The third letter stands for *attainable* and indeed this style is strong at setting goals that people feel they can realize. Instead of pursuing stressful stretch goals, that few in the organization believe are attainable, pragmatic leaders prefer to pursue achievable goals that will instill confidence in people that success is attainable. If a strategic plan is feasible given the capabilities of the organization and the external conditions, people will embrace it and feel engaged. This engagement in turn increases the chance of success, creating a virtuous cycle.

The fourth letter stands for *realistic* and indeed this style has the quality of setting goals based on a levelheaded assessment of the circumstances. Instead of formulating strategic goals on the basis of misplaced optimism, a disregard for the challenges and blindness to the inherent risks, pragmatic leaders take a practical and cautious approach to determining their strategic objectives. They avoid the feel-good fluffiness of dreams, preferring to take a more grounded and factual view of the situation and to set goals that are based on a realistic assessment of what is possible and likely. This sensible approach often gives people a more convincing picture of what to expect, leading to a higher confidence in the leader.

And last but not least, the fifth letter stands for *time-bound* and indeed this style is good at setting goals with clear "due dates." Instead of taking a long-term perspective without any fixed timescale for the required actions, pragmatic leaders translate long-term objectives into shorter-term goals, so that a schedule of milestones can be determined. With such a detailed blueprint, based on clear steps within clear time frames, everyone within the organization will know when what is due and will be able to more easily coordinate activities with one another.

However, the pragmatic leader can easily mess up as well. There are thousands of ways to make bad plans. Formulating a specific and actionable strategic plan is much more difficult than producing a shortsighted and bureaucratic one. Many pragmatic leaders stumble into the gaping pitfall of being ultra-pragmatic and ignoring strategy altogether, focusing on drawing up short-term operational plans. Not willing to be bothered with the complexities of looking further ahead, they shorten their horizon to the next months, weeks or days, going for the quick fix. This can generate much activity and give the satisfaction of immediate results, but can be strategically irrelevant: "rearranging of deck chairs on the Titanic." Worse, the emphasis on short-term targets might undermine long-term objectives, not only drawing away resources and attention, but actually blocking or frustrating necessary new developments. Pragmatically opting for short-term gain can readily lead to long-term pain. All this can leave people wondering where the organization is headed in the long run and whether the leader can be trusted to take them there.

Even where pragmatic leaders do throw in some strategic thinking, their plans can be so "realistic" that they lack all ambition and sense of possibility. Hiding behind their practicality, they are in fact unimaginative, compliant and timid. For fear of stretching the organization and themselves – and losing control – they can be overly cautious, preferring small steps and known terrain. For people with a sense of urgency to change, an overly pragmatic leader can seem part of the problem, not part of the solution. Such a meek pragmatist will not take the initiative to grab opportunities and will likely slow down necessary reforms, so many people will be unwilling to follow such an uninspiring person.

Pragmatic leaders' liking of clarity and control can also derail into overly specific planning. Many totally overdo the detailing of plans, bombarding people with meticulous instructions and leaving little room to do anything else

Qualities of Visionary Leadership Style	Qualities of Pragmatic Leadership Style
1. Outlines long term direction	1. Clarifies short term actions
2. Sensitizes people to the bigger picture	2. Focuses people on the next steps
3. Rallies team around a shared ideal	3. Rallies team around realistic goals
4. Instills confidence in tomorrow's success	4. Instills confidence in achieving today's targets
5. Stretches people to rise above themselves	5. Gives people predictability and security
6. Encourages people to think big	6. Encourages people to get things done
7. Requires team to co-create the future	7. Requires team to focus on execution
8. Leaves room for parallel initiatives	8. Makes measuring progress easy
9. Challenges people to leave their comfort zone	9. Challenges people to be disciplined
10. Inspires people to make a difference	10. Inspires people to get results

Pitfalls of Visionary Leadership Style	Pitfalls of Pragmatic Leadership Style
1. Leader seen as out-of-touch daydreamer	1. Leader seen as visionless bulldozer
2. Long-term goals lack concreteness	2. Short term goals lack perspective
3. People don't know what to do now	3. People don't see what comes next
4. Vague vision creates confusion	4. Detailed plans create bureaucracy
5. Unrealistic vision works disempowering	5. Shortsighted plans work disempowering
6. Danger of unrealistic big investments	6. Danger of overly cautious moves
7. Long-term focus hurts short-term results	7. Short term focus hurts long term position
8. Team interpret vision very differently	8. Team have little room to influence direction
9. Progress difficult to measure	9. Only implementers stay, others leave
10. People feel they are chasing a fata morgana	10. People feel like cog in the machine

Figure 7.2 Qualities and pitfalls of the visionary and pragmatic leadership styles

than implement. Some pragmatic leaders are so enthralled by the illusion of control that strategic plans bring, that they go full out in identifying exhaustive lists of key performance indicators, to measure and steer execution. All this micromanagement can leave people feeling dumbed-down and disempowered, like cogs in the corporate machine.

Profiling your leadership style

We all live under the same sky, but we don't all have the same horizon.

Konrad Adenauer (1876–1967)
Former Chancellor of West Germany

Have you already recognized your "default style?" Do you emphasize the possible or the probable? Do you shoot for the moon, or do you shoot at the target placed 50 paces away? Are you more a person of the big picture, looking to the horizon and instilling people with a yearning to set off on a great voyage? Or are you more of the detailed picture, looking to the travel itinerary and instilling people with the confidence to set off on a well-planned journey? Have you picked out some of your strengths, but also some of the pitfalls you occasionally fall in to? As before, below is a quick aid to identify the style you feel most comfortable using, so you can take along your profile to Chapter 13.

As for Esther, have you already decided what type of advice you should give her? Should she support Hans's visionary speech as a company-wide call to action, explaining to people that she doesn't have all the answers, but does know in which direction to look for them? Or should she support Walter's appeal for a pragmatic speech, pushing for more tangible programs and actions, giving people more specific and measurable tasks on which they can get started? Or do you think there is a third way, blending the two leadership styles in order to get the best of both worlds? As before, we have invited a number of senior managers to share their preferred approach on our website, www.leader ship-agility.com, but you will also find the ideas of other readers there as well.

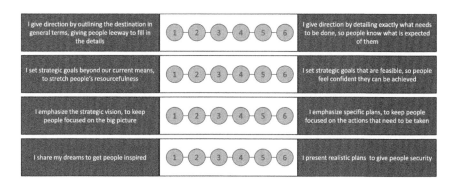

Figure 7.3 Profiling your leadership style: Strategic goal-setting

Notes

1 The abbreviation VUCA originates from the American military vocabulary. See Stiehm, J. and Townsend, N.W. (2002), *The U.S. Army War College: Military Education in a Democracy*, Philadelphia: Temple University Press, p. 6.
2 See Christensen, C. (1997), *The Innovator's Dilemma: When New Technologies Cause Great Firms to Fail*, Boston: Harvard Business School Press; Hamel, G. (2000), *Leading the Revolution: How to Thrive in Turbulent Times by Making Innovation a Way of Life*, New York: Penguin.
3 Meyer, R.J.H. (2014), "Strategy Development as Continuous Learning," in Rademakers, M. (ed.), *Corporate Universities: Driving Organizational Learning*, London: Routledge.
4 Collins, J.C. and Porras, J.I. (1994), *Built to Last: Successful Habits of Visionary Companies*, New York: Harper Business.
5 One of the few articles highlighting the pragmatic leadership styles also makes this point. See: Mumford, M.D. and Van Doorn, J.R. (2001), "The Leadership of Pragmatism: Reconsidering Franklin in the Age of Charisma," *The Leadership Quarterly*, Vol. 12, No. 3, pp. 279–309.

8 Strategic priority-setting

The paradox of exploitation and exploration

Drawing up a profile for the new commercial director was not as straightforward as Henry had initially thought. The previous director had suddenly left the company, lured away by a great offer outside the tough mail delivery business, so Henry wanted to find a replacement quickly. As CEO, Henry was acutely aware that the commercial challenges in the postal market were daunting and that the position could not be left vacant for long. Yet, in making his list of key qualifications, Henry recognized that he might be asking a lot – someone who could skate like Wayne Gretzky, jump like Michael Jordan and shoot like Lionel Messi, preferably all at the same time.

Being responsible for sales, the new commercial director would have to drive market share growth. Demand for the delivery of physical mail had been declining for years, so any increase in sales would have to be aggressively grabbed from the much larger former state-owned incumbent. In the volume business they were in, with high fixed costs and enormous economies of scale, getting more mail into the system was crucial for survival. For years they had suffered losses, as they clawed market share from their competitor, attempting to gain critical mass and now that they had finally reached break even, Henry couldn't afford to let volumes slip.

But not just any sales would do. The new commercial director would have to sell what could literally be delivered. As a company following a strategy of operational excellence, almost all variation had been squeezed out of the operational processes, focusing everyone on standardization and repeatability. The logistics machine was ultra-lean and very efficient, calibrated during years of continuous improvement. It was not the intention that a new commercial director would ruin the business model by adding complexity and unpredictability.

At the same time, Henry realized that expanding market share in a declining market was not going to be enough to keep his shareholders happy. More than once they had voiced their concern that the physical mail market was contracting faster than anticipated and that the company needed to look for new avenues of growth. Therefore, his new commercial director would also have to lead the search for new opportunities in the market place. This person would need to challenge the existing way of creating value and the current segment focus, opening up new horizons for growing the company.

More than just incrementally changing the existing business, the new commercial director would also have to be a driving force in business innovation. The company had already acquired a few disruptive start-ups, offering services such as package pickup lockers and data analytics, which the new person would also need to guide in their further development and market penetration. But besides these acquisitions, Henry had the ambition to stimulate the organization's own innovation capabilities, to be able to come up with new business models and launch these themselves. Preferably, his new commercial director would be at the forefront of these efforts, or at least a strong facilitator.

Looking again at the job profile, Henry wondered whether he had just drawn up a description of an ox that could fly. Maybe it would be better to focus on a safe pair of hands that could create stability and get things done. After all, running the existing business well and finally making money was key to survival. The company desperately needed someone who could perform, could execute. So, maybe it was best to find someone who could instill discipline in the sales team, optimize the current service offering and keep customers happy. Innovation could always be handled by a separate team.

Yet deep down Henry was concerned that a safe pair of hands could easily become a smothering pair of hands, rigidly holding on to the existing business model and suppressing all new ideas that might upset the status quo. Maybe it was better to have a bit of a rebel, willing to challenge "how things are done around here." After all, reinventing the postal business was essential to the company's long-term survival and this was not something that should be delegated to some staff department. The company desperately needed someone who could renew, could be entrepreneurial.

As Henry called in his HR director to discuss the job profile one last time, he again asked himself what had the highest strategic priority – finding someone who could run or renew the business?

The task of strategic priority-setting

> *The most successful business man is the man who holds on to the old just as long as it is good and grabs the new just as soon as it is better.*
>
> Robert P. Vanderpoel (1894–1955)
> American financial journalist

Who would have thought a generation ago that the delivery of physical mail would become a declining industry? That photograph film companies would be wiped out? Or that the encyclopedia salesman would be put out of business? All victims of the forces of creative destruction, as Schumpeter already explained back in the 1940s.[1] We can rest assured that many more will follow. Travel agencies? In steep decline. Newspapers? Fighting for their lives. Bookshops? Closing one by one. Music stores? Close to extinction.

Besides these cases of whole industries being wrecked by disruptive innovations, there are many more where new business models are upsetting the incumbents and changing the dynamics of competition. The entire retail industry is being challenged by new online players. Computer manufacturers are having to deal with cloud computing on the one hand and tablets on the other. Traditional taxi companies are seeing their livelihood threatened by apps matching potential clients to available drivers. TV channels are having to learn to compete against internet-based on-demand services. The list of rule breakers goes on and on. No industry is immune.

Knowing that competitors and potential new entrants are always on the prowl, looking to find ways of gaining the upper hand, companies have the choice of sitting still or innovating first – to disrupt or to be disrupted. They can continue to play by the rules or they can break the rules and establish a temporary strategic advantage. By exploring new possibilities and finding superior ways of creating value for customers, companies can be a step ahead of their rivals and win the favor of clients.

Even if there is no threat of someone else gaining a competitive edge through innovation – which never can be known for sure – it still makes sense for companies to look beyond their current business model and to explore opportunities for innovation, for two important reasons. First, because innovation can bring a company into a blue ocean[2] – an entirely new business area, with no, or only a few, competitors. Second, if the company does not innovate, its distinctiveness will diminish over time, becoming more and more like other companies, as characteristics that were once special become the industry norm. Not innovating, therefore, almost automatically leads to the withering of competitive advantage.

This process of losing distinctiveness we call the *commoditization* slide[3] (see Figure 8.1) and it happens in most industries. Over time, a value proposition that was once unique (a virtual monopoly) gets copied by others who see its

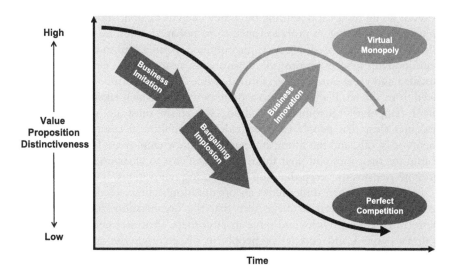

Figure 8.1 The commoditization slide

success (business imitation). As more and more similar offerings become available in the market, customers can increasingly play them off against one another (bargaining implosion). When the business is finally fully commoditized, only price competition remains (perfect competition).

The only way to avoid having to fight tooth and nail at the bottom of the commoditization slide is to introduce something innovative that will reestablish the relative distinctiveness of a company's offering. This rejuvenation can be based on some small innovations (which cumulatively can make quite a difference) or a big one, such as changing the entire business model. The company can try to be a first mover – the initiator of the innovation – or can be a close follower, quickly copying the innovation and rolling it out as one of the first.

Unfortunately for any innovator, successful renewal will only result in a temporary lowering of competitive intensity, as rivals will try to imitate useful changes, leading to a next decent down the commoditization slide. Therefore, the pressure to renew will remain. There is no such thing as a sustainable competitive advantage, only a succession of temporary ones.[4]

While innovation and imitation are at the heart of evolution in competitive industries, these forces are also felt in noncompetitive sectors, where governments and nonprofit organizations are predominant. They, too, often feel an urge to improve the effectiveness and efficiency of their organizations, either driven by their own ambition to do a better job, or pressured by external stakeholders to shape up. Often the upgrading is gradual, but sometimes they opt for big bang changes, basically reinventing the way they work. Sometimes their renewal is totally innovative, while at other moments they imitate developments led by other governments or nongovernmental organizations.

With all of this emphasis on the need for renewal, one might almost forget about the need for stability. Innovation and imitation mean upsetting current ways of doing things and learning how they need to be done differently. This is inherently disturbing, as processes need to be reshaped, often by trial and error. Plants need to be closed, products discontinued, partnerships disbanded, brands repositioned, services improved, departments restructured, new IT systems installed and cross-border teams formed, while at the same time customers still need to be served. People need to acquire new skills, which takes time, making them temporarily incompetent, while "the show must go on." Often it becomes clear that people can't upgrade their abilities, necessitating reassignments or layoffs, and the hiring and training of new employees. People become fearful for their jobs and their future, and resistance to change sets in. Yet, the pressure remains to "keep the shop open during renovations."

Too much change undermines an organization's ability to deliver. A level of stability is required to make sure that the organization can continue to perform its core activities and serve its customers. Processes need to be clear, outputs defined and competent people in place, otherwise the system will crash. Stability might sound boring, but anyone who has lived in a country with an unstable government will tell you that the uncertainty and volatility can be paralyzing.

So, companies need to combine stability and renewal. Leaders like Henry need to strike a balance between the needs for continuity and change.[5] As Robert Vanderpoel observes in his remark above, leaning over too much to one side or the other would be foolhardy. Yet, how much emphasis should leaders put on either side of the balance? What should be the relative importance of renewal activities, compared to stabilizing the current business? We refer to this leadership issue as *the task of strategic priority-setting*. Leaders need to determine whether primacy should be given to innovation, or whether consistent, predictable delivery should take precedence. As before, leaders are confronted with a perplexing paradox at the heart of the matter, making the answer to this question even more challenging than it first seems.

The paradox of exploitation and exploration

> *Part of human nature resents change, loves equilibrium, while another part welcomes novelty, loves the excitement of disequilibrium. There is no formula for the resolution of this tug-of-war, but it is obvious that absolute surrender to either of them invites disaster.*
> John Bartlet Brebner (1895–1957)
> Canadian historian

Deciding on the appropriate balance between organizational stability and renewal is in itself quite a testing challenge for strategists.[6] But from a leadership perspective there is an additional psychological angle making it even more difficult. As Brebner so eloquently states it in the quote above, in human nature there is an emotional tug of war between the love of equilibrium and the desire for novelty. People have a psychological wish to stay with the stable and known, but also crave the excitement of discovery and adventure. They want to get on with their existing business, but also scout around for stimulating new possibilities. They want to stick to their knitting, but also venture out in search of new opportunity.

While the love of equilibrium is often just seen as the fear of change, this doesn't do it justice. People aren't fond of stability simply because they are scared, conservative or lazy. Psychologically, something else is going on. People embrace stability because it allows them to get the job done. Organizational stability lets people perform in a way that satisfies them. It lets people use their capabilities to get results. People want to be able to do a good job. They take pleasure in delivering quality service to grateful customers. They take pride in being part of an organization that functions smoothly and lives up to expectations. Often, they are passionate about honing their skills and achieving mastery of their art. They build self-esteem by being the best they can be. They want to perform. All this points to the deep-seated need for *exploitation* – getting the best possible performance out of themselves and the organization under the existing circumstances. People want to exploit current resources and skills to achieve a satisfactory outcome. They want to hear the engine humming, nicely tuned, cruising down the highway.

At the same time, people have a desire for *exploration* – searching for new opportunities just over the horizon of the existing business. Their exploration can be directed at hunting for new client segments or geographic markets, developing new product lines, experimenting with new business models or diversifying into new business areas. It can involve incremental forms of renewal, or be about big bang innovations. Psychologically, this searching satisfies people's need for discovery. People enjoy the thrill of uncovering the unknown. They love a treasure hunt – there's a little bit of Indiana Jones in all of us. The excitement of finding something new is often only topped by the kick of inventing it oneself. Exploration also satisfies people's desire for variation. For many, repeatedly performing the same task turns mind-numbing and they blossom at the opportunity of finding a new way of doing things. And then there are people who revel in being a rebel. They savor the role of contrarian, doing things differently for the mere delight of being different.

For leaders, placing strategic priority on optimizing the current business will not be welcomed by people with a high need for exploration. As "hunters" these people will feel they are being forced to farm. They might enjoy eating tomatoes, yet hate the idea of watering and picking them all day. If they are told to toil in the fields, instead of chasing deer through the woods, they are going to be very disappointed, however important the tomatoes.

Yet, if leaders place strategic priority on innovation in the organization, this will not go down well with people with a high need for exploitation. They might feel like sailors who have just been told that a Mr. Columbus has chartered their ship to find a shorter route to India. They might enjoy the high seas, yet hate the idea of heading off into the big unknown. If they are told they are on a voyage of discovery, instead of a voyage of delivery, they are going to be very anxious, however important the new route.

The alternative of pursuing both priorities at the same time is not much easier, as CEO Henry already feared.[7] How can leaders communicate two opposite messages – "let's challenge the status quo" and "let's fine-tune the status quo" – at the same time? How can leaders champion iconoclasm and the irreverent questioning of company truths, while at the same time advocating reliability, predictability and efficiency? When you've just said: "If it ain't broken, don't fix it," it is tough to turn around say to someone else: "If it ain't broken, hit harder!"

It is not only communication that makes this tension between exploitation and exploration truly a paradox.[8] Money and attention can only be spent once, so all effort being put in to innovation will not be available for investment in optimizing the existing business. Moreover, the results of the exploratory efforts may upset existing practice, create cannibalistic products or undermine the very business model of the organization.[9] The very acts of doubting, experimenting and changing can trigger unrest, inefficiency and lower performance in the short run, while a drive to stabilize, standardize and synchronize can smother novel initiatives and bulldoze anything outside of the corporate mold. Performance measurement systems and incentives that are tuned to achieving tangible results in the current business will be ill-suited to appraise innovative efforts ("Most of it failed!") and reward people accordingly. And the values and beliefs required to foster a culture of invention and innovation will be at odds with a culture of concentration and optimization.[10]

It should not be surprising that leaders struggle with the paradox of exploitation and exploration, finding it easier to master one side than the other.[11] The leadership competences and mindset needed to focus people on exploiting the current business are very different than those needed to lead exploration efforts. Leaders capable of getting people to concentrate on optimizing the existing often have different skills, routines, approaches and ways of thinking than leaders capable of getting people to challenge the existing and search for innovative alternatives. For this reason, too, there is a tension between exploitation and exploration.[12] The consequence is that leaders tend to stress one over the other, strongly coloring their strategic leadership style.

The executive leadership style

> *We ought not to be overanxious to encourage innovation, for an old system must ever have two advantages over a new one; it is established and it is understood.*
> Charles Caleb Colton (1780–1832)
> British cleric and writer

Leaders leaning over to the side of exploitation have an *executive leadership style*, as they literally focus on execution – getting things done and getting results. They concentrate on implementing the existing strategy and optimizing the existing business. Top of mind is the efficient and effective functioning of the organization, by using, maintaining and extending the organization's existing capabilities, infrastructure and client base.

While not prioritizing innovation, that doesn't make executive leaders mere caretakers of the existing business. On the contrary, executive leaders are the ones that push to get as much mileage out of the current organization as possible. If there is potential value, they will capture it. Where growth is feasible, they will pursue it, rolling out the business model and building on the competences and systems already mastered. Where consolidation is required, they will drive the necessary cost-cutting, standardization and simplification. Where restructuring or downsizing is demanded, they will not shy away from the tough measures essential to restore viability. And where a business needs to be disposed of or closed, they will attempt to get as much value out of the remaining assets as they can.

Nor are executive leaders allergic to change. On the contrary, they generally love *kaizen* – continuous improvement.[13] They deeply appreciate the value of incremental enhancements that exploit current strengths and reinforce the existing business models. Most executive leaders will actively encourage optimization initiatives and renewal efforts that fit snugly with current practices and competences. Their change priority is *mastery* – getting continuously better at the same; as opposed to *breakthrough* – getting suddenly good at something new.

Achieving mastery and getting results can be very appealing to people in the organization. Executive leaders try to tap into people's desire to get things running smoothly and gradually grow the business from good to great. So, on the one hand, executive leaders establish the organizational stability in which people can get the job done, delight customers and earn a return on investment. This gives people a sense of professionalism and accomplishment. On the other hand, executive leaders nurture ongoing renewal by inviting people to build on their strengths and the strengths of the organization. This gives people a sense of advancement and confidence in the future potential of the organization to keep on developing.

If all this seems "sensible," it is. Leading "farmers" is not about creating excitement, but about appealing to their resolve. It is not about thrill and adventure, but about diligence and hard work. The executive leader gets people to put their backs into it…and love it.

The entrepreneurial leadership style

> *I can think of few important movements for reform in which success was won by any method other than an energetic minority presenting the indifferent majority with a fait accompli, which was then accepted.*
>
> Vera Brittain (1893–1970)
> British writer and feminist

Leaders emphasizing exploration over exploitation have an *entrepreneurial leadership style*, as they literally drive the entrepreneurial processes within the organization – ensuring the realization of new business opportunities. They concentrate on constantly rejuvenating the organization by getting people to challenge the existing business model and search for pioneering ideas and approaches. They continuously provoke innovation and might even themselves come up with new business concepts, novel products and improved processes.

There is a big difference between inventor and innovator that is of importance to point out here. An inventor is someone who explores and comes up with something new, such as a technology, product or process. An innovator is someone who explores, comes up with something new *and* gets it implemented. In other words, an inventor is someone who does the discovery, while an innovator is someone who puts the discovery into practice. Innovators can put their own inventions into operation, but they can also encourage other people to generate something novel and then champion these inventions and get them deployed in the field. To be able to rejuvenate, organizations need innovators, not only inventors.

To go a step further, there is also an important difference between innovator and entrepreneur. While an innovator puts a discovery into practice, an entrepreneur turns a discovery into commercial value. In other words, an innovator gets something novel into service, while an entrepreneur turns something novel into a commercial opportunity. An innovator will have an eye for an invention's practical feasibility, but to be an entrepreneur one also has to have an eye for commercial viability. To be able to rejuvenate in a strategically sound way, organizations need entrepreneurs who can tell the difference between a great idea with the potential of making money and one with the potential of being a white elephant.

Entrepreneurial leaders need to foster inventors and innovators, but always from the perspective of business sense. They need to find new possibilities outside of the current business, or even to overtake the current business, but their ideas eventually have to be operationally feasible and commercially viable. Of course, it is hardly ever clear at the outset how a novel proposal can be made to work and turned into something that will contribute to the bottom line. So, entrepreneurial leaders must not only stimulate the process of generating new ideas (ideation), but must drive ideas through all phases of the innovation pipeline, all the way to roll out. To ensure success, entrepreneurial leaders need to champion key innovations, putting their personal weight behind the efforts, shielding them from conservative forces and budget-cutters. And when innovations fail, as they often will for a variety of reasons, entrepreneurial leaders need to be there to draw the correct conclusion – not "that never again," but "let's keep trying" – and to sponsor the next project.[14]

Leaders with an entrepreneurial leadership style can be entrepreneurs themselves, taking the lead of a specific innovation project, but they can also lead the broader rejuvenation agenda, for example playing a role running the innovation pipeline. In whichever capacity, they lead people by inciting their sense of discovery. Sometimes entrepreneurial leaders need to challenge people to throw off their blinkers, while in other cases people will go into a creative frenzy at the slightest encouragement. Generally, it gets tougher for entrepreneurial leaders to keep people motivated during the long and arduous process of incubation. This is where leaders need to reiterate the importance of the renewal effort, keeping a sense of urgency alive and rekindling people's passion for chase and adventure.

The most daunting task for leaders with an entrepreneurial leadership style is to win the hearts and minds of people who prefer to hang out on the exploitation side of the paradox. Getting reluctant sailors to willingly sign up for a voyage into *mare incognita* is a rather tall order. This is where entrepreneurial leaders often combine push and pull – anxiety and hope. On the one hand, they create a burning platform, sketching the risk of not innovating or moving too slowly. On the other hand, they hold out a life raft, outlining a way forward at acceptable risk and tolerable instability. And then they wait for enough people to jump to create change momentum.

Not seldom, entrepreneurial leaders get disheartened by their inability to "get enough people to jump." They find it difficult to sway colleagues to embrace innovative initiatives and they get discouraged by the lack of rejuvenation they are capable of achieving. To their dismay, they also notice that many influential people in the organization see them as disruptive and blame them for wasting money on unsuccessful projects. For this reason, many leaders with an entrepreneurial bent give up on being "intrapreneurs," rejuvenating from the inside out, and leave their organization to set up a new business of their own, or to join a company with a more entrepreneur-friendly culture.

Table 8.1 Differences between the executive and entrepreneurial leadership styles

	Executive Leadership Style	*Entrepreneurial Leadership Style*
Emphasis on	Exploitation over exploration	Exploration over exploitation
Orientation towards	Optimizing the current organization	Creating the future organization
Leader needs to	Keep people focused	Keep people open-minded
Basic attitude	Let's run the business	Let's reinvent the business
Core quality	Getting results (harvesting)	Building potential (sowing)
Intended impact	Efficiency and effectiveness	Innovation and rejuvenation
Motivating people by	Delivering on promises (execute)	Discovering possibilities (experiment)
Underlying conviction	Continuity requires stability	Continuity requires disruption
Guiding principle/ motto	Build on your strengths	Grab the opportunity
Preferred tools	Planning and control systems	Innovation pipeline

Qualities and pitfalls of the executive leadership style

> *There is danger in reckless change, but greater danger in blind conservatism.*
>
> Henry George (1839–1897)
> American political economist

When looking at the qualities of the executive leadership style, they are all about providing the safe pair of hands you want to have running your business. The key strength of this style is already reflected in its name – execution. Executive leaders focus people on getting things done. They implement, effectively and efficiently. They ensure that people in the organization work in a disciplined fashion to provide the reliable delivery of goods and services in the marketplace. They create the steady and predictable organizational conditions that allow for excellent performance, leading to satisfied customers and healthy organizational returns. And besides these positive business results, followers also benefit, as they experience a sense of organizational and personal proficiency, professionalism and trustworthiness that is highly motivating.

But successful executive leaders are not merely caretakers, competently managing the existing business. They also strive to achieve their business's full potential, first pushing for growth and later milking it until dry. As with the owner of a truck, they are not only interested in driving effectively and efficiently, but also on getting the maximum mileage out of their vehicle. Executive leaders will constantly press people to look for ways of wringing even more value out of the business, exploiting it to the very last drop.

A powerful way to get the most out of the current business is to focus people on continuous improvement. Successful executive leaders encourage people to build on the existing competences, products and customer base, to see how the organization can be constantly upgraded through incremental steps. They stimulate the sharing of best practices and the honing of people's skills as ways to gradually move closer to excellence. Besides better business results, all this optimization also contributes to people's sense of steady, controllable and sustainable progress. It reinforces people's confidence that the organization is resilient and will be capable of adapting and developing in future.

Yet, in their drive to create stability and keep the business running smoothly, executive leaders can quickly establish themselves as unimaginative bureaucrats. In their desire to implement the existing strategy and get the job done, they can close their eyes to blatant new opportunities and inflate the risk of deviating from the set path. In their eagerness to deliver a dependable service to customers and a reliable financial performance to shareholders, they can inadvertently quash all attempts at even small-scale improvements. They are especially vulnerable to an unhealthy fixation on short-term performance indicators, particularly financial ones. Before you know it, in an effort to shore up financial results, the executive leader can turn into executioner, cutting all investment to innovative initiatives as nonessential costs.

As the organization continues to zip down the commoditization slide and the performance worsens, executive leaders will often only be reinforced in their belief that further cost-cutting is required, leading into a downward spiral. As Dr. Jekyll transforms into Mr. Hyde, the executive leader under pressure can become increasingly intolerant of nonconformists exploring new possibilities

Qualities of Executive Leadership Style	Qualities of Entrepreneurial Leadership Style
1. Provides a safe pair of hands	1. Provides a fast pair of feet
2. Focuses people on getting the job done	2. Focuses people on new opportunities
3. Drives optimization and performance	3. Drives invention and incubation
4. Supports delivering on promise to customers	4. Supports finding new promises and customers
5. Gets mileage out of the existing	5. Challenges future use of the existing
6. Encourages discipline and reliability	6. Encourages experimentation and trials
7. Backs sense of proficiency and professionalism	7. Ignites sense of adventure and discovery
8. Stimulates mastery and excellence	8. Stimulates rule-breaking and risk-taking
9. Strives for incremental improvements	9. Strives for breakthrough innovations
10. Inspires confidence in gradual adaptation	10. Inspires confidence in grabbing the next wave
Pitfalls of Executive Leadership Style	**Pitfalls of Entrepreneurial Leadership Style**
1. Leader seen as unimaginative bureaucrat	1. Leader seen as reckless risk-taker
2. Overly pessimistic about risk of change	2. Overly optimistic about future potential
3. Uninterested in new opportunities	3. New opportunities favored over current clients
4. Too few changes pursued	4. Too many changes pursued at once
5. Unwilling to invest in anything new	5. Unwilling to stop challenging and tinkering
6. Fixated on financial results	6. Disregard of financial realities
7. Prefers cost-cutting as solution	7. Prefers massive investments as solution
8. Backs suffocating planning and control system	8. Triggers debilitating chaos and lack of stability
9. Encourages conservative mindset	9. Encourages rebelliousness and flouting of rules
10. Intolerant towards "non-conformists"	10. Intolerant towards "non-believers"

Figure 8.2 Qualities and pitfalls of the executive and entrepreneurial leadership styles

and dissenters challenging the status quo. To reestablish control and stabilize the organization, the executive leader is often in danger of creating a "rational" business planning system that harks back to Soviet times, leaving no space for creative thinking, innovative initiatives or new business development.

Even in organizations where excessive cost-cutting has not led to corporate anorexia, executive leaders run the risk of reinforcing a conservative mindset, entrenching the current way of looking at the business model, with little room for exploratory deliberation. Like-minded old school thinkers will often be promoted to positions of power because "they get it" and "they get results," while more entrepreneurial types will be squeezed out, forced to leave after a failed innovation attempt or leaving voluntarily, frustrated by so little support and career perspective. Slowly but surely, executive leaders can shape a mono-culture of traditionalists, with a limited ability to see innovation opportunities and spot the danger of emerging business models. Sometimes these executive leaders even convince themselves that their modest efforts at continuous improvement are signs of vigorous innovative flair, soothing themselves with the thought that all is well. When a disruptive innovator enters their business and their days are counted, they are often the last to know.

Qualities and pitfalls of the entrepreneurial leadership style

> *The art of progress is to preserve order amid change and to preserve change amid order.*
> Alfred North Whitehead (1861–1947)
> British mathematician and philosopher

While the executive leadership style provides a safe pair of hands, the entrepreneurial leadership style provides a fast pair of feet. The key strength of this style is that it focuses people on grabbing new opportunities – getting people to find or invent new possibilities and then driving the process of incubation and roll-out. Entrepreneurial leaders get people motivated by appealing to their sense of adventure and discovery and by inspiring them to transform the organization. By stimulating people to be creative, to challenge the organizational orthodoxy and to come up with innovative proposals, this style encourages people to embrace disruption as a way of beating the competition and being at the leading edge of developments.

Entrepreneurial leaders go further than inciting rule-breaking and invention, supporting people on the tough path from idea to commercial success. Leaders using this style encourage experimentation and trials, ongoing tinkering and changing, calculated risk-taking, but also discontinuing projects that do not seem commercially viable. By guiding this process of constant exploration, entrepreneurial leaders contribute to people's confidence that the organization is capable of ongoing rejuvenation and is well-positioned to create, or grab, the next wave of innovation in the industry.

But just like executive leaders, entrepreneurial leaders often play their music too loudly. In their drive to champion pioneering products and revitalize the company, entrepreneurial leaders can easily go over the edge into reckless risk-taking. In their desire to be first-mover in the industry, they can be overly enthusiastic about a new business model's feasibility and overly optimistic about its future potential. They can become so enamored with a pet project that they lose sight of financial reality and are willing to throw heaps of cash at it, leading many people to joke that if a project is "strategic" it means that it won't make money any time soon.

In their eagerness to transform the organization, entrepreneurial leaders can quickly take on too many changes at once, triggering chaos, totally over-burdening employees and leading to poor service delivery to current clients. They can go on and on with their changes, constantly tinkering away, seeing new possibility, but thereby never finishing. It is not for nothing that a common rule of thumb for actually completing an innovation project is to make sure you "kill the inventor" on time.

There is a real danger that existing customers are ignored anyway, as the entrepreneurial leader is often bored with business as usual and seduced by the prospect of new liaisons. Leaders with this style can also adopt a condescending posture towards the executive "worker bees," busily implementing away, as the entrepreneur takes on the much more vital task of innovation. And where these executive types have the gall to question the bright new world conjured up or to doubt the wisdom of the investments and risks, the entrepreneurial leader will often be tempted to look down, or even humiliate, them.

Seeing themselves as a type of corporate revolutionary, challenging convention and breaking the rules, it is sometimes tempting for entrepreneurial leaders to overdo their countercultural role, reveling in provoking controversy and rubbing people the wrong way. Quoting Thomas Jefferson, they will often insist that "a bit of rebellion now and then is a good thing," sanctioning their followers to constantly flout the corporate rules and engage in activities "under the radar screen." Promoting such unashamedly undermining behavior will seldom make them friends, so when they slip up, as innovators are regularly wont to do, volunteers for the firing squad will be plenty.

Profiling your leadership style

> Wisdom lies neither in fixity nor in change, but in the dialectic between the two.
> Octavio Paz (1914–1998)
> Mexican poet and essayist

Have you already recognized your default style? Have you picked out some of your strengths, but also some of the pitfalls you occasionally fall in to? As before, in Figure 8.3 is a quick aid to identify the style you feel most comfortable using.

But let's not forget poor Henry at the beginning of this chapter, trying to determine the profile for his commercial director. Have you already figured out which strategic leadership style this person should master foremost? Should he be looking for the safe pair of hands or the fast pair of feet? Should he be looking for the "smooth operator" to get things done or the "contrarian

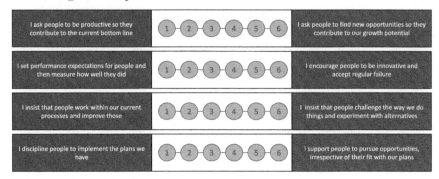

Figure 8.3 Profiling your leadership style: Strategic priority-setting

innovator" to shake things up? Or do you believe that he should try to find someone ambidextrous, able to switch flexibly between the two styles? Again, www.leadership-agility.com offers some interesting ideas how other people would advise Henry.

Notes

1 Schumpeter, J.A. (1934), *The Theory of Economic Development: An Inquiry into Profits, Capital, Credit, Interest and the Business Cycle*, London: Transaction Publishers.
2 Kim, C. and Mauborgne, R. (2005), *Blue Ocean Strategy: How to Create Uncontested Market Space and Make the Competition Irrelevant*, Boston: Harvard Business School Press.
3 Ron Meyer introduced this concept in 2011 to explain the generic path of industry evolution, all things being equal. Of course, it is a generalization, similar to the product life cycle, and many different trajectories are possible, depending on a variety of circumstances. Most importantly, the commoditization slide will be altered by "the visible hand" of companies trying to counteract "the invisible hand" of industry evolution.
4 Baden-Fuller, C. and Stopford, J. (1992), *Rejuvenating the Mature Business: The Competitive Challenge*, London: Cengage Learning.
5 Doz, Y. and Kosonen, M. (2010), "Embedding Strategic Agility: A Leadership Agenda for Accelerating Business Model Renewal," *Long Range Planning*, Vol. 43, No. 2–3, April, pp. 370–382.
6 The classic article arguing that organizations needed to do small and big changes simultaneously also coined the now widely used term ambidexterity (ability to use both hands interchangeably): Tushman, M. and O'Reilly, C.A. (1996), "Ambidextrous Organizations: Managing Evolutionary and Revolutionary Change," *California Management Review*, Vol. 38, No. 4, pp. 8–30.
7 Jansen, J., Vera, D. and Crossan, M. (2009), "Strategic Leadership for Exploration and Exploitation: The Moderating Role of Environmental Dynamism," *The Leadership Quarterly*, Vol. 20, No. 1, February, pp. 5–18; Andriopoulos, C. and Lewis, M. (2009), "Exploitation-Exploration Tensions and Organizational Ambidexterity: Managing Paradoxes of Innovation," *Organization Science*, Vol. 20, No. 4, July–August, pp. 696–717.
8 The terms exploration and exploitation were originally used by Jim March in a famous article: March, J. (1991), "Exploration and Exploitation in Organizational Learning," *Organization Science*, Vol. 2, No. 1, pp. 71–87. March argues extensively that the two phenomena are in tension with one another and are hard to combine.

9 See Christensen, C. (1998), *The Innovator's Dilemma*, Boston: Harvard Business School Press.

10 Gupta, A., Smith, K. and Shalley, C. (2006), "The Interplay between Exploration and Exploitation," *Academy of Management Journal*, Vol. 49, No. 4, August, pp. 693–706.

11 Lewis, M., Andriopoulos, C. and Smith, W. (2014), "Paradoxical Leadership to Enable Strategic Agility," *California Management Review*, Vol. 56, No. 3, Spring, pp. 58–77.

12 Rosing, K., Frese, M. and Bausch, A. (2011), "Explaining the Heterogeneity of the Leadership-Innovation Relationship: Ambidextrous Leadership," *The Leadership Quarterly*, Vol. 22, No. 5, pp. 956–974.

13 See Imai, M. (1986), *Kaizen: The Key to Japan's Competitive Success*, New York: McGraw-Hill.

14 Gordon MacKenzie has written a wonderful book describing the difficulty of this process, based on his years stimulating innovation at Hallmark Cards. His book is tellingly titled *Orbiting the Giant Hairball: A Corporate Fool's Guide to Surviving with Grace*, 1998, New York: Viking.

Part V
Leadership and mission

9 Purpose-setting

The paradox of wealth and health

This was not the way Mark had wanted to start his new job as CFO. The previous officeholder had quit in frustration, after needing to explain to the bank once again how the mounting losses would make it impossible to repay the extensive debts on time. The bankers had thrashed the company's strategy and made it absolutely clear that the company was on the last of its nine lives. Once the old CFO had cleared the field, the bank had insisted on parachuting Mark into the company to try to turn it around, before it went into receivership. Now, here was Mark across the table from the visibly shaken CEO, Jerry. As majority shareholder of his family-owned business, Jerry had run the company since taking over from his father nine years ago, but now he felt control slipping through his fingers. He was disappointed, confused, angry and desperate.

If only the bank had more patience, Jerry protested. Innovative players in traditional markets always need time to change customer behavior, he explained to Mark, while his company had the added challenge of selling its innovative water piping solutions to very conservative local governments and water utilities. When these customers need to renew their water pipes or extend their water supply network, they typically engage in a tendering process based on established terms of reference, picking the cheapest supplier. Jerry's firm had come up with high-tech flexible tubing that could be installed without ripping up streets. So, while more expensive to buy, it was cheaper to install, lasted a lot longer than old-fashioned pipes and was easier to maintain. However, few procurement managers were immediately enthusiastic about changing the existing tendering process and explaining why they were buying more expensive products.

The innovation that Jerry was most proud of, he immediately pointed out, was that the newest range of products had full cradle-to-cradle credentials. These products used only recycled materials and after an economic lifespan of about 50 years could easily be removed and recycled again. This was the crown on his work of becoming an entirely sustainable company, in which he had invested so much time, effort and money. Not only had he worked on all things green, but he had gone to great lengths to contribute to the local communities where the company worked, particularly at the manufacturing plants in California, Poland and Thailand. He was extremely proud to be one of the first companies to be certified as a B Corp (Benefit Corporation) and enjoyed being invited as guest speaker at Corporate Social Responsibility events.

Besides "taking environmental and social responsibilities very seriously," as he put it, Jerry was also intent on creating a healthy organization. Inspired by Ricardo Semler, he had decided to do away with hierarchy, instead organizing into self-steering teams. Local and cross-border teams had been formed and empowered to "do what is right given our mission to bring healthy water in a healthy way to as many people as possible." This move had drawn many idealists to join the company, including his own young son, Brian, who was at the forefront of developing the new product range.

"But hasn't doing away with hierarchy also created some chaos?" Mark asked. He continued to summarize what else he had heard in his first round of interviews: that country managers were suddenly demoted to team members, causing odd situations, multiple resignations and a general loss of market focus; that many self-steering teams, incited by the company mission, had started to spend money freely to "do what is right," raising wages and lowering prices for poor customers; that most units weren't selling much at all, as Brian's new green product line was hugely expensive, while he had insisted on discontinuing the cheaper older products because they didn't meet the company's sustainability requirements. "Isn't it true that in most of our 32 countries procurement managers actually show little interest in the green labels we stick on products, as they see it as a ploy to raise prices?" "All true," replied Jerry. "But who said that changing the world for the better was going to be easy? We have a mission! We have a purpose! We can't let short-term problems hold us back."

As Jerry left the room, Mark also stood up, weighing the words he had just heard ... "we have a purpose." Potentially powerful, he thought, but he doubted whether everyone agreed with Jerry's mission. The bank didn't, the minority shareholders didn't and many employees thought it sheer madness. As he also left the room, Mark was still wondering what to do – support Jerry's purpose, but bring in some financial discipline, or to push the company harder, to embrace profitability as its purpose, in order to save it from its impulses to avoid economic reality. Or was there some way to promote "doing good" and "doing well" at the same time?

The task of purpose-setting

> *Great minds have purposes, others have wishes.*
>
> Washington Irving (1783–1859)
> American writer

Do you notice that Mark is not only struggling with the *strategic* question of how to reposition the company, but also with an *existential* one? He is not only asking himself how to make the company a success, but also more fundamentally how success should be defined. He is concerned with the *how*, but even more with the *why* – why does the organization exist? What should the company be striving to achieve? While strategy is about "determining a course of action to realize the organization's purpose,"[1] Mark is wondering which organizational purpose should be pursued in the first place. He is contemplating the company's very reason for being.

Actually, Mark's doubts go even further than the firm's core purpose. He is also questioning whether its *mission* is viable. As the term "mission" is often misused and generally poorly defined, it is useful here to explore this concept in a bit more detail. An organization's mission is defined as "the enduring set of fundamental principles that forms the base of a firm's identity and guides its strategic decision-making."[2] To really understand what is meant by mission it helps to recognize the Latin origin of the word mission, which is *mittere*, that means "to send" – a mission is the assignment that sends people off in a particular direction. An organization's mission is the task it takes upon itself, launching it on its way, just as a missionary is also propelled by accepting a calling. In other words, a mission is the broad role that an organization sees for itself, while strategy is the tangible course of action inspired by this role definition.

Note that an organization never "completes its mission." A mission is not a goal to be reached, but a set of fundamental principles guiding choices and giving meaning to the voyage. Contrary to the military usage of the term, an organizational mission is never "accomplished," it is lived by. Just as with a philosophy, you have one and you behave according to one, but you never "finish" one. You carry your philosophy/mission with you. In the military, a mission can be over in a few hours, while an organizational mission is a lasting role definition with no time frame at all.

Note also how the concept of mission is entirely different than the concept of vision, although the two are regularly mixed up. As was discussed in Chapter 7, a vision is an image of what the future might be like. So, if Mark starts to consider what the company should look like in a few years' time, his picture of this desired long-term future will be his strategic vision. This long-term aim will give guidance to the required course of action and can eventually be achieved. Hence, a strategic vision is a very broadly defined strategy, giving general answers to *where* the voyage is going and a bit on *how* the voyage will take place. But a strategic vision says nothing about *why* the voyage will be undertaken in the first place – that is the task of the mission.

Sadly, in many organizations what passes as a mission statement is little more than a wooly platitude for the first page of the annual report, or a punchy slogan for the company website. When it is not an empty catchphrase for external consumption, the formulated mission is often the outcome of an internal feel-good session or the wishful thinking of the management team. In all these cases, what's put on paper is what people would like the mission to be, not what it truly is. The principles outlined in lofty sentences are what people wish for, not those that really drive the strategic choices made in the organization. Generally, the larger the gap between the official statement (the espoused mission) and organizational reality (the mission-in-use),[3] the greater the sense of confusion, frustration, disappointment and cynicism among people in the organization. This is unfortunate, as the whole idea of defining the organizational mission is to give people a shared sense of meaning, helping them to make choices, connect to one another and feel inspired. Much like a country's constitution, a mission should lay out the broad principles by which people will live. These "rules" need to be realistic enough to abide by, yet uplifting enough to engage people and create a sense of joint destiny. The defined role of the organization needs to be aspirational enough for people to want to join the community, without being so fanciful that people lose belief and view it as a corporate fairy tale.

With the definition of mission now clearer, it is also insightful to recognize what the constituent parts of a mission are. As suggested earlier, at the heart of an organization's mission is its purpose. An organization's *raison d'être* is generally a very strong impulse, justifying particular choices and driving people to behave in a specific way. Yet, as can be seen in Figure 9.1, there are three additional components that together shape the set of principles on which an organization's actions are based.

The first component of the mission is the *core business* – the activities at the center of the organization that are rarely called in to question. While the organizational purpose clarifies "why we do," the core business defines the essence of "what we do." It is a shared understanding of the type of work to which the organization is committed. It is the heartland of where the organization operates, which is taken as the starting point for strategizing, not as a variable to be easily changed while strategizing. As such, the core business encompasses all activity areas that are intrinsic to the organization's identity. So, for example, some organizations might fundamentally see themselves as car manufacturers and never consider dropping their automobile business in favor of anything else. Other companies might define their core business in terms of the required competences ("we are Lean specialists"), the type of tasks ("we are an engineering firm") or the focal customers ("we serve the healthcare sector") instead of the types of products ("we are a car company"), but in all cases, there

Figure 9.1 The organizational mission

is a strong sense of identity linked to the business definition that is embraced. For this reason, how people in an organization perceive their core business will to a large extent steer the strategic choices they are willing to consider.

The second component consists of the *core beliefs* – the fundamental convictions that are held to be true throughout the organization.[4] These shared beliefs are also called the organizational ideology, the collective worldview or the dominant logic.[5] Just as in the American Declaration of Independence, these shared truths "are held to be self-evident," not requiring any further justification. Actually, in the Declaration of Independence, at least the truths were spelled out, while in organizations most beliefs are so deeply engrained that no one realizes that they are merely collectively embraced assumptions.[6] Typical core beliefs can be "constant growth is essential," "never become dependent on others," "being demanding shows strength" and "the customer is king," to name just a few, but with a little bit of effort one can easily identify many more. Together they form a system of ideas that sometimes can be incoherent, but generally the stronger the internal consistency, the more powerful and persuasive the ideology will be. As a shared organizational faith, these views become part of the philosophy steering the choices made. If one believes deeply that success depends on putting the customer at the center of all organizational activities, this will be enshrined as a principle guiding all future choices. It might actually happen that this belief even influences the purpose of the organization and the perception of the organization's core business, as there will be a natural pressure to also bring internal consistency between all mission elements.

Besides what is seen as true, organizational missions are also shaped by what is seen as important. This brings us to the third additional component of a mission, namely *core values* – the qualities that are held in high esteem throughout the organization. Values are literally characteristics that people embrace as being of value. Core values are features that are collectively accepted as being worthy, justifying their pursuit and defense. Typical core values include competitiveness, freedom, responsiveness and decisiveness, but also their partial opposites, cooperation, responsibility, consistency and participation. As with the system of ideas, organizations usually have a more or less consistent system of values, which in turn tends to be consistent with their core beliefs, core business and organizational purpose. However, there is one big difference, which is that beliefs are held to be either true or not, leading opposite beliefs to be cast aside, while values are of higher or lower importance, allowing more room for opposite values to be embraced at the same time.

So, when someone like Mark calls the purpose of an organization into question, immediately doubt is cast on the entire organizational mission. If Mark disputes Jerry's purpose of bringing health to the world, he automatically also challenges the linked core values, the deeply held organizational beliefs and the very conception of the core business. Organizational purpose is at the heart of a mission, but intricately wrapped up in the whole. If Mark contests the purpose and tries to tinker with the "heart," he can expect the entire "immune system" to be triggered in response.

However, leaders like Mark can't escape the *task of purpose-setting*. If Mark wants to lead, he must realize that people will be looking to him for direction and meaning. People will want to know what he thinks the organization stands for and they will decide whether they want to be part of it or not. If he doesn't challenge the existing purpose, he will be seen as embracing it. If people see that Mark even implicitly accepts Jerry's purpose, they will conclude that the existing mission will remain in place, making them either relieved or frustrated. Yet, if Mark calls the purpose into question, other people will become highly alarmed, as such a challenge is truly existential – threatening the existence of the organization in its current form.

Therefore, ideally, Mark should try to tweak the organizational purpose in such a way that everyone is happy and inspired. Yet, unfortunately, there is a paradox at the center of organizational purpose, making it difficult to appeal to all people equally well. It is the paradox of wealth and health.

The paradox of wealth and health

The true worth of a man is to be measured by the objects he pursues.
Marcus Aurelius (121–180)
Roman emperor

What is the purpose of a hammer? Is it to drive nails or to build affordable housing? What is the purpose of a book? To share information or to facilitate human development? And what is the purpose of a football team? To win games or to promote social harmony? In all of these simple examples, both answers can be true. In each case, the first answer is the *functional purpose*, describing the direct effect that the item is intended to have. You could say that it is the straightforward *instrumental* purpose. Hammers, books and football teams can be seen as tools for doing something valuable and this is what can be achieved if you use them well. Each second answer, on the other hand, is a *higher purpose*, describing an indirect effect to which the item is intended to contribute. You could say that it is the *moral* purpose for which the item is being used. Hammers, books and football teams can have an impact beyond their immediate technical application, as stepping stones to the realization of something socially or ecologically virtuous.

The same is true for organizations. From an instrumental perspective, *organizations are tools for creating added-value*. Organizations function as vehicles for transforming inputs into more valuable outputs. On the input side resources go in, such as money, materials, labor, information and knowledge, while on the output side value propositions come out that need to be appreciated enough by clients that they are willing to pay more than the cost of the resources and of the intermediate value-adding activities. In competitive sectors, organizations will also need to do this value-creation job more convincingly than rival firms if they want to win over calculative customers.

From a moral perspective, *organizations are communities for creating added-virtue*. Organizations are platforms for bringing together individuals to cooperate towards achieving a purpose they feel is good and meaningful. People can collaborate to contribute to the well-being of other people, for example by helping the needy, supporting disadvantaged social groups, promoting education, backing scientific research, sponsoring musical performances or stimulating physical fitness. At the same time, people can complement these *social* causes with *ecological* ones, contributing to the well-being of all other life on the planet, for example by protecting fragile ecosystems, safeguarding endangered species, stimulating recycling, reducing carbon emissions, caring for stray cats and cleaning up the neighborhood.

These are two very different ways of seeing an organization. From an instrumental perspective, organizations are about creating value, on which a price tag can be hung. They are a means for generating economic *wealth*. In this way of looking at purpose, an organization is successful if it is better than competitors in drawing customers who are willing to pay more than the cost of the value proposition. The ultimate gauge of success will be profitability, but most people will realize that future profitability is strongly linked to such current factors as market share, customer satisfaction and operational efficiency, which is why these economically crucial aspects will also be tracked. If the game is played well and sufficient wealth is created, then enough financial resources will be available to share among the stakeholders and to reinvest in the future of the organization. Even not-for-profit organizations need to create added-value for their "customers" in this way, to generate enough funds to secure their long-term future. Their gauge of success will not be profit, but budget, which will allow them to keep stakeholders financially happy and invest towards future activities.

How different is the view on organizations if we look beyond their functional purpose to the higher purpose that they can serve? Then we see that organizations are not about *income*, but about *impact*. Making money is not an end in itself, but only a means to make a difference to others. Where organizations adopt a moral purpose, they are potentially a powerful force for doing good. Then they can be a means for generating social and ecological *health* – in the sense of bringing about more sound conditions in the environment surrounding the organization. In this way of looking at purpose, an organization is successful if it has a positive contribution to the well-being of people and the planet. At the same time, successfully driving sustainable external health can be a major factor in promoting internal organizational health. As doing good makes people feel good, contributing to external health often strengthens internal stakeholder's physical, mental and spiritual well-being. If the game is played well, a virtuous cycle can be started, whereby people internally feel better because they are doing good externally – and the more good they feel, the more good they do.

Yet, despite the great slogan "People, Planet, Profit,"[7] pursuing health and wealth simultaneously is rather tricky. Promoting the health of people and the planet usually comes at a cost that reduces profit, while promoting wealth generally causes collateral damage to some people and parts of the planet. So, to a certain extent, wealth and health come at each other's expense – more of the one will necessarily lead to less of the other. Moreover, not only do the two conflict with each other in practice, they also contradict each other in theory. The logics of the two just don't fit together easily. Wealth uses an economic rationale and focuses on the direct business environment, while health uses an ethical rationale and highlights the broader social and ecological environment. It is for this reason that we speak of *the paradox of wealth and health*.

As these two types of organizational purpose – wealth and health – pull in opposite directions and seem difficult to reconcile with one another, it should come as no surprise that most leaders tend to emphasize one side over the other. Either by character, by habit or by conviction, leaders generally exhibit a preference to stress the importance of either wealth or health, resulting in two very different types of leadership – the *value-driven* and the *virtue-driven leadership styles*.

The value-driven leadership style

> *I have no complex about wealth. I have worked hard for my money, producing things people need. I believe that the able industrial leader who creates wealth and employment is more worthy of historical notice than politicians or soldiers.*
>
> J. Paul Getty (1892–1976)
> American industrialist

Where leaders place more emphasis on wealth than on health, they are said to have a value-driven leadership style. As this name implies, a value-driven style focuses on *value creation* as the key driver of the organization's activities. To value-driven leaders, the core task of organizations, on which everyone should be relentlessly fixated, is to realize superior value for customers and as a payoff to reap part of this value as profit for the organization. In this view, organizations exist to get a job done, to the mutual benefit of the customer and the producer. If the work done by the producer results in a product and/or service that is valued more than alternatives offered by other suppliers, customers will be willing to pay a premium reflecting this superior value. Customers will be satisfied with the value for money they receive, while the organization will earn a margin over the total costs incurred – a profit.

This is basic business sense, you might say, and the value-driven leader will readily agree. To the value-driven leader it is not rocket science that the purpose of business is to make money by serving clients well. By creating value and sharing the proceeds between the customer and the organization, both sides benefit. Both increase their wealth – the customers materially and the organization financially. Within the organization, the wealth can be further distributed between the various internal stakeholders, such as the employees and the owners. Even in not-for-profits and the public sector, this value-creation logic usually holds true, as organizations need to perform value-adding activities for some client groups and must ensure that they do the job well enough to receive further funding.

It is important to point out that value-driven leaders aren't blind to the significance of social, ecological, physical and mental health. On the contrary, they are often willing to invest in organizational health as a means towards success and they can be called on to contribute to social and ecological causes, if these help to create the necessary conditions to achieve results. It's just that they don't consider dealing with these health factors as the purpose of the organization. Where promoting health is a necessary precondition to creating value, they will be willing to consider investing. In other words, value-driven leaders are willing to do "good," where that is required to do "well."

For value-driven leaders it is usually not difficult to explain this whole line of reasoning to people in the organization since the economic logic is quite compelling. The true challenge is keeping people focused on this purpose. Knowing that value creation is key is one thing, but concentrating on value creation every day in all one's behaviors is quite something different. To most people in organizations it is totally opaque how their work contributes to superior value creation. How does filling in forms all day add value? And how about going to meetings? Or drawing up reports? Especially for activities that are not customer-facing it is often very difficult to see how and when they truly add value. Yet, even when the impact on the customer's value experience is recognizable, people will often be concerned with other things than creating value, such as finishing the conversation with their colleague, trying to realize the agreed Key Performance Indicators, leaving on time to beat the traffic jams or completing their to-do list. Customers can be such a disturbance in getting your work done on time.

For this reason, successful value-driven leaders go beyond repeatedly preaching the value-creation purpose of the organization. To win hearts and minds, they infuse people with a broader sense of mission. They typically stimulate reinforcing organizational beliefs such as the beneficial influence of being customer-centric and the impact of getting strong Net Promoter Scores. They also emphasize supportive organizational values, such as responsiveness, efficiency and/or service-orientation, while simultaneously projecting an attractive core business definition. All these aspects of the organizational mission are tied together and strengthened by such means as organizational storytelling, highlighting positive role models and celebrating joint successes.

Where people are still left with a sense of why, value-driven leaders will ultimately point to the bottom line, as the final gauge of how well the organization is doing. Where enough wealth has been created, there will not only be a good basis to face the future, but also some financial resources available to reward those who have contributed to the success. After all, value-driven leaders know that if you want people to focus on creating joint wealth, then it is very motivating that there is a prospect of sharing in that wealth. If you want people to create value, you have to be willing to share it.

The virtue-driven leadership style

> *Virtue is its own reward.*
>
> Cicero (106–43 BC)
> Roman philosopher, politician and orator

Leaders who emphasize the importance of health over wealth are said to exhibit a virtue-driven leadership style. As the name implies, virtue-driven leaders are propelled by their desire to do good. They are motivated by a strong inner drive to do what is ethically just. They have a well-developed moral compass that guides them in their choices, pushing them to do what is noble, truthful and fair. In their view, organizations are communities of people who together also have a moral obligation to do good, but have the added benefit of their collective strength, which enables them to have a significant impact. Organizations have the potential to be a powerful force for good, if they know what good they are striving for.

Most virtue-driven leaders believe that one of the most worthwhile ways of being good is to contribute to the well-being of others. This includes supporting the well-being of other people, as well as the well-being of the natural environment. This is usually summarized as promoting the health of "people and planet." To virtue-driven leaders it is obvious that every individual has the moral responsibility to safeguard the health of the social and ecological environment, as well as the duty to advance their long-term sustainability. This responsibility also collectively rests on the shoulders of groups of people working together in organizations.

Yet virtue-driven leaders go a step further than expecting people in organizations to accept the *responsibility* to do good. To them, it should be an organization's very *purpose* to do good. Morally, the only reasonable goal for organizations is to contribute to the well-being of others – all else is self-centered. If organizations aren't oriented towards benefitting others, then they obviously only exist to benefit themselves. They are about taking, not giving, and this can hardly have been seen as virtuous. Therefore, for virtue-driven leaders, people in organizations need to be very clear on the good they want to *do*, and the good they want to *be*, as these are the ultimate reasons justifying the organization's existence.

Of course, virtue-driven leaders are not blind to economic reality and realize that organizations need to be financially viable. To be able to do good, organizations have to do well. They have to create value and secure sufficient income to be able to survive. But earning money is only a means, not an end in itself. Money enables, it doesn't ennoble. Money is like food, as it provides sustenance to get other things done. And as with food, you can even enjoy money, but if you become overly obsessed with it, ill-health is just a step away. There is a natural inclination towards excess, leading to gluttony and greed.[8] As the famous Greek shipping tycoon, Aristoteles Onassis, once remarked: "A rich man is often only a poor man with a lot of money." Financially rich, but morally poor.

Money doesn't provide meaning. Wealth is a useful tool, but it isn't fulfilling in itself, as it doesn't provide a moral answer to the question "why?" Getting rich is only "a poor man's" meaning in life. To virtue-driven leaders meaning in life should be sought in being virtuous and pursuing a just cause. Only by serving a higher purpose than simply making money will people find long-term contentment. Personal health – physical, mental and spiritual – can only be found in supporting the health of others.

While virtue-driven leaders are literally driven by the desire to be virtuous themselves, their message and their very behavior will inspire many people to follow. Not only will these leaders' purpose be appealing to others, providing meaning to the organization's activities, but their broader mission will also win hearts and minds. Many people will be attracted to the virtuous organizational values that these leaders stand for and the compelling organizational beliefs that they propagate. People will also be drawn to the positive organizational identity, preferring to be a part of a "good" organization instead of a "grubby" one. To a certain extent, this positive organizational identity will reinforce their personal identity, making them also feel good about themselves.

In conclusion, virtue-driven leaders are able to mobilize people because their mission is uplifting. They offer an inspiring view that there is more to life than just the material side. Life and organizations are not about exploiting others and hoarding money, but about harmony with others and using money to do good. This message touches the heart-strings while convincing the mind, and is therefore a powerful motivator for people to come along on the voyage. In this sense, virtue-driven leaders really are missionaries.[9]

Qualities and pitfalls of the value–driven leadership style

> *Business or toil is merely utilitarian. It is necessary, but does not enrich or ennoble a human life.*
>
> Aristotle (384–322 BC)
> Greek philosopher and scientist

With such huge differences between the value-driven and virtue-driven leadership styles, it is useful to delve a layer deeper, to uncover their underlying qualities and pitfalls. Starting with the qualities of the value-driven leadership style it can be said that its main strength is that it focuses people in the organization on surviving and thriving in the here and now. Every organization has a job to do and the value-driven leadership style concentrates hearts and minds on doing that job extremely well. Organizations need to create tangible value for customers otherwise there will be no future: that's simply the economic reality. Organizations need to beat off rival organizations that are vying for the same client's money: that's how the world works. Winning each match and going on to the next round is how the competitive game is played. Value-driven leaders focus people on this joint task as the defining challenge that the team needs to tackle together. They rally their troops to win the next battle, because that is the nature of the struggle for survival they are caught up in.

Besides facing up to the *competitive reality* in which organizations need to perform, the value-driven leadership style also keeps people alert about the *financial viability* of everything they do. Is every activity being undertaken truly of value to customers and will they be willing to pay enough extra to offset the additional costs? This financial discipline is essential to determine whether activities are justified or just someone's hobby. Such cost/benefit analysis is key

Table 9.1 Differences between the value-driven and virtue-driven leadership styles

	Value-Driven Leadership Style	*Virtue-Driven Leadership Style*
Emphasis on	Wealth over health	Health over wealth
Motivating people by	Realizing financial rewards	Realizing moral rewards
Core value	Doing well	Doing good
Orientation towards	The business environment	The social and ecological environment
Basic attitude	Strive towards economic viability	Strive towards ethical vitality
Core quality	Creating added-value	Creating added-virtue
Intended impact	Focus people on customer satisfaction	Focus people on noble contributions
Underlying conviction	People work to make money	People work to make a difference
Guiding principle/motto	Money makes the world go around	Meaning makes the world go around
Preferred tools	Performance targets and profit-sharing	Impact and sustainability reports

to ensuring that investments are only made if there is a good chance that they will be recouped at a later moment. For value-driven leaders, emphasizing the organization's mission to create wealth helps in weeding out all spending that is value-destroying, even if it is meant to do good. Spending money is easy; spending it profitably is hard work.

Furthermore, as value-driven leaders are less distracted by issues in the social and ecological environment, they are able to concentrate attention on the two key stakeholder groups in the value-creation equation – customers and producers. So, on the one side, they focus everyone in the organization on the fundamental objective of achieving *customer satisfaction*. The purpose is to keep the customer, not save the planet. This helps enormously in getting people to direct their energy towards the right activities. On the other side, value-driven leaders also focus everyone in the organization on the beauty of the value-creation activities being performed. People should not only take pride in a satisfied customer, but also in a job well done. Recognizing how value-adding activities contribute to a fantastic product or service amplifies their value and importance, giving people a sense of dignity and fulfillment. People see how their efforts and mastery lead to great outputs and delighted customers. Customer satisfaction and *employee satisfaction* go hand in hand. In this way, value-driven leaders give meaning to the everyday work of people in the organization.

In all of the above, it is not the value-driven leader who determines what is good and what is bad. "Value is in the eye of the beholder," to rephrase the old saying, which in this case is the customer. Customers determine what they value and it is up to the organization to find a way to realize this value in a financially viable way. It is not up to value-driven leaders to pass judgment on the customer's wishes – value-driven leaders are *morally neutral*. They will have their ethical boundaries, but they won't impose their moral preferences on others. Their purpose is to please, not to preach. As such, it is a quality of the value-driven leadership style that it is tolerant to all different types of higher purposes that people might have, as long as they don't expect the organization to take sides. If people want to save the rainforest or alleviate regional unemployment, they are welcome to do so, but value-driven leaders do not see it as their role to make this decision on behalf of the organization. Everyone in the organization is only held to one objective standard – do they contribute to value creation? – not whether they agree with the political and social preferences of the leader.

Last, but not least, Aristotle might have thought that business doesn't ennoble a human life, but that sounds rather self-serving coming from a philosopher who doesn't like to toil. Why shouldn't striving for wealth be satisfying to many people? Why shouldn't making money and increasing one's material comfort be motivating? The British author Patrick O'Brian once joked that: "Although wealth may not bring happiness, the immediate prospect of it provides a wonderfully close imitation." So, maybe the most obvious quality of the value-driven leadership style is that it appeals to many people's strongly felt desire to be financially and materially better off. It might not be morally highstanding in some individuals' judgment, but many people are greatly inspired by the prospect of achieving greater wealth. Value-driven leaders tap in to this formidable motivation.

However, it must be noted that tapping into people's craving for increased wealth can easily go wrong. It is a slippery slope from "wealth is welcome" to "greed is good." Once people develop a taste for financial rewards, they will often become addicted and want more and more. In the beginning this may only involve working increasingly hard, to the detriment of one's own physical and mental health. Yet soon addiction leads to a shift of perspective, whereby ethical boundaries are more easily crossed. A white lie here, a few changed numbers there…it might be necessary to make the financial case. Putting undue pressure on colleagues here, neglecting the interests of the client there… you need to be tough to get things done. Slowly but surely moral hesitations wither as the logic of winning at any cost takes over. Finally, the person is willing to brutally exploit any situation, as long as there is money to be made. Child labor? It's not formally forbidden. Burning down a rainforest? Technically, it wasn't us who did it. Paying less than minimum wages? Well, strictly speaking it's an internship. Sadly, the addict is the last to notice how profoundly the addiction has taken over their worldview. This is a huge pitfall of a value-driven way of thinking, for both leaders and followers.

Most of the other pitfalls of the value-driven leadership style also affect both parties, as leaders pull their followers along in their fall. As people's perspective shifts from value-driven to financial-driven, all aspects of organizational life tend to be reduced to a financial number. An employee is no longer a human, but a human resource that costs a particular amount. Each customer has a net present value and becomes an account. Brands can be bought and sold. But as the old saying goes, not all that counts can be counted, and many important things can definitely not be expressed in Dollars, Yen or Euros. Team spirit? Can't buy it, so it's probably not that important. Trust? Never saw it on a balance sheet, so I doubt it's really valuable. Leadership? No idea how to price that, so let's leave it out of the business plan. Clearly, one-sided financial thinking can blind people to what is essential for value creation.

A knock-on effect of this money-centric thinking is the further *financialization* of the organization. As only money counts and is counted, departments will fail to work together, unless they can send each other an invoice. Actually, given the choice between an internal and an external supplier, most will prefer the external party because the arm's length financial arrangements are much clearer and you're not dependent on such squishy qualities as cooperation and goodwill. While value-driven leaders might try to get people and units on board for a new project to serve the clients even better, few will be motivated to follow unless their cooperation is purchased by more budget or at least part of the spoils. Individuals, too, will demand to be incentivized to do their work – without a bonus no one will be motivated to go a step beyond their agreed performance level.

If the value-driven leader does not beware, the money-centric culture that takes root will be one in which each individual runs their own personal profit and loss account, with no one feeling responsible for each other or the whole. Deals will be done internally, but on the basis of negotiation power, with each person looking after their own interests. The strong will secure a large part of the wealth for themselves and their department, while the weak will complain but be ignored. Internal inequality will grow and people's status will depend largely on how much money they make. Needless to say, the overall organizational health will be weakened, with receding engagement, lower involvement, higher sick leave and increasing turnover. Everyone will complain about the silos in the organization, but no one will know what to do about it until a desperate value-driven leader suggests that maybe more cooperation needs to be incentivized – after all, won't people do anything for money?

Qualities and pitfalls of the virtue-driven leadership style

> *Virtue has never been as respectable as money.*
>
> Mark Twain (1835–1910)
> American writer

When it comes to the qualities of the virtue-driven leadership style it is important to avoid mixing them up with the qualities of particular virtues. One might think highly about promoting cancer research, protecting the habitat of Adelie penguins or supporting journalistic freedom, but different people will have different definitions of what constitutes "good." It is very interesting to get into moral debates about what contributes to social and ecological health, but that is not the point here. The question is how leading on the basis of a particular set of virtues has certain advantages and potential downsides. We need to evaluate the leadership style, not the virtues themselves.

The clearest quality of the virtue-driven leadership style is that it appeals to people's deeply felt passions and therefore can result in a high level of engagement. If people feel strongly about a particular topic, tapping into these values and convictions can unleash an enormous amount of energy. If people are involved in activities they truly believe in, their intrinsic motivation will be extremely high. If they invest their hearts and minds in realizing something they embrace as being profoundly important, they will be highly committed to do their best and pour all their discretionary effort into achieving success. In other words, virtue-driven leaders are in a position to make a connection with people's ideals and fears, mobilizing them to exceptional levels of persistence and performance.

Besides engaging current organizational members, virtue-driven leaders will also be a magnet for like-minded people outside the organization, who will want to join in. Virtue-driven leaders typically have an outspoken profile, as they promote certain causes and exhibit the good for which they stand. This leads to a self-selection of exceedingly dedicated enthusiasts who feel attracted to the mission and will vie to become part of the team. This allows the virtue-driven leader to select above average candidates and to ensure a tight fit with the culture of the organization.

Moreover, once people join, virtue-driven leaders generally find it easy to shape them into a high performing team, because everyone passionately shares the same mission and there is a natural alignment of interests. While in other organizations people compete for budgets and tend to focus on their own local agendas, virtue-driven leaders can rally everyone around the compelling common interest of realizing the higher purpose. People will be strongly inclined to cooperate to support the joint cause and even sacrifice their own interests, if that's what it takes to achieve success. As everyone is working towards the same goal, it is also easier to build trust and team spirit, while joint successes and failures will further reinforce the sense of "being in this struggle together."

In this sense, it could be said that for virtue-driven leaders it is not only about *doing* good, but equally about *being* good – not only promoting external health, but also nurturing internal health. Besides contributing to the well-being of society and the environment, virtue-driven leaders have the opportunity to walk the talk and advance internal well-being as well, stimulating individual and organization health. Instead of treating people like expendable human resources, virtue-driven leaders are generally keenly aware that people should be given room to develop themselves as healthy individuals, physically, mentally and spiritually. And instead of treating organizations like money-driven machines, virtue-driven leaders place great emphasis on building healthy relationships and a virtuous culture.

Last, but not least, it could be said that virtue-driven leaders not only encourage people to *do* good and *be* good, but also to *feel* good. By enabling

Qualities of Value-Driven Leadership Style	Qualities of Virtue-Driven Leadership Style
1. Rallies people around joint welfare	1. Rallies people around joint well-being
2. Inspires by pointing to higher prosperity	2. Inspires by pointing to higher purpose
3. Emphasizes surviving and thriving	3. Emphasizes supporting and sustaining
4. Encourages hard work and performance	4. Encourages healthy work and impact
5. Focuses on competitive realities	5. Focuses on contextual realities
6. Concentrates on serving customers	6. Concentrates on serving people and planet
7. Guides via financial standards	7. Guides via ethical standards
8. Finds meaning in doing good work	8. Finds meaning in working to do good
9. Tolerates a variety of worldviews	9. Attracts people with specific worldview
10. Motivates by sharing monetary rewards	10. Motivates by sharing moral rewards
Pitfalls of Value-Driven Leadership Style	**Pitfalls of Virtue-Driven Leadership Style**
1. Rallies people around joint greed	1. Rallies people around joint vanity
2. Stimulates self-enrichment	2. Stimulates moral arrogance
3. Glorifies people who profess to be wealthy	3. Glorifies people who profess to be virtuous
4. Brutal to people with 'poor performance'	4. Brutal to people with 'wrong values'
5. Reduces people to human resources	5. Reduces work to development opportunity
6. Blind to everything that can't be counted	6. Blind to financials that should be counted
7. Ignores the cost of unhealthy externalities	7. Ignores the impact of unprofitable activities
8. Willing to exploit anyone to gain a profit	8. Willing to exploit customers to gain impact
9. Perverse incentives trigger unethical behavior	9. Unchecked hobbies trigger unfunded behavior
10. Promotes 'every person for themselves' culture	10. Promotes 'others will pick up the bill' culture

Figure 9.2 Qualities and pitfalls of the value-driven and virtue-driven leadership styles

people to contribute to a higher purpose and to behave in a virtuous way, virtue-driven leaders let people feel good about themselves. People feel proud to be part of something admirable and develop strong self-respect for "doing the right thing." The very nobleness of the cause and the impact of the actions undertaken give people a sense of meaning and fulfillment that could never be bought with money.

Yet, in this feeling good about themselves lies one of the worst pitfalls of the virtue-driven leadership style. As with most pitfalls, the danger is found in a strength's exaggeration – in this case an excessive amount of pride. As virtue-driven leaders beat the drum of their cause and emphasize how to do good and be good, there is a big risk that leaders and followers alike will start to feel really good about themselves, verging on the border of smugness. As they look around and see others with "wrong beliefs and values," smugness easily slips into moral arrogance. The more these passionate true believers speak to each other and shake their heads at the dimwitted sheep around them, the more their attitude turns into a holier-than-thou posture. Ultimately, their pride transforms into vanity and their prejudice into intolerance. Only *they* see the light. Only *their* virtues are truly good.

This air of ethical superiority often goes beyond just a few individuals, spreading through departments to the whole organization. The aforementioned virtuous cycle of attracting and hiring new believers who reinforce the positive culture can quickly degrade into a vicious cycle, as only hard-core believers join the organization, further speeding up the descent into a cult-like culture. As the pressure grows to prove your goodness, a certain level of competition arises as to who is the most virtuous, leading some people to advertise their moral credentials, while others actually radicalize. Slowly but surely the atmosphere of self-righteousness becomes stifling.

Yet, even where this excessive emphasis on virtuousness doesn't take hold, the concern for society and the environment can heavily overshadow the concern for the customer. As serving the customer is only seen as a means for achieving the organization's higher purpose, the customer is easily taken for granted or approached with a measure of arrogance. Often customers "don't yet see the light," valuing a product or service that isn't "good," so they need to be ignored or at most educated, as with Jerry's water piping clients, who didn't yet realize that expensive cradle-to-cradle solutions should be more desirable than cheap throw-away products. In the same way, virtue-driven leaders often tend to be dismissive of competitors that only sell "bad" products, sometimes even demanding that governments step in to protect them from unfair competition from such "unethical competitors."

While virtue-driven leaders are often blind to the wishes of customers and the threat of competitors, probably their biggest blindness is to financial realities. Of all of the pitfalls that virtue-driven leaders can fall into, a lack of attention to basic economic feasibility is the one that enjoys the highest popularity. Somewhere deep down virtue-driven leaders often feel that they shouldn't be held back in their mission by such a trivial detail as financial resources. As they are engaged in issues of a higher order, they feel they shouldn't have to worry themselves with mere commercial nitty-gritty. They should have their hands free to concentrate on the truly important challenges, not on the vulgar business of chasing after other people's cash. Money shouldn't have to be earned, it should just be available. Yet, while not wanting to concern themselves with securing sufficient income, virtue-driven leaders commonly do have highbrow plans requiring significant funding. In their drive to make an impact they have plenty of virtuous initiatives they would like to launch, but only a shaky grasp of how they should be paid for. A view on financial viability is often missing, not to mention a real interest in achieving an acceptable level of profitability. Not surprisingly, financial analyses are seldom carried out and a culture of "let others pick up the bill" prevails.

Even where this financial blindness is less pronounced, it is seductive for virtue-driven leaders to passionately believe in their "good" schemes and to overestimate the likelihood of commercial success. As they are not morally neutral and emotionally detached they typically are too optimistic that what is good will also do well. Therefore, they are too quick to fund proposals to boost external and internal health. They may have high ethical standards and moral discipline, but their investment standards and financial discipline are often their Achilles heel.

Profiling your leadership style

> *An aim in life is the only fortune worth finding.*
>
> Robert Louis Stevenson (1850–1894)
> Scottish novelist and poet

Do you recognize that Jerry, the CEO in the introductory case, is a stereotypical virtue-driven leader? While he has been able to leverage some of the qualities of the virtue-driven leadership style, he has unfortunately fallen face-first into each of the pitfalls described above. At the moment of writing the future of his company is still up in the air. Do you already know what you would do if you were in Mark's shoes, as CFO? Would you lurch the company over to the side of wealth, by taking a strongly value-driven leadership style? Refocusing the company on profitability as a purpose would be a revolution, but it might be the medicine the company requires. Or would you build on the current mission, sticking with health as its purpose and adopting a virtue-driven leadership style? If so, what would you do to pull Jerry and the company out of the pitfalls in which they find themselves? Or do you see a third way, making a combination of styles, getting the benefits of wealth and health at the same time? Make sure you go to www.leadership-agility.com to share your solution and to read up on the ideas that others have about dealing with this case.

And what about your own style preference? Do you recognize your own default leadership style? And have you spotted some of the pitfalls that you've been in before? As in the previous chapters we have included a few opposite statements in Figure 9.3 that you can use to profile your general inclination. If you prefer to map your purpose-setting leadership style in more detail, you can always consult the Leadership LEAP App. It requires only a modest investment and provides a lot of meaning, so independent of your leadership persuasion it might be a worthwhile action to take.

The final question, as always, is how agile you judge yourself to be along this dimension of leadership. Is this an area where your style flexibility could use a

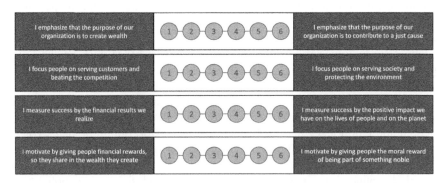

Figure 9.3 Profiling your leadership style: Purpose-setting

boost? If so, ensure you make a mental note and come back to this issue in Chapter 13 on developing leadership agility.

Notes

1 De Wit, B. and Meyer, R. (1998), *Strategy Synthesis: Resolving Strategy Paradoxes to Create Competitive Advantage*, London: International Thomson Publishing.
2 This definition was first proposed by Meyer in De Wit, B. and Meyer, R. (2005), *Strategy Synthesis: Resolving Strategy Paradoxes to Create Competitive Advantage* (2nd ed.), London: International Thomson Publishing.
3 For this distinction between espoused theory and theory-in-use, see: Argyris, C. and Schön, D. (1974), *Theory in Practice: Increasing Professional Effectiveness*, San Francisco: Jossey-Bass.
4 Meyer, R. (2007), *Mapping the Mind of the Strategist: A Quantitative Methodology for Measuring the Strategic Beliefs of Executives*, Rotterdam: ERIM.
5 The term dominant logic was coined by C.K. Prahalad and Richard A. Bettis to describe the mental maps developed by managers through experience in their core business. See Prahalad, C.K. and Bettis, R.A. (1986), "The Dominant Logic: A New Linkage Between Diversity and Performance," *Strategic Management Journal*, Vol. 7, No. 6, pp. 485–501.
6 This is not only true at the organizational level. Yuval Noah Harari also powerfully makes this point, but at the level of civilizations. See Harari, Y. (2014), *Sapiens: A Brief History of Humankind*, London: Vintage Books.
7 For the argument that companies should seek a balanced approach to planet, people and profit, see Elkington, J. (1997), *Cannibals with Forks: The Triple Bottom Line of 21st Century*, Oxford: Capstone.
8 Note that these are two of the seven deadly sins held up to people since the Middle Ages.
9 One particular strand of virtue-driven leadership thinking emphasizes spiritual health as the overarching theme. For follow-up reading, see: Fry, L.W. (2003), "Toward a Theory of Spiritual Leadership," *The Leadership Quarterly*, Vol. 14, No. 6, pp. 693–727.

10 Interests-setting

The paradox of self-actualization and service

Peter was fast on his way up the corporate ladder and the new position as country manager had sounded like an ideal next step on his route to becoming CEO one day. His career within the company had been stellar, but so far, he had lacked the international experience needed to have a shot at the top job. So, when he was asked to head the company's biggest foreign subsidiary, it seemed like a golden opportunity. But now that he had been on the job for two weeks he was starting to wonder whether in reality the "golden opportunity" was fool's gold.

Running this huge subsidiary of 3,500 employees in a country he had never visited before would have been challenging under the best of circumstances, but his actual assignment was outright intimidating. His task was to close two of the four pharmaceutical production sites and shift the work to cheaper locations offshore. In parallel, the two remaining sites would need to radically cut costs, probably resulting in job losses for about a quarter of their workforce. Taken together, more than two thousand people would need to be laid off, which would not be easy as employment regulations were very strict and the unions extremely militant.

The logic for the restructuring had sounded compelling to Peter. In the past, the pharmaceutical industry had been highly profitable, focusing on developing new products and getting them to market quickly. But as the number of blockbuster products coming out of the development pipelines had steadily declined, firms had become more dependent on older drugs, many of which were no longer protected by a patent and therefore had to compete with lower priced generic drugs. As for the increasingly expensive new drugs, these had caught the attention of budget-sensitive governments and insurance companies, looking for means to keep rising healthcare costs under control. The result had been tough price negotiations and often an imposed maximum price, seriously reducing the pharmaceutical companies' returns.

To shore up their profitability, pharma firms had taken an axe to their cost structures, trimming some marketing spending, but mostly slashing production expenditures. Manufacturing had traditionally been close to where R&D had taken place, at scattered locations, so savings could be found by integrating plants to achieve economies of scale and transferring activities to cheaper locations. Furthermore, there was plenty of scope for process reengineering to achieve more efficiency, to automate in order to cut labor costs and to out-source to low cost outfits. All these interventions were on Peter's agenda. And as an extra incentive, he had even been promised 10% additional bonus for each 1% reduction in production cost that he would be able to realize.

Peter's initial worry was how to deal with the hard-nosed unions. They and their members had a lot to lose and it seemed likely that they would not accept the intended measures without putting up a fight. But Peter was also con-cerned about keeping the highly qualified employees on board, as they would have the best opportunities elsewhere and might be the first ones to jump ship if they saw stormy weather ahead. Losing his top talents would jeopardize production continuity in the short run, but more importantly make the upgrading of the facilities in the longer run more difficult. Getting people to follow him through this transformation process and support him in making it a success was not going to be easy.

But after two weeks of talks with all key stakeholders in the subsidiary, Peter's mental state had migrated from worry to guilt. Many of the two thousand people who would be laid off had worked their entire lives for the company and particularly the older employees would have considerable difficulty finding new jobs. The local communities would be devastated. Didn't Peter have a responsibility towards these people – the people he wanted to lead? It also became clear to him that the subsidiary had enormous untapped potential, but for years lacked the leadership to bring it to a higher level. Shouldn't he champion their cause?

But at the same time, he feared that serving their interests would be against his own. He had accepted the restructuring task and not sticking to his assign-ment would threaten his standing as "golden boy." Choosing between his own interests and the interests of the people around him was a bitter pill, and one he was not yet ready to swallow.

The task of interests-setting

The shepherd always tries to persuade the sheep that their interests and his own are the same.
Stendhal (Marie-Henri Beyle) (1783–1842)
French writer

If you focus on the factual side of the case, Peter's conundrum can be framed as a strategic puzzle. On the one hand, the company must cut production costs to safeguard profitability, while on the other hand, the subsidiary has competences and other human capital that could be leveraged to contribute to future prof-itability. From a strategic point of view, these are opposite pressures and the challenge for Peter is to come up with a solution that reconciles the two, cutting cost and leveraging subsidiary capabilities simultaneously.

Yet, if you shift your focus from the factual side to the values side of the case, it is not about the company's strategy, but about the company's mission. It is about determining what is most important to the company and what it ultimately wants to achieve. It is about the organization's purpose. What weighs more heavily, profitability or moral responsibility?[1] What should Peter emphasize, wealth or health – striving to maximize value creation by cutting cost or exhibiting virtuous behavior by caring for employees and local communities? This was the discussion in Chapter 9, which explored the different types of organizational purpose.

But intertwined with the question of *which purpose* to pursue is the question of *whose purpose* to pursue. Who should determine the organizational purpose and whose organization is it in the first place? Does Peter's subsidiary "belong" to him, allowing him to decide its fate, or does the subsidiary belong to the people working there, giving them a moral right to co-determine the future? If the subsidiary exists as a tool to further Peter's (and headquarters') interests, then it is his prerogative to establish the organizational purpose, but if the subsidiary exists to serve the interests of all stakeholders involved, then the mission should reflect this "co-ownership." In other words, the question "for whom does the organization exist" largely boils down to the issue of *cui bono?* – for whose benefit?[2] Whose interests should shape the mission and drive strategic choices?

Dealing with the interests of different stakeholders and weighing which should predominate is an essential part of being a leader.[3] We call this *the task of interests-setting* – determining whose interests will be kept in mind, which will be served and which will ultimately prevail. The task is essential because leaders need to bring people together to get things done while their interests are hardly ever entirely aligned. More often than not, leaders need to mobilize stakeholders whose interests point in different directions or even conflict.[4] This is not because people are inherently difficult, but because organizations by their very nature embody tensions that bring people into collision with one another. Because of the way organizations work, there is just plenty of potential for disagreement.

Take, for example, the difficulty of dealing with what economists would call scarcity and the rest of us would call limited resources. Budget going to the one department can't be given to another, while a vacant management position can only be won by one candidate if the others lose. What is to the benefit of one person or department is at the expense of the other, leading to disputes about who should get what. Game theorists call such a situation a "zero-sum game,"[5] since the win of the one is balanced out by the loss of the other. In organizations, there are many decisions that are zero-sum, such as spending time and money on product A or on product B, or getting the IT department to work on front office or on back office systems first. Peter's challenge also seems to be a zero-sum game, as costs saved by headquarters are at the expense of people at the subsidiary.

Even where there is a "positive-sum game" and more than one person or department could benefit simultaneously, there is still room to fight about relative gains. Even when you make the pie bigger so there is more to go around, people can quarrel about the relative size of their piece. If higher profitability allows more investment budget to be made available, trench warfare can easily break out about who should get what, until leaders can broker an armistice. If a success in the market has been realized, people and departments will often dogfight and shoot each other down, in an attempt to claim as much of the triumph for themselves as possible. And ask any HR manager about salary and bonus discussions and you'll be told that tensions are less about the absolute amount of people's increase and more about their increase compared to others. As these examples show, especially when it comes to interests such as status and power, relative positions are extremely important.

Not only do people squabble about the amount of benefits distributed, but also about the types of benefits that are most important. What should be valued more – protected jobs, increased profitability, lowered cost, higher innovativeness, social responsibility or labor market reputation, to name just a few? To a certain degree your personal values will come in to play, but political scientists will be quick to point out that to a large extent "where you stand depends on where you sit" – the types of benefits you appreciate will strongly depend on your position in the organization.[6] Interests are tightly linked to the role played and less to the specific player, as in sports, where any goalie's interest is to prevent a goal, while all forwards' interest is to make one.

With so much potential for conflicts of interest, it is clear that leaders are constantly engaged in negotiating between people and departments to get enough support to get things done. Yet leaders need to think further than only the people and departments with whom they directly interact, to be aware of stakeholder interests in the broader environment, with whom they might also align or clash. In other words, leaders need to look beyond their *primary stakeholders*, that is, beyond the people they want to lead.

As depicted in Figure 10.1, there are three levels of stakeholders of importance to leaders. The primary stakeholders include all potential followers. These are the people identified in Chapter 1, whom leaders may want to engage to move in a certain direction. *Secondary stakeholders* include all people, departments and organizations directly impacted by the behavior of the leader, although the leader is not trying to lead them. They are outside the "leadership circle" but still experience the consequences of what the leader does. Typically, this includes company-internal groups such as other departments and units, as well as many external groups such as customers, suppliers, unions, banks and regulators. This is a potentially troubling group, as the leader is not consciously trying to lead them, but their interests are affected by what the leader does, which might provoke them to take countermeasures. In terms of stakeholder management, it is wise for leaders to know who these secondary stakeholders are, how much power they can wield, what their interests are and to what extent these interests overlap or conflict. This analysis can result in keeping one's distance, striking arm's length deals or deciding to treat the party as a primary stakeholder, drawing them into the leader's circle of potential influence.

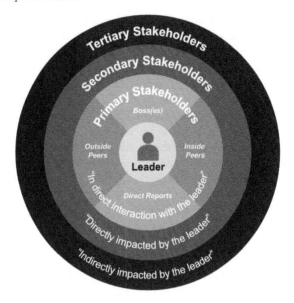

Figure 10.1 A leader's stakeholders

Tertiary stakeholders include all people, departments and organizations indirectly impacted by the behavior of the leader. This is the remaining group touched by the "footprint" of the leader. They are the group that experiences the knock-on effects of what the leader does. Inside the organization, they can include people inspired by the example of effective leadership they witness at a distance and units enabled by the cooperative organizational culture fostered by the leader. But this group can also contain people disengaged by leaders' infighting at the top and units hindered by the organization's tainted reputation, resulting from the leader's unreliable behavior. Externally, typical tertiary stakeholders include local communities impacted by (dis)investments, researchers inspired by new developments, governments challenged by ecological degradation, universities stimulated by growing demand and citizens enraged by extravagant bonuses.

In dealing with all three levels of stakeholders the question for leaders is not only who should get how much attention, but whose interests should prevail. To whose ultimate benefit should the organization be run? Whose interests should the leader be serving? The primary stakeholders? The secondary or tertiary stakeholders? Or none of the three? It turns out there is quite a paradox at the heart of interests-setting.

The paradox of self-actualization and service

> *I must follow the people. Am I not their leader?*
>
> Benjamin Disraeli (1804–1881)
> British Prime Minister

As Disraeli seems to suggest, leaders must be attuned to the needs of their followers. You can march out front, but if no one follows you, you are not a leader. If you want people to move with you, you must know what will win their hearts and minds. You must know their values and beliefs and sense their hopes and fears. And you must be aware of their interests, because it is next to impossible to get people to act in direct contradiction to their own benefit. In short, to mobilize your followers, you have to give them what they need – you must serve them.

Service is all about fulfilling the demands of the other. Service is about *giving*, not *taking*. It is about providing people with what they require to willingly follow. It is about respecting the interests of followers and ensuring that these are looked after. By offering followers their service, leaders can win their trust and entice them to invest their time and energy in a joint journey. In this sense, service is the leader's side of the bargain – it is what the leader gives to get the follower's cooperation.

But this is a very instrumental definition of service. It is a bit like saying that people are friendly to others so they will be treated politely themselves, or that parents love their children because then the children will love them back. This is a *calculative* way of looking at giving, as an exchange in which givers should receive something in return. Yet many people are friendly because they want to be and it feels like a kind thing to do. Parents generally love their children unconditionally and find joy in making them happy. In the same way, leaders can also serve their followers because it makes them feel good and because they genuinely care. Leaders can literally love their followers and want the best for them. This is an *affective* way of looking at giving, in which the warmhearted emotions of givers motivate them to serve without expecting anything in return, except for the satisfaction of being able to help.

There is a third reason why leaders "give" – because they believe they ought to. Many leaders are convinced that it is their responsibility to serve others and to ensure that the interests of their followers are protected. They operate on the notion that they should take care of their fellow human beings and accept the obligation to serve the interests of those around them. For many leaders, this "duty of care" is particularly acute if the followers are less powerful and dependent on the leader. As the old French phrase goes, "noblesse oblige," higher station comes with obligations. Being in a position of power brings the ethical imperative to be the guardian of the weak. This is a *moral* way of looking at giving, in which leaders as a matter of principle have the responsibility to be of service to those in their environment.

So, whether inspired by calculative, affective or moral reasons, leaders serve their followers. The constant challenge for leaders is to balance the differing interests of each of these primary stakeholders, as no two people or units will want the same thing. Leaders continuously need to negotiate and compromise to ensure that everyone feels they are being treated fairly. The complexity of this balancing task only increases where leaders feel they should also serve secondary and tertiary stakeholders. If leaders approach these stakeholders in a calculative way, the complexity will be moderate, as leaders will only need to take care of the powerful, who could potentially push back (e.g. "We need to treat those customers well, otherwise they'll leave" or "We need to stay within the formal rules, otherwise the regulator will be all over us"). But leaders can feel affectively or morally compelled to serve the interests of certain secondary or tertiary stakeholders (e.g. "We believe the customer should truly be king" or "We want to be an essential part of the local community"). In these cases, juggling all of the various interests can be a circus-worthy acrobatic act.

In the discussion so far, one person's interests haven't yet been mentioned, namely the leader's. We have focused on the need for leaders to serve the interests of others, but of course they should also serve their own. Leaders should be clear on what they want to get out of being a leader and what they want to achieve. What is their ambition, motivating them throughout years of hard slog and constant setbacks? What is their dream, driving them to work long hours and go the extra mile? What makes them proud, filling them with energy and the enthusiasm to recruit others to join them in their quest? What do they passionately believe is worthwhile, strengthening their perseverance in the face of resistance and their resilience to overcome disappointments?

Becoming a leader is hard work, and remaining one over a prolonged period of time even more, so something has to make it worthwhile. What's in it for the leader, justifying the considerable investment in "blood, sweat and tears" that leaders need to make? For some people becoming a leader allows them to attain *benefits through* the organization, such as knowledge, experience, money, positions, recognition, relationships, status and power. For other people, becoming a leader enables them to achieve *results with* the organization, such as developing innovative products, building a business, disrupting an industry and improving society. It will vary from person to person which specific set of motivations spurs them to strive for a leadership role, but in all cases their motivation will need to be consistently strong over time to be successful.

The only way to keep one's motivation high in the long run is to stay close to one's inner desires, while striving to realize one's full potential. This is called *self-actualization* – activating one's inherent capacities and aspirations, becoming what one potentially could be.[7] In other words, leaders need to be attentive to their own drivers and dreams, letting these come to fruition, instead of living up to social expectations or living someone else's dream. They should be aware of their own hopes, fears, ambitions and pleasures, setting their course based on these, instead of following someone else's mold. They should focus on activities that will help them to grow and satisfy their inner desires, instead of sticking to cultural conventions or fulfilling the wishes of parents, spouses or friends. This means that leaders need to be keenly aware of "what makes them tick" and to pursue self-actualization as their primary interest.

However, self-actualization is difficult to combine with service. If leaders place significant emphasis on self-actualization, they will put their own interests ahead of their stakeholders, pursuing their own ambitions and dreams over and above the needs of the people around them. Yet, if leaders highlight the importance of service, they will put the interests of their stakeholders ahead of their own, giving the people around them what they need, to the detriment of their own development. It is for this reason that we speak of *the paradox of self-actualization and service*. These two positive requirements placed on leaders pull in opposite directions, making it seemingly impossible to do both equally well at the same time. On the contrary, leaders seem forced to lean over to one side or the other, resulting in two very different types of leadership – the *sovereign* and the *servant leadership styles*.

The sovereign leadership style

> *A leader has two important characteristics; first, he is going somewhere; second, he is able to persuade other people to go with him.*
>
> Maximilien Francois de Robespierre (1758–1794)
> French lawyer and politician

Where leaders emphasize the importance of self-actualization over service, we say they have a sovereign leadership style. To the sovereign leader, the organization (or smaller unit) exists to support them in achieving their dreams. Followers are there to serve them, not the other way around. Sovereign leaders know where they are going, have set a course and only need others to come along on the voyage to "man the oars."

King Louis XIV of France is often misquoted as saying: "*L'état, c'est moi!*" (the State, that's me), but although historically incorrect it does succinctly encapsulate his view and that of other sovereign leaders. They are at the head of the organization and it should be an extension of their will. The organization is a tool which they are allowed to use to realize their ambitions, a means to their ends. It is their interests that determine the mission of the organization, their purpose that prevails.

All this doesn't mean that sovereign leaders are dictators and blind to the interests of others. On the contrary, sovereign leaders are very aware that they must recruit others to join them on their journey, because they can't accomplish their objectives on their own. Like an adventurer attempting to reach the South Pole, sovereign leaders need to find people willing to join them on their expedition. Preferably these people already have a shared interest in trekking across Antarctica and are motivated to become members of the team, but sovereign leaders are also well-positioned to sell their mission because they fervently believe in it themselves. Sovereign leaders with a strong sense of mission can be very charismatic.

To push the expedition metaphor just a bit further, sovereign leaders wouldn't necessarily call all the shots on the way to the South Pole, as their decision-making style could just as easily be democratic as opposed to autocratic. Nor would sovereign leaders always tell people what to do, as their interpersonal steering style could just as easily be facilitative instead of supervisory. The only point on which sovereign leaders would certainly put their foot down would be on the ultimate purpose of the team – it is their ambition to go to the South Pole and the team is there to serve this purpose. There is no chance a sovereign leader would turn around and say: "But those are my dreams...where would all of you prefer to go?"

So, sovereign leaders do understand that they need to give followers enough to get them to come along, but this service is of a calculative nature – sovereign leaders give just enough to keep people on board and committed to the cause. Sovereigns are the principles, but they need to motivate their agents to serve on their behalf.[8]

The servant leadership style

The administration of government, like a guardianship, ought to be directed to the good of those who confer, not of those who receive, the trust.

Cicero (106–43 BC)
Roman philosopher, politician and lawyer

Leaders who place more emphasis on service to stakeholders than on their self-actualization have a servant leadership style.[9] As in Cicero's quote, they behave like guardians, placing the interests of those in their care above their own. They are selfless, striving to do what is best for all involved. It is not about the leader's dreams and desires, but about assisting followers to realize their own. They give without expecting anything in return, helping others to thrive and shine, and supporting new leaders to develop, so they too can serve others.[10]

As their mission is to be of service, these leaders position themselves among their followers, not in front of them. Instead of saying "Follow me," servant leaders will say "I'm behind you all the way," supporting and enabling others to move forward. Still people will follow, as they trust the servant leader's intentions and sense that their interests will be cared for. Precisely because servant leaders have no other agenda than pursuing the common good, they can be counted on to keep an eye on everyone's stake. Because they make themselves the willing tool of their followers, they are trusted as custodians of their followers' interests.

As it is not about them and they don't need to stand out front shouting "Follow me," servant leaders are often humble and not that conspicuous. They tend to be modest and have no urge to stand in the spotlight themselves. On the contrary, they excel at letting other people look good. In general, it is not unfair to say that: "Behind every strong individual, stands a strong servant leader," invisible to the outside world, but vital to success. It is not that servant leaders avoid stepping forward and taking the floor, it is only that this is rarely the best way to serve. Servant leaders don't need the glory, don't feed on the admiration and don't chase the stardom of a hero leader, preferring to play the "supporting actor" role. In sports terms, the servant leader rarely scores the goal, but is usually essential in providing the assist.

All this doesn't mean that servant leaders do exactly what stakeholders want them to do. Just as caring parents don't always give children candy when they ask, servant leaders sometimes have to resist the demands of the people around them, deciding it is not in their best interest. Servant leaders are not butlers, there to fulfill people's every wish, but guardians, there to protect people's fundamental well-being. Their purpose is not to give people what they want, but what they need. If servant leaders were merely straightforward servants, doing what they were told, they would forfeit their role as leaders. They would not be the sense-makers we would expect them to be, helping people to find the right direction. However, servant leaders are well aware that this "I know what's good for you" posture can easily tip over into perceived or real paternalism, so they are constantly engaged in dialogue with their stakeholders to establish where to go and what will truly be to their benefit.

A second reason for intense dialogue and not giving people what they want is that servant leaders can never make everyone happy at the same time. Although in principle servant leaders would like to be of service to all individual stakeholders, people's interests seldom fully overlap, forcing leaders to choose or strike a balance. At the same time, the "common good" of the whole is never equally good for all and often even at the expense of some, again requiring leaders to make hard choices between different people's interests or engineer difficult compromises.

However, in the end, servant leaders accept this painful balancing of interests as a vital task of leadership that someone needs to burden themselves with. Actually, it is the ultimate service to the stakeholders to ensure that interests are constantly aligned in a peaceful, orderly and legitimate fashion, as opposed to a brutal, chaotic and antagonistic one. Having an altruistic leader willing to channel the process of interests-setting in an impartial manner is a valuable service indeed, to the whole organization, but especially to the less powerful, who would otherwise be trampled on while the elephants fight.

Table 10.1 Differences between the sovereign and servant leadership styles

	Sovereign Leadership Style	*Servant Leadership Style*
Emphasis on	Self-actualization over service	Service over self-actualization
Motivating people by	Striving to fulfill the leader's ambitions	Striving to fulfill shared ambitions
Core interests are	The good of the individual	The good of the group
Orientation towards	Satisfying one's own needs first	Giving priority to collective needs
Basic attitude	What's in it for me	What's in me for it
Core quality	Willpower and charisma	Caring and humility
Intended impact	Followers support the leader	Followers are supported by the leader
Underlying conviction	The organization is a tool to serve me	I am a tool serving the organization
Guiding principle/motto	Follow me!	I am behind you!
Preferred tools	Compelling speeches	Intensive dialogue

Qualities and pitfalls of the sovereign leadership style

So long as men worship the Caesars and Napoleons, Caesars and Napoleons will duly arise and make them miserable.

Aldous Huxley (1894–1963)
British novelist

There is a reason why ships don't have two captains. If one captain wants to find a new western route to India across the Atlantic, while the other wants to trade along the African coast, there is no compromise that is going to satisfy both ambitions. Either one captain needs to leave the ship or they will get "stuck in the middle," fudging some type of half-baked in-between deal that satisfies neither. If a venture needs to go somewhere, there needs to be unity of purpose – everyone on board needs to want to strive towards the same objective. This is most easily achieved with one captain, one ultimate authority who determines the mission of the vessel. The crew can take turns at the steering wheel, can debate which islands to stop at and which sails to hoist, but only the captain decides where the voyage is headed and why it is being undertaken. The crew didn't have to join, they signed up voluntarily because the journey appealed to them.

This is the main quality of the sovereign leadership style – people are asked to "join me on my quest." Sovereign leaders advertise their dreams and ambitions and then enlist people who want to support the realization. People don't join a community and then shape a purpose together; they join a purpose and then become a community together. They self-select, buying into the project and the leader they want to serve. And if after a while they decide they don't like it any more, they can quit and join another quest or even start their own.

It is important to note this essential difference between living under a sovereign leader and serving under a sovereign leader. If you are born into a community or country and have no choice but to live under a ruler you don't like, didn't choose and can't influence, this can be highly frustrating. An important historic reason for revolt against absolute monarchs and tyrants, however well-intended they were, has been that lack of freedom to withdraw from the sovereign's dominant influence. Once a subject, always a subject. But signing up to serve a sovereign leader is a choice, usually because the purpose is inspiring or the leader exudes a particular charisma that is attractive to the follower.

And how inspiring these dreams can be! Just think of entrepreneurs starting their own companies, philanthropists building a new museum, managers conquering new markets, humanitarians saving homeless kids from poverty, innovators bringing new business models to life and swashbucklers "putting a ding in the universe."[11] Society needs people who dream big dreams and then exhibit the "get up and go" to make them happen. It is rather difficult to dream-by-committee and then come up with something gripping. The opposite usually happens, whereby multiple interests are balanced to arrive at a complex, convoluted compromise – much like too many cooks in the kitchen crossing an Indian curry with Austrian Sachertorte and Camembert cheese, topping it off with American ketchup. No, clear, crisp, compelling ambitions belong to individuals, who as sovereign leaders mobilize the like-minded to join their cause.

And yes, it is true that sovereign leaders serve their own ambitions and interest first and expect to be supported. But this makes them focused, driven and competitive, enlarging their chances of success, so people who jump on their bandwagon are more likely to be joining a winning team. And by pursuing self-actualization, sovereign leaders are more likely to be persistent and resilient in their quest in the long run, again making them a good locomotive to hitch your wagon to.

Yet, offsetting these appealing qualities, there are some unpleasant shadow sides to the sovereign leadership style that can easily slip to the fore. Unsurprisingly, many sovereign leaders have difficulty sticking to "my purpose first" and quickly slide into "my everything first." Instead of treating the organization as a tool to pursue their mission, the organization becomes a personal playground to fulfill their every need. It is no longer only about realizing their dreams and ambitions, but also about stroking their ego and having everything their way. They go from self-made to self-centered, treating stakeholders as the Sun King used to treat his courtiers and servants – as stage props for his one-man show, with everything revolving around the sun.

Unfortunately, this tendency to become preoccupied with "me, myself and I" is only reinforced if sovereign leaders have no strong check on their power, but can indulge themselves without restraint. "Absolute power corrupts absolutely," and in this case, it happens to them affectively and morally, as sovereign leaders can start to care less about what stakeholders think and experience, while increasingly not feeling responsible for their plight. Before long, self-centered behavior degenerates further into outright egotism, with the sovereign leader taking an undeservedly large piece of the company pie, while neglecting the needs of others. Especially secondary and tertiary stakeholders will be totally outside the leader's field of vision, with little regard given to their interests. But even the interests of primary stakeholders will be easily trampled on, particularly if they can't wield any power to defend themselves. Followers will be seen as expendable pawns, easily disposed of and replaced by others, not as individuals with their own personality and interests.

In the worst cases egotists deteriorate even further in to outright egomaniacs, when their self-indulgence becomes linked to self-adoration. This form of narcissism happens when sovereign leaders become convinced that they deserve all of the benefits they accrue, not only because they have power, but because they are so much more brilliant than the rest. They persuade themselves that the success of the organization is all due to their genius, while failures are all attributable to the bumbling idiots they need to put up with. If your mental picture of this sovereign leader is close to a James Bond villain, you're actually not that far off the mark.

Qualities and pitfalls of the servant leadership style

Avoid putting yourself before others and you can become a leader among men.
Lao-Tzu (605–531 BC)
Chinese philosopher

To servant leaders "self-actualization" sounds like the delusional mantra of the self-absorbed me-generation. Yet they realize that it is just a new reincarnation of old-fashioned egotism, dressed up to sound less selfish. To them, it is a good excuse to blatantly promote one's own interests, while ignoring any responsibility for the people and society around them. It often surprises servant leaders that people are willing to follow such self-enriching types and accept being used as pawns in their chess games. The charisma of such "Caesars and Napoleons" eludes them.

To servant leaders, it is clear that they do have a responsibility for the people and society around them. To take the lead is to take the burden of caring for all. To aspire to leadership is to ask people to place their trust in you and to have faith that their confidence will not be betrayed. It is building a relationship in which followers agree to come on board because they have become convinced that the leader can be counted on to recognize their interests and act accordingly. This earned trust is the key quality of the servant leadership style – by accepting the duty of care, leaders persuade followers to in turn accept them.

But servant leaders go beyond attending to each stakeholder's specific desires and needs. Instead of only serving the individual interests, servant leaders also try to find the common interest. They attempt to identify goals and solutions that align the interests of all those involved, striking a balance between the costs and benefits flowing to each of the stakeholders. It is precisely because servant leaders are impartial and have no stake to defend that they are trusted as mediators and bridge-builders in this process.

Not only do servant leaders avoid promoting their own interests, but they also avoid promoting their own egos. As true servants, they prefer to be "neither heard nor seen," letting followers take the stage and claim the successes. It is their strength that their egos are not in need of constant stroking, so they can let others shine. They actually actively enable followers to take the initiative and allow them to feel that they have "done it themselves." This empowers, while at the same time building followers' self-confidence and encouraging them to grow as leaders in their own right.[12]

So, how do servant leaders keep up this altruistic style? How do they downplay their own needs in favor of those around them? Largely by finding satisfaction in service itself. As Albert Schweitzer once said to a group of graduates: "I don't know what your destiny will be, but one thing I know: the only ones among you who will be really happy are those who will have sought and found how to serve."

Yet, despite Schweitzer's aspirational words, one of the gravest pitfalls of the servant leadership style is to lose sight of one's own interests and to become the doormat of the organization. Servant leaders can be so good at serving others and staying in the background that followers take them for granted, imagining they have achieved everything themselves. And where the servant leader's help is explicitly needed, it is often assumed to be part of the organizational infrastructure, to which the follower is naturally entitled. The more that stakeholders are served, the more spoilt they become, expecting the service to be snappy, tailor-made and preferably with a smile. "They want it all and they want it now."[13] Before servant leaders know it, they will have slipped from service to servitude, and yet they will continue to sacrifice themselves for others, because morally and emotionally they feel that is the right thing to do. If your mental picture of this servant leader is close to the worn-out parent of a teenager, you're actually not that far off the mark. And just as parents are only really appreciated decades later, so too servant leaders are often only valued once they are gone.

Some servant leaders can be so invisible or diplomatic that it is unclear what they contribute and what they stand for, triggering many followers to have low confidence in them. And even when they do speak up, servant leaders can seem so submissive or appeasing that even followers' respect for them will waver, undermining their ability to actually lead. To retain their standing, leaders need to take a stand and prove their value, but this is something that servant leaders are hesitant to do. The consequence can be a self-inflicted wound to servant leaders' influence and a career-limiting underestimation of their contribution.

Qualities of Sovereign Leadership Style	Qualities of Servant Leadership Style
1. Gets followers to serve the leader	1. Gets the leader to serve followers
2. Establishes unity of purpose	2. Establishes balance of interests
3. Asks people to embrace the mission	3. Asks people to determine the mission
4. Enlists people to participate	4. Enables people to initiate
5. Focuses people on leader's goal	5. Involves people in finding common goal
6. Clarifies what is expected of people	6. Clarifies what people can expect
7. Shows people the goal is valuable	7. Shows people they are valuable
8. Inspires respect and admiration	8. Inspires trust and connection
9. Establishes leader as figure head	9. Allows followers to figure prominently
10. Promotes leaders everywhere	10. Creates leaders everywhere
Pitfalls of Sovereign Leadership Style	**Pitfalls of Servant Leadership Style**
1. Takes followers for granted	1. Is taken for granted by followers
2. Feels no duty of care for stakeholders	2. Feels excessive duty of care for stakeholders
3. Self-actualization slips into self-centeredness	3. Service slips into servitude
4. Loses sight of followers' interests	4. Loses sight of own interests
5. Shows willingness to sacrifice pawns	5. Shows willingness to sacrifice self
6. Unable to accommodate others' interests	6. Unable to balance conflicting interests
7. Enriches self at expense of stakeholders	7. Fails to compromise between stakeholders
8. Egotistic purpose inspires no one	8. Convoluted purpose inspires no one
9. Excessive visibility undermines others' growth	9. Lack of visibility undermines respect
10. Narcissistically believing the leader is best	10. Paternalistically believing the leader knows best

Figure 10.2 Qualities and pitfalls of the sovereign and servant leadership styles

Another pitfall awaiting servant leaders is that they can easily fail to align stakeholder interests and find a common good that will unite them. As an envoy shuttling back and forth between opposing forces, the servant leader can be unsuccessful and then get blamed for the lack of a joint result. As all stakeholders feel that the servant leader should understand and serve their needs, they will be reluctant to compromise and quick to fault the servant leader for being a poor mediator.[14] But even where a compromise between all stakeholders can be achieved by the helpful leader, the chances are high that it will be convoluted and uninspiring, receiving only feeble commitment from those involved.

To help stakeholders to achieve real unity of purpose, servant leaders often need to push them to find the middle ground. This means not being stakeholders' errand boys, but rather being arm twisters. Instead of giving stakeholders what they want, servant leaders must focus on giving them what they need, persuading them to see things differently and accept a good compromise instead of remaining adamantly rigid. The pitfall here is that servant leaders can quickly start to believe they know better what followers' interests are than the followers themselves. As with the civil servant manipulating the minister, they feign humble serve, but stop listening and push their own agenda. In the longer run, such paternalism backfires, as stakeholders catch on to the servant leader's lack of real effort to understand and protect their interests. Here, too, the old maxim holds: you get the trust you deserve.

Profiling your leadership style

> *My precept to all who build, is, that the owner should be an ornament to the house, and not the house to the owner.*
>
> Cicero (106–43 BC)
> Roman philosopher, politician and lawyer

Back to Peter at the start of this chapter, who needs to decide whether he will pursue his own agenda and restructure the subsidiary, or whether he should serve the interests of all stakeholders and try to find a compromise that would be beneficial to all. Have you already figured out what you would do if you were in his shoes? Have you also considered a number of alternative approaches, using the opposite styles as a starting point? If you are curious how others suggest you deal with Peter's paradox, you will find a rich set of answers at www.leadership-agility.com.

And what does this say about your own preferred leadership style? Do you recognize yourself generally leaning over to the sovereign side of the scale, or are you a diehard servant leader at heart? Or do you see yourself switching back and forth between the opposite styles depending on the circumstances that you encounter? As before, we close this chapter with a few simple short profiling questions in Figure 10.3, to assist you in determining your default style. To further develop your style repertoire, building on the qualities you recognize and those you want to enhance, we encourage you to go to Chapter 13 and to make use of the Leadership LEAP App.

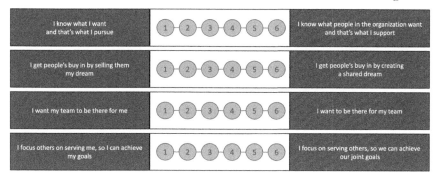

Figure 10.3 Profiling your leadership style: Interests-setting

Notes

1 De Wit, B. and Meyer, R.J.H. (1998), *Strategy: Process, Content, Context: An International Perspective*, London: International Thomson Press.
2 *Cui bono* was attributed by Cicero to Lucius Cassius. In their classic work, Peter Blau and Richard Scott used this expression to distinguish between different types of organizations based on who the primary beneficiary is. See Blau, P.M. and Scott, W.R. (1962), *Formal Organizations: A Comparative Approach*, Redwood: Stanford University Press.
3 The classic text in this field is by Richard Freeman. See: Freeman, R.E. (2010), *Strategic Management: A Stakeholder Approach*, Cambridge: Cambridge University Press.
4 Zakhem, A.J. and Palmer, D.E. (eds.) (2008), *Stakeholder Theory: Essential Readings in Ethical Leadership and Management*, Stoll: Prometheus Books.
5 Neumann, von J. and Morgenstern, O. (1944), *Theory of Games and Economic Behavior*, New Jersey: Princeton University Press.
6 Cleveland, H. (1977), "Interdependence: Where You Stand Depends on Where You Sit," *California Management Review*, Vol. 20, No. 1, pp. 93–96.
7 Although originally coined by Kurt Goldstein in 1939, the term "self-actualization" was made famous by Abraham Maslow. See: Maslow, A.H. (1954), *Motivation and Personality*, New York: Harper & Brothers; Goldstein, K. (1939), *The Organism: A Holistic Approach to Biology Derived from Pathological Data in Man*, New York: American Book Company.
8 Eisenhardt, K.M. (1989), "Agency Theory: An Assessment and Review," *Academy of Management Review*, Vol. 14, No. 1, pp. 57–74.
9 Greenleaf, R.K. (1970), *The Servant as Leader*, Indianapolis: The Greenleaf Center for Servant Leadership. But also see Jill, G.W. (1991), "Servant-Leadership in Organizations: Inspirational and Moral," *The Leadership Quarterly*, Vol. 2, No. 2, pp.105–119.
10 For a good overview of the servant leadership literature see Dierendonck, D. van (2011), "Servant Leadership: A Review and Synthesis," *Journal of Management*, Vol. 37, No. 4, pp. 1228–1261.
11 With a respectful bow to Steve Jobs.
12 Not only do servant leaders grow new leaders, but they also show everyone how to serve. See Hunter, E.M., Neubert, M.J., Perry, S.J., Witt, L.A., Penney, L.M. and Weinberger, E. (2013), "Servant Leaders Inspire Servant Followers: Antecedents and Outcomes for Employees and the Organization," *The Leadership Quarterly*, Vol. 24, No. 2, pp. 316–331.
13 With an equally respectful salute to Queen.
14 Karpman, S. (1968), "Fairy Tales and Script Drama Analysis," *Transactional Analysis Bulletin*, Vol. 7, No. 26, pp. 39–43.

Part VI

Leadership and self

11 Leadership problem-solving
The paradox of thought and action

Agnes was in a tight spot and had to say something. Despite the hustle and bustle of the trade show floor, she was concentrated on the anxious face of the client standing at the company's booth. Again, the client prodded: "The product line your competitor is exhibiting is absolutely stunning, it must have taken you by surprise! Will your company be coming out with something similar very soon or do we need to consider taking our business to them?" Agnes could sense the client's sudden doubt and need for affirmation that her company was the right partner. "We're working on it," Agnes tried. "Our next product line is going to blow them away." But the client wanted more than just this vague promise that something wonderful was somewhere in the pipeline. "Agnes," he said with a firm voice, "you are head of R&D and I trust your judgment. Can I count on something similar being delivered in the next twelve months?" She had to say something more concrete.

To her right Agnes could see Harold, the company's sales director, who had been listening in on their conversation. His eyes screamed: "Say yes!" The client had purchased many of the company's automation systems in the past and during some years was good for more than ten percent of their sales. Their relationship had been quite tight, as the client was heavily dependent on their fast repair service and ongoing maintenance program. It would be a blow to Harold if this client was lost, not only because of future product sales, but because the lucrative service side of business would probably also be transferred to the competitor. It was this stable repeat income that had saved the company a few times before, when the cyclical project side of the business had been in the dumps.

Agnes knew the importance of the client and knew that overall sales were behind target, given the intensity of the competition. Process automation systems were a tough market, with many suppliers and a high rate of innovation, so keeping up market share was a constant battle. Trade shows, like the one she was attending, were important to confirm a company's reputation as cutting edge and as a dependable partner for the future. So, any sign that the company was falling behind needed to be vigorously refuted, lest clients defect to hotter competitors, triggering a self-fulfilling prophesy. Her very reason to be present, as head of R&D, was to strengthen the company's standing as trailblazing innovator.

In reality, however, it seemed they *had* fallen behind. Agnes truly *was* stunned by the new product line being shown off by the company's reinvigorated rival. Their new approach hadn't occurred to Agnes and her team before, but it was patently obvious to her that this type of automation system was superior to their own. She had no choice but to quickly return to her lab and redirect development efforts to counter this imminent threat. However, it wasn't yet clear to her whether the competitor's approach would become the dominant standard to which she would need to adapt herself, or whether the 43 people in her team could come up with an alternative that could place the company ahead of the pack again.

Agnes had already sent a few pictures to her R&D colleagues back at the lab and a few had expressed dismay at their blindness to this new possibility. Others voiced their frustration that the R&D budget had been scaled back in the previous years and that vital colleagues had felt impelled to leave. Agnes's major concern was the company's rigorous decision-making process, which was heavy on spreadsheets and analysis, while more often than not slow on results and implementation. Getting the budget she would need to catch up was not going to be a walkover.

All this flashed through her mind as she fixed her gaze on the client across the counter, eagerly awaiting her pronouncement. She had to say something. Should she honestly admit that she needed to look into the development timeline and would get back to him as quickly as possible, or should she courageously seize the moment and commit the company to delivering a comparable product line within a year? Should she carefully think it through and then present a realistic plan, or should she boldly jump into the unknown and trust that she and her team would find a way of meeting the deadline. She was in the business of automation, but how to deal with this problem didn't come to her automatically.

The task of leadership problem-solving

> *In the arena of human life the honors and the rewards fall to those who show their good qualities in action.*
>
> Aristotle (384–322 BC)
> Leadership problem-solving Greek philosopher

Agnes actually has two problems to solve. First, she must decide what to tell the client, then and there, on the spot, under time pressure. Not only what she says, but also how she says it, will influence the perception of the client. His trust in her depends on how she says she will tackle the challenge that he poses. Her reputation rests on whether her answer is convincing.

Her second problem is what she factually needs to do when she gets back to the company. She and her team quickly need to come up with a new product line, although they only have a vague idea of where to look for a solution. If you add in to the mix a limited budget, a shortage of R&D skills, slow corporate decision-making and high expectations, it is fair to say that Agnes has a Gordian knot of a problem on her hands.

Leaders constantly need to tackle issues, big and small. We call this their *task of leadership problem-solving*. Note that not all of these problems are negative, in the sense of a difficulty or an obstacle. As in mathematics, a "problem" is any type of puzzling issue that needs to be resolved. A problem is a situation requiring action that is not known yet,[1] so prospects and opportunities are also problems that leaders are faced with. Basically, any question challenging someone to come up with a feasible response is a problem.

Problem-solving is also not something limited to leaders. Everyone, every day, is engaged in problem-solving. Some problems are tiny, such as choosing a dish from a restaurant menu, while other problems are huge, such as finding food during a famine. Some problems are individual, such as quitting smoking, while other problems are collective, such as limiting global warming. Some problems are simple, such as fixing a flat tire, while others are complicated,[2] such as filing your tax return. And some problems are tame, such as winning a game of chess, while other problems are wicked, such as eradicating poverty.

This last pair[3] requires a bit more explanation. Tame problems are those whereby the nature of the problem is stable and understood, the problem-owner and other stakeholders are known, all influencing variables can be mapped, all potential solutions are given, all consequences can be predicted and the problem-owner has the power to decide and implement a solution. Chess is a good example, because while complicated, the problem is still tame, and therefore easily solved, even by a computer. Wicked problems are the absolute opposite. In the case of a wicked problem it is difficult to even pin down what the problem is, because it shifts over time and depends on how you look at it and even who looks at it. Wicked problems have many stakeholders but not one problem-owner, and while the stakeholders have opposing interests, no one has the power to impose a solution. Wicked problems are influenced by many variables that are volatile and uncertain, while interacting in complex and ambiguous ways.[4] There is no menu of solutions to choose from, but a limitless number of options, depending on the inventiveness of the problem-solver. And what the consequences will be of any intervention is unclear, but it will be impossible to turn back time and undo what has been done. In this way, wicked problems constantly mutate as problem-solvers try to grapple with them. Needless to say, people generally prefer to deal with tamer problems, leaving the more wicked ones for others to solve. The people who nevertheless step forward to try to tackle these more tricky issues we recognize as leaders.

Where leaders engage in problem-solving together with others in the organization, we call this *organizational decision-making*. In Chapter 6 this process of understanding issues and deciding what needs to be done was described in detail, focusing on the question who should be involved in which phase of the decision-making cycle. It was discussed whether leaders should take decisions autocratically or whether multiple stakeholders should be asked to participate in the process. But that was at the level of organizational leadership. If we descend to the level of the individual, we see leaders and all other people go through the same decision-making cycle themselves every time they want to solve a

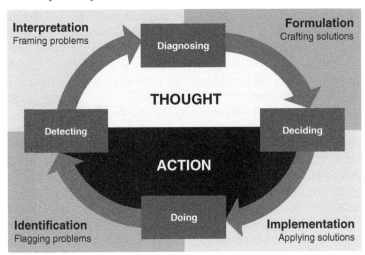

Figure 11.1 The problem-solving cycle

problem, whether big or small. The four steps of problem-solving (see Figure 11.1) are basically the same, whether an individual goes through them to decide on lunch, or an organization goes through them as a decision-making process to determine a new product line.

Any individual attempting to solve any type of problem will necessarily engage in all four problem-solving activities. Typically, the first step is *identification*, whereby the individual will move from a state of *doing* current activities to *detecting* a problem. This realization that something probably requires attention can be a conscious observation, but it can also be based on an intuitive sensing that something needs to be addressed. The second step is *interpretation*, whereby the person will move from a state of *detecting* the problem to *diagnosing* the nature of the problem. This determination of the character, importance and urgency of the problem can again be based on a conscious framing of the issue, but can also be driven by more intuitive sense-making. Together these first two steps are more inductive, oriented towards defining the problem.

The next two steps are more deductive, oriented towards solving the problem. The third step is *formulation*, whereby the individual moves from a state of *diagnosing* the problem to that of *deciding* on an appropriate solution. This process of coming up with a favored answer to the problem can include a conscious review of various options, but it can also be the result of an intuitive jump to a preferred solution. The fourth step is *implementation*, whereby the individual moves from *deciding* on what should be done to actually *doing* it in practice. This deployment of the intended solution can again be very consciously planned and structured, but can also be more intuitively improvised and unfolding. As can be seen in Figure 11.1, the bottom two steps, implementation and identification, are both rooted in doing and as such are more action-oriented activities, while the top two steps, interpretation and formulation, are tightly tied to diagnosing and as such are more action-oriented activities.

As said, this process of combining thought and action to achieve tangible results is the same for any individual or group of people engaged in problem-solving. But if problem-solving is such a universal task, why is it specifically mentioned here as a leadership task? Isn't it a task for everyone? The simple answer is: "Yes, leaders like other people need to solve problems, there is no real difference." Yet, because they are leaders their approach to problem-solving does indirectly impact the people around them. People look to leaders dealing with problems and weigh whether this inspires trust or undermines their confidence. Like the client judging Agnes's response, it is how leaders handle issues that increases their authority or chips away at their credibility. So, while the task of leadership problem-solving is about how leaders *relate to problems*, not how they *relate to followers*, their behavior still has leadership consequences. How leaders conduct themselves when faced with a problem is what shapes how followers see them and whether followers are willing to be influenced by them. The way leaders hold up under pressure, show courage, take initiative, display restraint, search for alternatives, remain open-minded and exhibit tenacity are all aspects of problem-solving that can be clustered under the heading "leaders leading themselves," but all have ripple effects towards the standing of leaders.[5]

There is a second reason why leadership problem-solving is different than the "what should I wear to work?" type. While leaders also constantly sort out everyday issues,[6] they often need to grapple with more complicated and wicked types of problems than many other people. And it turns out that wrestling with these nine-headed monsters places different strains on leaders than wrestling with their pet Labrador. When dealing with more complex problems a paradox emerges. Leaders need to combine thinking and acting, but it becomes increasingly difficult to establish in which order they need to do what. Thought and action are opposite yet complementary activities, so both are required, but the leader must determine in which sequence each needs to be undertaken and how much emphasis each requires. Thus, out of complicated and wicked problems comes the *paradox of thought and action*.

The paradox of thought and action

> *Think like a man of action and act like a man of thought.*
>
> Henri Bergson (1859–1941)
> French philosopher

Put simply, "thought" is everything that goes on in your conscious mind. It refers to mental processes that can't be seen but result in having ideas, opinions, daydreams, analyses and associations. Thought encompasses all of the activities of the brain that we are aware of, as opposed to the activities that take place unconsciously.

Our brains are a fascinating type of apparatus, studied by neurologists, psychiatrists, psychologists, philosophers and artificial intelligence scientists, to name just the most obvious ones. Much could be said about how the brain functions,[7] but for our purpose here the key point is to realize that over time our brains are "programmed" to think in a particular type of way. During our lives, we build up mental maps of the world around us that help us to explain reality. These so-called "cognitive structures" gradually evolve as we interact with our environment and try to make sense of how things work.[8] We call this pro-gramming of the brain "learning" and it leads to an ever more detailed mental map supporting us in understanding what we experience on a day-to-day basis.

But once we have a mental map, this becomes the filter through which we view the world. We can't look at the world objectively and then adapt our mental maps, but rather our mental maps subjectively determine how we look and what we see. We become the captives of our own worldview. We still learn, but through the lens of our existing beliefs. And the more our beliefs are echoed by those around us, the more deeply engrained our convictions become. This is the essence of culture – shared beliefs and values that clarify how the world works and how we should behave. To a large extent individuals have been shaped by the cultures to which they belong, such as their national, corporate, professional and family cultures.

Besides cognitive structures, that tell us *what to think*, our brains also for-mulate "cognitive scripts" that tell us *how to think*. Over time we build up such thinking routines because they help us to reason more quickly and efficiently. We learn how to think like an economist or an engineer because this makes us more capable. We learn how to play chess and how to approach relational difficulties, so that we don't have to remain poor amateurs all our lives. Actu-ally, many of these thinking routines help us to solve problems. But as with mental maps, once we have acquired certain thinking routines, they become our norm and we unwittingly apply them to every situation that comes on our path. They form the comfort zone within which we prefer to linger.

The opposite of thought is action, which encompasses all activities that take place outside of one's mind. Action includes all behaviors potentially visible to external observers, such as presenting, coaching, budgeting, investing, produ-cing and selling. All these actions are tangible conduct, generally directed at putting things into motion and achieving a result. Action is about effecting some type of outcome. Note that there is one odd type of activity that some-times is more like thought and sometimes more like action, which is speaking. We sometimes speak as an aid to thinking, making it tangible, but still largely directed at facilitating the mental process. Yet, in other instances, speaking has the intention of putting things into motion. If the spoken word is used with this mobilizing intention, we say that people are engaged in a "speech act."[9]

Thought and action are obviously each other's complementary opposites. To be able to solve problems, the two need to be combined. But how? If we go back to the definition of a problem as "a situation requiring action that isn't known yet," it seems logical that one first needs to understand the problem before one can solve it. In other words, thought should precede action. A doctor should start with a diagnosis before prescribing medicine. A mechanic should begin by examining the sputtering engine before deciding to take it all apart. A utility should first analyze electricity usage before building a huge new plant. And a government should start with insight into why unemployment remains high, before throwing money at the problem. First think, then do.

But starting with thought assumes that the solution is knowable upfront. It only makes sense to do all the hard thinking if the answer can be deduced from the information available. But what happens if we can't know the solution ahead of time? What happens if we lack the data or it's impossible to know what's going on and what could potentially work? Yet this is exactly the case when dealing with complicated and wicked problems. Then the issue at hand is too volatile, uncertain, complex and ambiguous to be well-understood and a solution needs to be imagined or painstakingly invented. Under these circum-stances, it seems more fitting to learn by trial and error, so first do and then think. Only by experimenting with potential solutions and experiencing the results in practice will insight in to the problem grow.

Yes, but learning-by-doing seems a rather costly and high-risk way of wrestling a nine-headed monster. Giving a patient pills in the hope that one will work takes time, is expensive and can potentially kill the person before having the opportunity to get better. Building a plant as a form of trial and error can easily bankrupt a company. Spending money on public policy in the hope that it will have some impact is not only wasteful, but it is doubtful whether anything will be learned, as the cause and effect relationship between "doing" and "result" will be tenuous at best. At the same time, such gung-ho action-first behavior will detract attention from rigorous thinking about policy choices. So, maybe it is still better to first think and then do.

Not so fast, you might say, learning-by-thinking can also be costly and highrisk. Not only are the solutions to complicated and wicked problems unknowable upfront, but most of the thinking about solutions will probably be done in the wrong direction. As we are all captives of existing mental models and thinking routines, we generally keep on thinking the way we always have and will "jump to solutions" with which we are familiar. Ask a marketer about a problem and you get a marketing solution, but ask a finance person about the same problem and not surprisingly you get a financial solution. So, often the only way to find a novel solution is to approach the problem without any pre-conceived ideas. Open-mindedly see what happens. So, back to first do, then think. As the aphorism goes: "It's easier to act your way into a new way of thinking, than to think your way into a new way of acting."

By now, this whole question of whether thinking or acting comes first should remind you of the "chicken and egg" paradox – both are needed, one leads to the other, but surely one must be at the start of the cycle. This is a slightly different type of paradox than in previous chapters, where two oppo-sites conflicted with one another. In the case of the paradox of thought and action the two opposites complement each other and are both required: it is a matter of which comes first and foremost. And just as in its poultry equivalent, where some favor the chicken side, while others are more partial to the egg argument, here too leaders tend to lean over to one side or the other, as both can't be true at the same time. Leaders placing more importance on thought and exhibiting a preference to start there, we say have a *reflective leadership style*. Leaders who see more value in action and show an inclination to begin there, we say have a *proactive leadership style*. Let's reflect on both.

The reflective leadership style

> *Don't just do something, stand there.*
>
> Dean Acheson (1893–1971)
> American Secretary of State

When confronted with a problem, reflective leaders prefer to step back and think before they act. In their perspective, first comes perspective – they start by coming to grips with what is going on, understanding the problem, and then they move to exploring potential solutions, deciding on the best one and putting that into action. To them, it is essential to take the time to become fully convinced that they have crafted the best possible solution before proceeding towards implementation. They want to complete their thinking, before taking the next step of execution.

Many reflective leaders take a thoroughly analytical and orderly approach when going through the problem-solving cycle, moving from detecting to diagnosing to deciding and only then doing. Starting with detection means they like to begin by considering what the nature of the problem is and whether it is actually even a problem. They have a penchant to extensively observe what is happening in practice and mull over these reflections, trying to nail down the essence of each issue, often searching for the problem behind the problem. They also have a fondness of collecting data and intelligence, to feed their analysis and problem structuring. The more complicated and wicked the problem, the more value these reflective leaders see in trying to map out its complexity and figure out what influences what. As they are aware of the bias of their worldview, they like to search out different perspectives and explicitly spend time looking at issues from different angles.

However, not all reflective leaders are necessarily analytically-inclined – there are multiple ways of being "thoughtful." Many reflective leaders will take a more intuitive approach to detecting, trusting their "gutfeel" to identify issues, while their diagnosis will also be more subjectively based on their impressions and hunches. To them, reflecting is about soaking up the situation, letting it brew a bit and then allowing a sense of what is going on emerge in their minds.

As reflective leaders move from diagnosing to deciding, again the more analytically-oriented will follow a structured approach, examining multiple angles, envisioning a general direction and then formulating a variety of solution options, before zeroing in on the optimal one, often asking others to field alternative possibilities to avoid falling in the trap of favoring "pet solutions." Typically, the vetting of the options will be on the basis of rigorous criteria, including implementability and the risk/return profile. Once the best possible choice has been selected, these reflective leaders will prefer to draw up an implementation plan before continuing on to doing.

But again, not all reflective leaders are focused on analytical rigor. Some take a more creative approach to coming up with solutions, by skipping past extensive diagnosis and using their imagination to dream up new ideas. Often, they start with a notion of a possible solution even before they have fully understood the problem. Sometimes they even loop backwards from formulation to do some follow-up interpretation or even rethink the identification of the problem. To them, thinking is not a rational and linear process, but a creative and iterative one. And the solution doesn't have to be a detailed plan, but can also be an attractive picture of the future situation – not a blueprint, but a vision.

Whichever way the thinking is done, reflective leaders believe it should be concluded before progressing to action – it makes sense to go through this cycle thoroughly, thoughtfully and only once. It might take a bit longer but the quality of the outcome is key and it should be done right the first time. And the reflective leader also knows that pacing the problem-solving process – not too fast and not too slow – allows insights and solutions to mature, just like a good beer needs to ferment. Some reflective leaders will even make a point of sleeping on a problem, because with a little bit of distance and a fresh demeanor the next morning, the problem often looks quite different.

All in all, it can be said that reflective leaders like to take the time for a problem-solving process. They want to get on top of the problem and conquer it mentally before conquering it in practice. They want to stand above the problem and see the solution in their mind's eye, before intervening and seeing it in reality.

The proactive leadership style

> *The right man is the one who seizes the moment.*
> Johann Wolfgang von Goethe (1749–1832)
> German scientist, writer, philosopher and statesman

Proactive leaders are less hung up on this desire to see the solution before getting up out of their chairs. Reflectiveness is for bookkeepers and scientists, not for leaders grappling with real world problems in real time. To them the best way of dealing with a problem is not to step back, but to step forward, and to grab the bull by the horns. You can study a book on bulls, talk to a variety of people who have dealt with bulls and even do a bullriding course online, but the quickest and most insightful way to learn is to courageously go out and engage the bull. You won't know what he'll do and you won't know what will work, but you must trust yourself that you'll learn fast and figure it out along the way.

Typical of proactive leaders is that they dare to start before they have all the data and the end in sight. In their view, most problems can't be solved sitting behind your desk thinking, but must be experienced and explored to arrive at the necessary insights and to invent a workable solution. The more complicated and wicked the problem, the more difficult it will be to map out in abstraction, looking at it from a distance. Perfecting a solution will only lead to procrastination, so proactive leaders dive in, trying to understand enough to reach a satisfactory approach. They often don't get it right immediately, so they keep on trying until the result is acceptable.

This learning-by-doing approach is not only faster and more effective, but it has the added effect of bringing people into motion and creating momentum in the organization. Proactive leaders are good at stirring things up, getting people off their chairs and instilling an attitude of "get up and go." The first step is often the most difficult one for people to take, but proactive leaders are good at taking initiative and pressing people into action. This creates a buzz and a willingness to change, making the organization less rigid and set in its ways. People are often inspired by a sense of opportunity as they see the dynamism around them. It strengthens their confidence that the organization is capable of getting things done in practice, not only good at making lengthy PowerPoint presentations.

In terms of the problem-solving cycle, the approach taken by proactive leaders is that they start by "deciding" to try out a particular type of solution, based on a quick and dirty, intuitive understanding of what the problem is. As the solution they explore is not yet fully developed, the "doing" they engage in doesn't resemble classic implementation, but looks more like hands-on experimentation. They then rapidly carry on to "detecting," reflecting on what seems to be working and what isn't. A bit of "diagnosis" follows, to gain a first understanding of the successes and failures of the experiment, leading to a quick decision to adapt the doing, tweaking the experiment a bit. This cycle is repeated multiple times, constantly learning and adapting along the way.

Table 11.1 Differences between the reflective and proactive leadership styles

	Reflective Leadership Style	*Proactive Leadership Style*
Emphasis on	Thought over action	Action over thought
Motivating people by	Knowing how	Showing how
Competent leaders are	Considered and generally right	Hands-on and generally learn
Orientation towards	Being sure	Being swift
Basic attitude	Correct is better than quick	Actions speak louder than words
Core quality	Putting things in perspective	Taking the initiative
Intended impact	Doing it right the first time	Making things happen
Underlying conviction	Insight leads to success	Movement leads to success
Guiding principle/motto	Think before you act!	Just do it!
Preferred tools	Workshops and plans	Experiments and feedback

So, while reflective leaders want to be sure about making the *right* decision, proactive leaders want to be sure about making a *timely* decision. While reflective leaders want to avoid jumping into the wrong type of action, proactive leaders want to avoid getting stuck in inaction. They see problem-solving as an ongoing learning process, not something that can be achieved in one bold stroke. They don't want to be right, they want feedback, so that insight into the problem can gradually grow and a solution will progressively emerge. All it takes is the confidence to get started and take the first step.

Qualities and pitfalls of the reflective leadership style

He who considers too much will perform little.

Johann Friedrich von Schiller (1759–1805)
German poet, philosopher and historian

The paced approach that reflective leaders take to problem-solving is first and foremost *considered*, as opposed to fast and furious. Reflective leaders want to get their arms around the problem and refuse to be swept along by emotional appeals and first impressions. They are convinced that the best way to tackle a problem is to step back and do your homework, taking the trouble of collecting and structuring information and ideas. Generally, more can be known than first meets the eye, but it does require the desire to seek out data and intelligence, and to creatively explore ideas, instead of accepting lazy observations and falling back on simplistic perceptions. To reflective leaders, tested hypotheses should be leading, to avoid basing their understanding of problems on rumors, superficial assumptions, prejudices and superstitions.[10] Even where problems are complex and information is missing, reflective leaders believe that chewing on a problem will release more insights and make it more easily digestible than quickly swallowing the problem in one gulp.

Closely tied to the reflective style's strength at going deeper is its quality of going broader – reflective leaders are often good at being *thorough*. They seek to approach problems by taking a bird's eye view, identifying which variables are in play and closely examining what influences what. In mapping out causal relationships, they are interested in determining which factors can be influenced and which risks there are lurking. They also want to pinpoint where assumptions have been made and where a different angle might result in a different understanding of a problem or a potential solution.

The reflective style also allows leaders to apply their considered and thorough thoughtfulness in a *diligent* manner – they first patiently and persistently complete their thinking before moving on to implementation. The most disciplined are the analytically-inclined leaders, who prefer to go through the entire problem-solving cycle in an orderly fashion, completing each step in a proper way before advancing to the next. To them it is crucial to first have a fixed grip on the problem before advancing to the formulation of possible solutions, decision-making and eventually implementation. But for all successful reflective leaders it is essential to scrutinize multiple solution options, teasing out the advantages and disadvantages of each, to find the optimal answer, instead of picking the first acceptable solution that happens to come their way. In the same vein, reflective leaders also favor a diligent approach to learning, stimulating reflection, analysis, idea generation and discussion, leading to explicit conclusions.

Together with their diligence, reflective leaders also have a *measured* approach to problem-solving. In the beginning of the process they are keenly aware that they are not yet on top of the problem, so they are careful to declare early victory and jump to implementing solutions. As they develop a more thorough understanding of the problem they face and a more vivid image of the potential solutions, they increasingly gain an intimate insight into what is volatile, uncertain, complex and ambiguous, again making them watchful to draw quick and clear conclusions. And once it is time to select a solution for deployment, they will have already considered the execution challenges ahead and the risks involved, making them deliberate and level-headed implementers.

Taken together, these qualities of being considered, thorough, diligent and measured thinkers cause leaders with a reflective style to seem calm, cool and collected, which often inspires followers to have confidence in them. Especially followers who value the impression that a leader is on top of the problem-solving process will more easily place their trust in such a considered person.

But leaders using this style are on a very slippery slope and many regularly slide into being too thoughtful. Take the pitfall of being too considered and too thorough, which many reflective leaders get stuck in. It sometimes starts with a preference for rationality and "hard facts," which easily becomes a bias against "soft facts." For these reflective leaders, evidence-based decision-making often is the same as spreadsheet-based decision-making, in which the hard numbers tell the story. But this means they tend to neglect hunches, intuition, informed opinions, feelings and most other forms of qualitative information, cutting themselves off from a richness of sources. Even more common is that they overestimate how much hard objective information can really be found and they overrate their ability to know the future and to collect facts about other unknowns. The essence of "unknowns" is that people don't know them and all of the rationality in the world will not reveal them. The more compli- cated and wicked the problem, the more unknowns one must assume there will be, so trying to map out a complex issue is an exercise in futility. All that happens to these reflective leaders is that they get stuck in a morass of detail. Instead of gaining the bird's eye view they wanted, they get sucked into the swamp of data, collecting more and more, but sinking deeper and deeper.

The twin brother of paralysis-by-data-collection is paralysis-by-analysis, whereby reflective leaders repeatedly mull over a problem, each time finding new layers, different angles, additional stakeholders and unexpected risks. As soon as reflective leaders threaten to converge on the optimal solution to a problem, new questions are posed and doubts are raised about the completeness of the analysis, throwing reflective leaders back into another round of delib- eration, often requiring renewed data collection and number crunching. This

maddening tendency to overanalyze is further reinforced by too much proce-
dural discipline, whereby the reflective leader feels uncomfortable moving to the
next step of the problem-solving cycle without having completely finished the
previous one. To remain in control of the process, order must be maintained, as
it is felt that making quick and dirty steps invites a descent into sloppy thinking.

There is actually even a third brother completing the triplet – paralysis-by-
perfection. Where reflective leaders get past the hurdles of paralysis-by-data-
collection and paralysis-by-analysis, they often tumble into the pitfall of being
overly ambitious at crafting the ultimate answer to all challenges. It is often just
too alluring to come up with the perfect solution instead of merely an acceptable one. "Why settle for good if you can be great?" is the siren call that
seduces leaders to continuously fine-tune their plans. As they polish their ideas
again and again, each blemish sticks out like a sore thumb, triggering a new
round of intense polishing. And the longer reflective leaders wait to act, the
more they feel the anticipation that the actions should be great, again sending
them back to do further polishing.

At the same time, reflective leaders are often overly cautious, weary of risk
and afraid of making mistakes. All this results in an excruciatingly slow problem-solving process, whereby action is constantly postponed and the window
of opportunity is usually long shut by the time a decision is finally made. To
followers the reflective leader's thought often seems like an excuse not to act.
Reflecting looks more like procrastination. Thinking seems like a "security
blanket" to sooth the hesitant and unsure leader. This air of timidity doesn't
help followers to have confidence in such a leader.

Where reflective leaders are not stuck in endless procrastination, they can
easily get lost in endless imagination. Because of their passion for reflection,
conceptualization and invention, it is very seductive to delay deciding, preferring to dig deeper or come up with even more ideas. Instead of consciously
working towards a conclusion, many reflective leaders are more inclined to
linger in the maze of complex analysis, generating an increasingly sophisticated
understanding of the issues and envisioning ever more angles for a potential
solution.

And then there are the reflective leaders who believe that their task is completed as soon as they have reached a decision. They are decision-makers, not
foot soldiers. Sometimes they will go to the trouble of communicating their
decision, but often once they have decided in their mind the rest is incon-
sequential and not high on their priority list. To them implementation is
uninteresting, or beneath them, or something that is not really their responsibility. Hence, they fail to engage in action, leaving the problem factually
unsolved. The PowerPoints will look great, but nothing will actually change in
practice. And they definitely won't change themselves, even though they are
often part of the problem and without personal commitment to adjust their
own behavior the problem will remain unsolvable.

In all these cases, reflective leaders can seem disconnected from the organizational reality where action is needed. They can give the impression of living

in an ivory tower, unaware or uninterested in what is going on in practice. This can make them appear theoretical and aloof, or even cold and calculating. Either way, they can quickly be seen as emotionally detached from the problem and the people around them, making them difficult to "warm" to, thereby creating distance and lowering trust.

Qualities and pitfalls of the proactive leadership style

> *Mark this well, you proud men of action! You are, after all, nothing but unconscious instruments of the men of thought.*
>
> Heinrich Heine (1797–1856)
> German poet, journalist and essayist

While the qualities of reflective leaders are centered on how they employ thought, the qualities of proactive leaders revolve around how they employ action. First and foremost, proactive leaders use action to drive *discovery*. To them, problem-solving is not about figuring out, but about finding out. It is not about analyzing and calculating the optimal solution on the basis of known facts; it is about searching and distilling a satisfactory solution despite the lack of vital facts. Sometimes the solution is "out there," yet hidden and in need of uncovering. But often the solution still needs to be invented, requiring experimentation and learning. Proactive leaders know that to discover, one has to go out and look. In the beginning, it might seem like groping in the dark, but that is the nature of searching. After a while, on the basis of experience and feedback, the searching can be narrowed until finally an acceptable solution is discovered. The quality of proactive leaders is that they are skilled at driving this process of guided search, using facts and analysis where possible, but intuition and hunches where necessary. They open-mindedly scan around, generate possibilities, try things out and improvise, while the entire time not committing themselves to only one line of inquiry, because they "know that they can't know" whether it will be a fruitful one. This is truly learning-by-doing.

Closely linked to this "action as discovery" is how proactive leaders use action to drive a sense of *adventure*. Instead of earnestly and gravely reflecting on problems and identifying risks and barriers, proactive leaders use action to lower people's fear of the unknown and to see the fun side of exploration. They optimistically focus on the possibilities and the joy of the chase. While trying out new things might feel a bit daring, proactive leaders highlight that it can be thrilling and enjoyable as well. And they further lower any feelings of trepidation by emphasizing the playful nature of learning and the acceptability of making mistakes. "Failure Fridays" and other lighthearted tools are often used to signal that "failing fast" is okay and should be embraced instead of dreaded.

Another quality of leaders using the proactive style is that they employ action to drive *momentum* in their organizations. Proactive leaders know that extensive contemplation, meticulous analyses and dragged out decision-making are exhaustive and sap the energy out of people. And the longer there is no action, the more it feels like that is the normal state of affairs. Inactivity is contagious. People settle in, stagnation spreads and any proposed change will have to go through numerous committees. But proactive leaders know that you should never let people settle in. Just as meetings are much shorter if people are standing, so too change goes much faster if people remain on their feet and are active. So, proactive leaders use the discovery process as a way of triggering movement and creating a sense of dynamism. By letting people take the initiative and try out new solutions, the organization's ability to adapt and transform is improved. In this way, it is action that becomes contagious.

Next to "action as discovery," "action as adventure" and "action as momentum," a fourth quality could be called "action as audacity." Proactive leaders often use action to quickly and courageously jump at an opportunity, before it slips away again. As the Roman philosopher Publilius Syrus already said more than two thousand years ago: "The opportunity is often lost by deliberating." Or as the Dutch philosopher Desiderius Erasmus said more than five hundred years ago: "Fortune favors the audacious." Proactive leaders know that if you reflect too long and want to have absolute certainty, opportunities will not wait and neither will competitors. In many circumstances, leaders simply don't have the luxury of unhurried contemplation, but must make a quick judgment call and rapidly come into action. That requires some nerve, but this challenge comes with the role of leader.

Taken together, these qualities of using action to drive discovery, adventure, momentum and audacity cause leaders with a proactive style to seem courageous and can-do, which often inspires followers to have confidence in them. Especially followers who value the impression that a leader is able to make things happen will more easily place their trust in such a dynamic person.

But proactive leaders, just like their reflective counterparts, are vulnerable to the slippery slope of exaggeration, making them slide towards a number of gaping pitfalls. The most obvious danger is that their approach to discovery can easily degenerate into clueless drifting. They can be so action-oriented, that they give themselves little or no time to think. Instead of taking some time to reflect on their next step, many proactive leaders prefer to behave like real-life "action figures," coming out shooting and seeing where their daring-do will take them. Instead of contemplating the facts and taking aim at the true problem, they are inclined to trust their gut and shoot from the hip. Instead of learning from their doing, they simply keep on doing, hoping that their frantic activity will get them somewhere. And it often does – it gets them into trouble. They are then pressed to fall back on their improvisation ability to deal with the poorly thought out situation and avoid the consequences of the unfolding mess they create. The result is that they get no closer to solving the problem, but actually add to it, forcing them to muddle through and try to survive.

This naïve, impulsive, approach to solution discovery often goes hand in hand with a rather cavalier disdain for facts and disciplined reasoning. In their drive to promote curiosity and a sense of adventure, proactive leaders can easily promote a disregard for information gathering and planning ahead. As they stimulate playful and open-minded exploration, they give their blessing to ignoring all the data and insights that are already available. Such proactive leaders often don't challenge the biases picked up elsewhere that implicitly push people to jump to certain solutions. They tolerate uninformed initiatives and even glorify foolish failures that could have been prevented with a bit of healthy analysis and respect for the facts.

All this undisciplined rambling about is commonly justified because of the dynamism it unleashes. Proactive leaders are enthralled by the energy and movement that can be triggered by their emphasis on action. However, this vibrancy often decays into frenzied commotion, as people are off in all directions, undertaking action that is not thought through and not coordinated. The "animated atmosphere" is generally just plain unrest, as people's initiatives collide, fights for budget break out and dim-witted errors wreak havoc. In reality, the buzz created is that of irate bees, angry that someone has entered their hive and threatens to steal their honey. The momentum that proactive leaders assume they are building is just a wave of chaos that will frustrate lasting problem-solving.

And then there is the audacity on which proactive leaders pride themselves. Unfortunately, there is a very fine line separating courageous audacity and cocky brazenness, and the line is almost impossible to distinguish. In the name of "grabbing the bull by the horns," many proactive leaders imprudently jump into the streets of Pamplona and end up being impaled. In the name of "seizing the moment," they arrogantly jump into the quicksand of a poor decision, from which it is difficult to free themselves. Arguing "no guts, no glory," they will take irresponsible risks, that with a bit more thought would be seen to be foolhardy. And if they are nevertheless successful, their learning will be that rashness pays, so they will continue their high stakes game until disaster eventually catches up with them.

Taken together, being impulsive, naïve, chaotic and brash is not a way to reinforce confidence among followers. By letting discovery degenerate into drifting, letting adventure spin into laziness, letting momentum collapse into unrest and letting audacity grow into recklessness, proactive leaders lose the trust of those around them. People will see an erratic individual, driven more by emotions than by logic, which will seriously undermine such a leader's credibility.

Profiling your leadership style

> *I never worry about action, but only about inaction.*
>
> Winston Churchill (1874–1965)
> British Prime Minister

Have you already spotted on which side of the continuum you tend to hang out? Are you the thinker, calmly reflecting before moving into action, or the doer, trying solutions out to see what works? Do you first read the instructions before putting together IKEA furniture, or do you immediately get going and

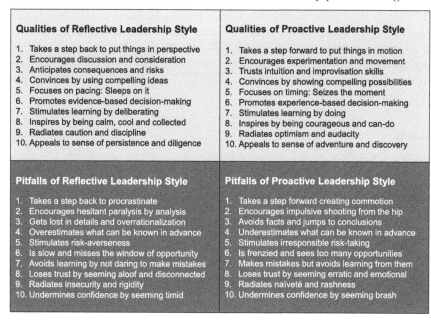

Qualities of Reflective Leadership Style	Qualities of Proactive Leadership Style
1. Takes a step back to put things in perspective	1. Takes a step forward to put things in motion
2. Encourages discussion and consideration	2. Encourages experimentation and movement
3. Anticipates consequences and risks	3. Trusts intuition and improvisation skills
4. Convinces by using compelling ideas	4. Convinces by showing compelling possibilities
5. Focuses on pacing: Sleeps on it	5. Focuses on timing: Seizes the moment
6. Promotes evidence-based decision-making	6. Promotes experience-based decision-making
7. Stimulates learning by deliberating	7. Stimulates learning by doing
8. Inspires by being calm, cool and collected	8. Inspires by being courageous and can-do
9. Radiates caution and discipline	9. Radiates optimism and audacity
10. Appeals to sense of persistence and diligence	10. Appeals to sense of adventure and discovery

Pitfalls of Reflective Leadership Style	Pitfalls of Proactive Leadership Style
1. Takes a step back to procrastinate	1. Takes a step forward creating commotion
2. Encourages hesitant paralysis by analysis	2. Encourages impulsive shooting from the hip
3. Gets lost in details and overrationalization	3. Avoids facts and jumps to conclusions
4. Overestimates what can be known in advance	4. Underestimates what can be known in advance
5. Stimulates risk-averseness	5. Stimulates irresponsible risk-taking
6. Is slow and misses the window of opportunity	6. Is frenzied and sees too many opportunities
7. Avoids learning by not daring to make mistakes	7. Makes mistakes but avoids learning from them
8. Loses trust by seeming aloof and disconnected	8. Loses trust by seeming erratic and emotional
9. Radiates insecurity and rigidity	9. Radiates naïveté and rashness
10. Undermines confidence by seeming timid	10. Undermines confidence by seeming brash

Figure 11.2 Qualities and pitfalls of the reflective and proactive leadership styles

figure it out along the way? Do you worry about ill-considered action, or are you more like Churchill, worried about inaction? Do you catch yourself "sleeping on" an issue, or do you prefer to come at a problem "with your guns blazing?" To continue the firearms metaphor, do you recognize your pitfall as "ready, aim…aim…aim…," or as "ready, fire, fire, fire!?"[11] To aid you in establishing your preferred leadership problem-solving style, we have again provided a few profiling statements, which you can find in Figure 11.3.

In the meantime, you have also had the opportunity to consider what Agnes should say to the client putting her on the spot at the trade show. If you are

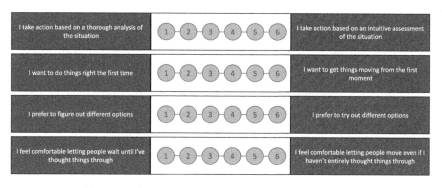

Figure 11.3 Profiling your leadership style: Leadership problem-solving

still reflecting on what she should do, that just might tell you something about your default problem-solving style. If, on the other hand, you didn't even have to read this chapter to know what you would do, that too gives you an important clue to your preferred style. Whichever it is, if you want to read up on other people's approach to Agnes's predicament, the website will offer you some inspiring solutions.

Notes

1 This is Karl Weick's well-known definition of a problem. See: Weick, K. (1989), "Theory Construction as Disciplined Imagination," *Academy of Management Review*, Vol. 14, No. 4, pp. 516–531.

2 For a good description of the difference between complicated and complex phenomena see Sargut, G. and McGrath, R. (2011), "Learning to Live with Complexity," *Harvard Business Review*, Vol. 89, No. 9, pp. 68–76. Complex is closer to the older concept of wicked problems.

3 See Rittel, H., and Webber, M. (1973), "Dilemmas in a General Theory of Planning," *Policy Sciences*, Vol. 4, No. 2, pp. 155–169.

4 This is the VUCA world discussed in Chapter 7.

5 While the leadership tasks in the previous eight chapters all dealt with the relationship between *leaders and their followers*, you might have noted that the task of leadership problem-solving is about the relationship between *leaders and their problems*. That makes this chapter quite different than the previous ones. If you reflect on it, "thought" and "action" aren't activities that leaders do with their followers or to engage their followers – they aren't really *leadership activities* at all. They are only *activities that leaders do*, as we all do. Leaders breath, but that doesn't make it a leadership activity. In other words, leadership problem-solving is of a different order than all of the other tasks covered in the previous chapters. We say that leadership problem-solving is at the level of *leadership and self* – how leaders behave themselves, even when they are not trying to lead.

6 Mintzberg, H. (1973), *The Nature of Managerial Work*, New York: Harper & Row.

7 For a recent example see: Herculano-Houzel, S. (2015), *The Human Advantage: A New Understanding of How Our Brain Became Remarkable*, Cambridge: MIT Press.

8 For a good overview of the role of cognitive maps and cognitive structures in managerial decision-making see Walsh, J. (1995) "Managerial and Organizational Cognition: Notes from a Trip Down Memory Lane," *Organization Science*, Vol. 6, No. 3, pp. 280–321.

9 Searle, J.R. (1969), *Speech Acts: An Essay in the Philosophy of Language*, Cambridge: Cambridge University Press.

10 Daniel Kahneman would say that reflective leaders have the quality of supplementing their System 1 thinking (which is "quick and dirty" intuition) with System 2 thinking (which is slower conscious analysis). See: Kahneman, D. (2011), *Thinking Fast and Slow*, New York: Farrar, Straus and Giroux. This argument is similar to Malcolm Gladwell's argument on the advantages and disadvantages of human intuition. See: Gladwell, M. (2005), *Blink: The Power of Thinking Without Thinking*, New York: Little, Brown & Company.

11 Peters and Waterman quote Ross Perot using similar terms to distinguish the approach taken by EDS and GM. See: Peters, T.J. and Waterman, R.H. (1982), *In Search of Excellence: Lessons from America's Best-Run Companies*, New York: Harper-Collins.

12 Leadership attunement

The paradox of authenticity and adjustment

"I quit!" Robert bellowed, as he threw his ID badge onto Jeffrey's desk. "No, you're fired!" Jeffrey shouted back. "Robert, you are impossible! You don't listen to what I tell you. You show no respect…you didn't even knock, you just barged in!" After a short moment of silence, Robert drew a deep breath and said in a slightly calmer voice: "Look Jeffrey, that's the way people work around here. This isn't Singapore. If you can't deal with me, good luck finding another German operations manager you will be able to get along with. I'm not impossible, I just don't like being commanded by someone who doesn't know what he's talking about."

As Robert stormed out the door, Jeffrey sank back in his chair fuming. He had been in Hamburg now for more than a year, setting up the new assembly plant that was going to serve the entire European market. Progress had been slow and it had frustrated Jeffrey greatly. And now this. How was he going to explain this new setback to the company directors in Singapore? Not only was he going to lose face, but so would the people who had supported his nomination as head of European operations. As only son of the company's founder, few had been willing to question his appointment, but many would delight in his failure. Especially his retired father and uncle had carefully pushed for Jeffrey to be given this opportunity to shake off his image of spoiled playboy and gain essential foreign business experience. It was facing his father that Jeffrey dreaded most.

The project had started well a year back. After the decision had been made to move assembly activities from Malaysia to Europe, the harbor of Hamburg had been selected as plant location because of the excellent connections over water to Singapore and over rail and road to the European hinterland. Moreover, plenty of highly qualified engineers and production workers would be available as employees, it was believed. Jeffrey had identified approximately twenty experienced hands from the Malaysian site to come with him to Hamburg, to ensure that vital knowledge and skills would be transferred to the new facility. In accordance with company policy, Jeffrey was also accompanied by a seasoned company finance director, Elizabeth, and a number of Singaporean employees for the control function.

Jeffrey's first priority after hitting the ground in Germany was to hire a local HR manager, with whom he could start recruiting people for other key posts.

Claus had been responsible for HR in China for a German company earlier in his career, so had been an enthusiastic pick to join Jeffrey in bridging the cultural differences between Asia and Europe as fresh head of HR. Once in place, Claus had helped to sign up the other three members of the management team: Robert as operations manager, Ingrid to run IT and Helmut to head logistics. With this core team of six set, attention subsequently passed to taking on the next layer of personnel and getting the project started.

But irritations soon surfaced. Jeffrey set tight deadlines, was very disciplined and worked long hours, and expected the same of others, sometimes demanding evening and weekend meetings. Being slightly perfectionist, he was adamant that high quality standards should be upheld and he complained bitterly if he felt that anyone was not meeting performance norms, often showing his displeasure in public. He was distanced and direct, almost blunt, towards others, displaying a touch of arrogance, but was easily insulted if he felt that others didn't treat him with the respect he believed he deserved. But what irked Ingrid and Robert most was that he insisted on making the final decision on even the smallest of issues. Although Jeffrey lacked any experience in building and running an assembly plant, he wanted to call all the shots himself, leaving others no decision-making authority.

Both Ingrid and Robert had tried to give him feedback, but he had shown little interest in their grievances, so Robert had elected to occasionally ignore Jeffrey and make some necessary minor decisions himself. That "insubordination" had lead Jeffrey to call Robert to his office, resulting in their quarrel and Robert's dramatic exit.

As Jeffrey sat reflecting on what had just happened, Claus came in, drawn by the racket. "Jeffrey, if you want to lead these people, you're going to have to adjust your style," Claus ventured. "Maybe," Jeffrey responded. "But I am who I am. And don't forget that our Singaporean staff are also watching me, so I have to be consistent. We just need to find a new operations manager who fits with me." Jeffrey watched Claus's face. "You don't agree with me, do you?" Jeffrey surmised. "OK Claus, so what would be your advice?"

The task of leadership attunement

> I suppose leadership at one time meant muscles; but today it means getting along with people.
>
> Mahatma Gandhi (1869–1948)
> Indian politician

In line with Gandhi's observation, Jeffrey's challenge is how to get along with the people he seeks to lead. To be accepted as their leader, not merely as their boss, Jeffrey needs to connect with those around him and win their confidence. He needs to align his behavior with the needs of those he wishes to influence, in order to entice them to willingly follow. This we call *the task of leadership attunement* – creating a fit between the leader on the one hand and the followers and their circumstances on the other.

To ensure that leaders are constantly in tune with their environment, ongoing adjustment is required. Creating fit is a dynamic process and can go in two directions; leaders can adjust themselves to their followers, or vice versa, followers can become adjusted to their leaders. Where the followers are the ones doing the aligning, there are four ways in which this can take place. First, followers can *voluntarily adjust* their behavior because they become convinced that this is more effective. Second, followers can be indirectly *nudged to adjust* their behavior, by changing the conditions under which they function. Third, followers can be *compelled to adjust* their behavior, under pressure of potential disapproval or incentivized by carrots and sticks. And fourth, followers can be *replaced* by other people who show a better fit with the leader in question.

Where leaders are the ones doing the adjusting, this is generally a display of *leadership style flexibility*, as they switch to leadership behaviors in their repertoire that they deem more effective. But sometimes they even exhibit *leadership style adaptability*, learning new behaviors that are better suited to the circumstances. Taken together, the capacity to flexibly shift between leadership styles, and adaptively master new ones, can make leaders potentially very adjustable to the specific needs of the people and situation they want to influence.

But it is not easy for leaders to constantly adjust themselves to achieve fit. Leaders are not endlessly malleable. Just as with all people, leaders have been shaped by nature and nurture to have a relatively stable profile and are largely set in their ways. Leaders don't wake up in the morning asking themselves "who shall I be today," but have a sense of who they genuinely are. They have established personal characteristics that are not easily changed and determine "who is me." All this makes attuning themselves to the requirements of others at the very least a challenge.

So, what is it about leaders that limits their adjustability? To answer this question, we must delve into the self of leaders, examining their "inside," to find the elements that make them more or less shapeable. To avoid making this voyage of inner exploration unnecessarily complicated, we have formulated a simple layered model of the individual.[1] This model, depicted in Figure 12.1, takes the globe as a metaphor for understanding "the world of each person."

Just as earth is extremely complex if you zoom in, so are people if you study them in detail. But if you zoom out, to take in the big picture, the globe can be understood as consisting of four general layers – the crust, the mantle, the outer core and the inner core. If this image is transposed onto an individual, all aspects of a person can be mapped into four similar categories. On the surface is the crust – the thin layer that is visible from the outside, where all the action takes place. In the case of people, the crust is made up of the positions and roles that they fulfill. Positions are all of the formal stations that an individual occupies, such as manager, captain of a football team, physician at a hospital, member of the orchestra, inhabitant of Spain or government official, while roles are all of the informal functions taken up by an individual, such as leader, community organizer, philanthropist, band member and friend.

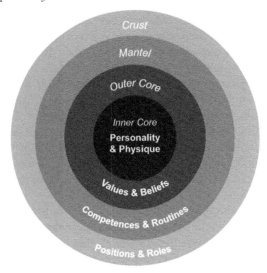

Figure 12.1 The layered model of the individual

To a certain extent individuals "are" these positions and roles. Ask someone at a party who they are and they will answer lawyer, New Yorker, neighbor, member of Amnesty International or employee of Google – and potentially all at the same time. Clearly, the positions and roles people occupy are a key determinant of how each individual behaves, as they bring people into particular situations to which they need to respond. As an ambulance medic, an individual needs to respond differently than as a garbage collector, CEO, Justin Bieber fan club member or grandmother.

If we dig one level deeper, we get to the mantle on which the crust is afloat. In the case of people, the mantle consists of competences and routines – everything that allows an individual to act. The competences and routines enable people to perform the required behavior and thus fulfill their positions and roles. Competences are all of the learned abilities that individuals can consciously employ to enact the behavior they have in mind, while routines are all of the learned scripts that have been internalized and are unconsciously activated to get things done. People can have competences in mathematics, car repair, language interpretation, dog grooming and building design, which they can use at will to achieve some result, while much of their walking, car driving, speaking, typing and body language will be almost automatically driven by ingrained routines. Habits and customs are typical routines – we have been programmed to do things in a particular way and will follow this set script without consciously knowing why.

To a certain extent individuals "are" their competences and routines. Ask people at the same party as before who they are and they will answer an accomplished pianist, a speaker of Japanese, a fast runner, someone who can hold their liquor or a person who tends to mumble. And again, chances are that all answers are mumbled by the same person. Clearly, the competences and routines that people learn during their lives are a key determinant of how they behave. Being proficient at something, or being programmed to do things automatically, significantly enlarges the likelihood that certain behavior will be favored over other types of action.

If we go yet a layer deeper, we get to the outer core of individuals, which is shaped by their values and beliefs. As discussed in Chapter 9, people's values are what they hold to be important, while their beliefs are what they hold to be true. Together these elements shape the cognitive structure, or mental map, of the individual (as outlined in Chapter 11), clarifying how the world works and how it preferably should work. This is the level where we find people's opinions, ambitions, expectations, knowledge, intuition and superstitions. And similar to the previous levels, individuals "are" their values and beliefs. At the proverbial party, people might declare themselves to be liberal, Hindu, in favor of more empowerment, against quantitative easing, a supporter of the monarchy and slightly apprehensive towards black cats. And these values and beliefs will be a key determinant in shaping their behavior, by informing them about what is wise, just, respectful, correct and crucial.

At the inner core of the individual we find their personality and physique. While the outer core and especially the mantle were molten, the inner core is solid and hard. These are the aspects of the individual that are hardly malleable. To use a different analogy, if an individual were a computer, this would be the level of the hardware and operating system on which the higher-level programs are run. A person's physical body, like the physical layout of a computer, can't be greatly changed, nor can their personality traits, which as an operating system drive how the hardware interacts with higher-level applications. Personality traits are the enduring characteristics underlying people's thoughts and feelings, largely shaped at an early age by an interplay between nature and nurture.[2]

Here again, individuals "are" their personality and physique. They will call themselves tall, brown-eyed, extroverted, agreeable and trusting. And their personality and physique will be a key determinant in shaping their behavior, by forming the basis of their senses, feelings and thoughts.

Taken together, these four layers determine who people are and drive how they behave. The closer to the center, the more solid and difficult to change, while the closer to the rim, the more fluid and easy to change. At the same time, these are the four levels at which people define themselves – four levels of *identity*. All four provide us with a sense of self, clarifying to ourselves who we genuinely are. These are the four types of elements that we perceive of ourselves and help us to "identify" who we truly are. We might not always be right in our self-image, as we look at ourselves through a subjective lens, but these are the four types of characteristics that we use to paint our self-portrait.[3]

The closer we stick to these elements of identity, the more we feel *authentic*, close to our true selves. Authenticity is the quality of being real and people have a sense of being authentic when they act in accordance to their self-image. Yet the closer they stick to the existing aspects of their identity, the less they will be willing to adjust to external demands. In other words, striving for individual authenticity seems at odds with the need for individual adjustment to achieve leadership attunement. This is what we call the *paradox of authenticity and adjustment*.

The paradox of authenticity and adjustment

> *We are what we pretend to be, so we must be careful about what we pretend to be.*
> Kurt Vonnegut (1922–2007)
> American novelist

When you ask friends whether the watch they are wearing is an authentic Rolex, they should be able to give you an objectively verifiable answer. It was either produced by the Rolex SA company, making it a genuine Rolex, or it was produced by someone else, making it an imitation. When it comes to people, however, authenticity is in the eye of the beholder. When you behave in accordance to your own sense of identity, you will feel authentic – you will feel faithful to your real self. Still, your behavior can be perceived as fake by others, if they have different assumptions about you. If they have built up a picture of the real you that predicts different behavior, your sudden deviance from their expectations can make you seem fake or even scheming. In other words, authenticity is perceived genuineness. We feel authentic ourselves if our behavior matches our identity, but others see us as authentic if our behavior matches the image they have of us.[4]

Both sides of this "authenticity coin" are important – we want to *be* genuine and we want to *be seen* to be genuine. We want to be genuine because faking it is tiring and stressful. Behaving contrary to our physique, personality, values and beliefs costs enormous amounts of energy and is difficult to keep up. Playing a part that is very different than the positions and roles to which we are accustomed can be very draining, all the more because we often miss the required competences and routines to make it a success. Staying close to true selves actually gives us energy, as we don't struggle with inconsistencies and weaknesses, but behave in ways that build on our strengths and reinforce who we are. We don't have to "lie and cheat," but can be honest and sincere.

At the same time, being seen by others to be honest and sincere is essential for building trust. If people believe that you are behaving authentically, they will conclude that they are not being manipulated. By showing the real you, warts and all, people will gain an impression that you are transparent, truthful and predictable, which all help towards building your trustworthiness. If, on the other hand, they get the impression that you are hiding certain personality traits, faking values, pretending to have certain beliefs and feigning important competences, confidence in you will quickly plummet.

Yet, staying close to your current authentic self is diametrically opposed to the demand for adjustment to the needs of followers and the circumstances they are in. Adjustment by leaders means that they should be willing to move out of their comfort zone to close the gap with followers, instead of leaving the gap and assuming that followers should do all the adjusting. Some adjusting by leaders can be relatively easy, particularly where in the past they have stretched themselves to learn new leadership styles, thus broadening their existing repertoire of accessible behaviors. Leaders who have a range of leadership styles generally have a default preference that is most comfortable and feels most authentic, but will be able to switch over to less comfortable styles where necessary. The more easily they can shift to an alternative leadership style, the less it will feel inauthentic and the more truly flexible they will be. However, some leadership styles will remain uncomfortable for a long time, even if they are often required and often used.

Adjustment by leaders is generally more difficult if it means adaptation instead of flexibility – learning new leadership styles instead of employing ones that are a bit rusty or uncomfortable. Adaptation literally means altering the way one is structured or functions. If leaders adapt, that means making changes to themselves or adding something that is not currently part of themselves. Sometimes an adaptation in leadership style will snuggly match a person's personality, values, beliefs, competences, routines, positions and roles, making it feel like a natural extension of who that person is. But adaptation that fits like a glove from the start and feels entirely authentic is the exception. As all leadership styles are opposites and conflict with one another, almost all adaptation means learning styles that are at odds with a person's existing preference. Adaptation means learning styles that contradict your comfortable default style and thereby clash with your authentic self.

Taken together, this presents leaders like Jeffrey with a paradox. Should Jeffrey emphasize the importance of authenticity, staying true to himself and remaining predictable to the people around him? Or should he emphasize the importance of adjustment, switching to some styles he feels less comfortable using and even learning new styles that might be more fitting to the people he wants to lead and the situation they are in together? Leaning over to authenticity would mean sticking to his default styles on all of the previous nine leadership style dimensions and requiring his team to do all the adjusting in order to achieve attunement. We call this the *consistent leadership style*. But if Jeffrey leans over to the side of adjustment, it would be him taking responsibility for closing the gap and achieving attunement. It would require Jeffrey to employ a wider variety of styles along most of the previous nine leadership style dimensions. We call this the *responsive leadership style*.

Note how these two opposite styles are of a different order than the previous nine sets of opposites. The consistent leadership style is based on the assumption that leaders *shouldn't* vary their leadership behavior along the other nine dimensions – it is a style that advocates that all other leadership styles should be kept consistent, in order to be authentic. The responsive leadership style is based on the assumption that leaders *should* actively vary their leadership behavior along the other nine dimensions – it is a leadership style that promotes style variation, in order to adjust to situational requirements. As such, these are the two *meta-styles:*[5] the two styles for dealing with leadership styles.

The consistent leadership style

Be yourself. Ape no greatness. Be willing to pass for what you are.
Samuel Coley (1825–1880)
American Methodist preacher

Coley summarizes the essence of the consistent leadership style crisply – be yourself. Don't be a fake, stick to your genuine you. Don't act – be. As Coley implies, it can be seductively appealing to constantly live up to the expectations of the outside world and lose sight of your true self in the process. You start to "play a role," but it is not really you. It is what others would like you to be, or even what you yourself think you need to be. Before you know it, you are performing a part that has very little to do with your deeper character and desires. You adopt an invented persona, a mask that you wear, hiding the real you from sight. You play along with the rules of the game, but cut the connection with your inner drives and being.

It is this danger of disconnection with oneself that motivates many leaders to emphasize the importance of authenticity over adjustment. They believe that it is better to "pass for what you are" than trying to "play what you aren't." This means asking *others* to accept and respect the real you, but also getting *yourself* to accept and respect your actual self. To be authentic means that you must be willing to show your true self to others and have the confidence that you will not be rejected, while at the same time feeling comfortable with who you are yourself.[6]

All this stimulates adherents of the consistent leadership style to avoid "acting a role," instead preferring to behave "straight from the heart." They want to be honest and straightforward, doing things in accordance to who they really are, not in accordance to expectations.[7] Instead of pandering to external demands, they want to stay true to their internal compass. They want to lead in a way that fits with all four levels of who they are – their personality and physique, their values and beliefs, their competences and routines, and their positions and roles.

The consequence of attuning their leadership actions tightly to these four levels of identity is that their behaviors will be more consistent than varied. By staying close to themselves they will prefer the leadership styles that fit them best. These leaders will tend to focus on the leadership styles that correspond most closely with their identity – their default styles. They will consistently use this fixed set of leadership styles, not because they are what the situation requires, but because they feel most authentic. It would go too far to say that consistent leaders behave in exactly the *same way* under all circumstances, but they do behave in a *predictable way*. They don't blindly copy their approach from one situation to the next, but they do consistently tap into the same narrow repertoire of favorite leadership styles that closely match their identity.

Once you get to know consistent leaders, their style of leading will be immediately discernable. You will instantaneously note the common threads running throughout everything they do. You could say that consistent leaders generally have a distinct *leadership brand*, with a number of conspicuous attributes, rooted in a few fundamental characteristics typical of the person. In this way, their consistent style is far from being bland and boring, but rather, it functions as a highly recognizable and reliable trademark. Consistent leaders have a well-defined profile, promising that what you see is what you get.

The responsive leadership style

> *It is not the strongest species that survive, nor the most intelligent, but the ones most responsive to change.*

Charles Darwin (1809–1882)
British naturalist and geologist

Darwin's quote[8] can be directly translated to leaders. It is not the strongest or most intelligent leaders that are successful, but the ones who are the most responsive to the changing demands in their environments. This is the essence of the responsive leadership style – success is not about building on one's strengths, but about following and fitting the needs of the situation. Dinosaurs were powerful, but are understandably extinct. Polar bears can rip you to pieces, but are struggling to survive as the conditions around them change. Tigers can remain true to their genuine self, but that won't help much in securing a future for their species. For all these wonderful animals, it seems extremely unfair that they are not prospering, but this is the mechanism of "survival of the fittest" in action, and fairness hardly comes into play.

The same mechanism is seen in industries, where brilliant products are competed away in changing markets. Some companies cling to small niches making fabulous products, like Rolls Royce in limousines and Morgan in sports cars, but they have long been left behind by more nimble rivals such as Mercedes-Benz and Porsche, who *have* been adaptable. Calling themselves "authentic" might make them sound like heroic holdouts, but it seems more like putting a positive twist on a terrible failure to keep up. Now the next round of change has announced itself, with autonomous driving and electric engines as the new demands to which car makers must respond. Petrolheads and slower companies complain that this will be the end of the "genuine driving experience" and some even vow to resist adapting, but as before this sounds more like a psychological coping mechanism to deal with loss. Here, too, there is a sense of unfairness that change is happening to them and forcing them to adjust, while they are quite happy with who they are and quite content to remain so.

Responsive leaders don't suffer from such inside-out conservatism, but prefer outside-in realism. The outside world is in constant flux, so adjust or die. But it is not merely *survival* of the fittest, it is actually *prospering* of the fittest – those who are able to match the needs of the environment most closely will be the most effective and therefore the ones to flourish. So, companies that are the best at meeting the needs of their customers will be the ones that thrive, while leaders who are the best at meeting the needs of their followers will be the most successful. As firms need to be customer-centric, leaders need to be follower-centric.

Responsive leaders will typically adjust the leadership styles they employ depending on the specific people they want to lead and the specific situation these people are in. As they value adjustment highly, responsive leaders tend to want to build a broad repertoire of leadership styles, so they have the options at hand to switch over to different leadership styles if the circumstances require them to do so. And as they often hop from one leadership style to the next to fit with the variety of people that they deal with, responsive leaders often have developed a high level of leadership style flexibility, much as a yoga practitioner who switches positions a lot gets increasingly pliable. At the same time, responsive leaders realize that they will continuously come across new people and new situations that will require them to adapt and to add new styles to their repertoire. But while leaders embracing the consistent leadership style see opposite styles as being at odds with their true self, adherents of the responsive leadership style see opposite styles as an opportunity to stretch and renew their true self. Learning new leadership styles isn't felt as being at odds with their identity, but as a possibility to reshape their sense of identity. In their view, you can be much more fluid and dynamic than many people think – you can become who you want to be. Your genes may be fixed, but everything on top of that can be shaped over time if you are truly willing to learn and change. And you can learn to learn, getting better at adaptation the more you actually adapt.

All this adjustment willingness, however, has to be directed. Responsive leaders must know to what they must adjust. That is why responsive leaders focus significant energy on identifying and interpreting the needs of their followers and the developments in the broader context. We also call this *sensing* and *sense-making* – first picking up signals of what's going on and what people are doing and saying, and then trying to understand what this means and how important it is. You might recognize these two steps as the left (inductive) half of the problem-solving cycle as discussed in Chapter 11, with the leader responding to the "doing" of followers by moving through the phases of identification ("What do I observe?") and interpretation ("What do I understand?"). Once they have a picture of the situation, responsive leaders continue through the cycle, going from formulation ("What should I do?") to implementation ("How should I do it?"). We also call this *selecting* and *applying* – determining which leadership style needs to be accessed and then employing it in an appropriate fashion.

Where leaders are good at going through this cycle of sensing, sense-making, selecting and applying, we say they have a high level of *leadership style responsiveness*. They show mastery at picking up on follower needs and selecting the most suitable response. As with other capabilities, the more often they practice, the better, the faster and the more gracious they get at it. And if at the same

Table 12.1 Differences between the consistent and responsive leadership styles

	Consistent Leadership Style	*Responsive Leadership Style*
Emphasis on	Authenticity over adjustment	Adjustment over authenticity
Motivating people by	Behaving predictably	Responding appropriately
Identity is	Stable over time	Dynamic over time
Orientation towards	Self-expression	External understanding
Basic attitude	Build on your personal strengths	Respond to the situational needs
Core quality	Remaining true to oneself	Continuously renewing oneself
Intended impact	Build reliability	Develop agility
Underlying conviction	Nature is leading	Nurture is leading
Guiding principle/motto	I am who I am	You can be who you want to be
Preferred tools	Making clear statements	Asking open-ended questions

time they have a broad repertoire of styles that they can easily and quickly select from (*leadership style flexibility*) and the learning capability to swiftly and smoothly acquire new ones (*leadership style adaptability*), then we speak of *leadership agility*. This is the capacity that successful responsive leaders have and employ to constantly keep attuned with the people and situations around them.

Qualities and pitfalls of the consistent leadership style

> *Consistency requires you to be as ignorant today as you were a year ago.*
> Bernard Berenson (1865–1959)
> American art historian

The consistent leadership style has many qualities, starting with its ability to convey *consistency as honesty*. By being consistent in their behavior, leaders with this style are seen as real, straightforward and transparent. As they don't adjust their behavior, but unfailingly act in the same way, they are perceived as truthful and sincere. Being unadjusted is interpreted as a sign that leaders are not playing a game, but openly showing their true selves. Often the more distinct and recognizable this consistent leadership behavior is, the more people will sense that it truly must be a reflection of the leader's inner self – the more "characteristic" it is, the less it will seem fake. It is this impression of authentic honesty that greatly contributes to the trust that people have in consistent leaders.

Confidence in consistent leaders is further strengthened by the fact that their behavior is stable and dependable. Not only are they honest, but consistent leaders can be counted on to act in a constant and reliable manner. This is the quality of *consistency as predictability*. Instead of confusing people by showing a different face under different circumstances, the consistent leader is steadfast, offering people certainty. Instead of making people apprehensive and anxious by flip-flopping between different behaviors, the consistent leader is reliable, offering people security. It is this track record of authentic predictability that further reinforces the confidence that people have in consistent leaders.

Another advantage of being a more consistent leader is that sticking to a smaller repertoire of leadership behaviors allows people to truly get good at them. This is the quality of *consistency as specialization*. By consequently focusing on just a few styles, leaders more quickly and deeply develop their competence in these areas. Instead of spreading their efforts across multiple leadership styles, consistent leaders direct their attention and energy at the styles that most closely fit with their natural inclinations. By building on their strengths, consistent leaders can achieve style excellence, instead of trying to learn every style a bit, resulting in across the board mediocrity.[9] The added benefit of staying close to one's authentic strengths is that followers generally have more confidence in leaders exhibiting high competence in a few styles than in leaders adjusting poorly, bungling styles they don't really master.

But maybe the most important quality of the consistent leadership style is that it allows leaders to stay true to themselves. Taking on a leadership role is demanding under the best of circumstances, but "playing a leadership role" that is far away from your actual self can be exhaustive and usually unsustainable. The stress of acting in a way that doesn't feel authentic can nibble away at one's energy and self-worth. Never mind whether others believe you are fake, but if you feel like an imposter yourself, then your behavior will be untenable. The consistent leadership style encourages leaders to stay close to their identity, reducing the risk that they lose themselves along the way. This is the quality of *consistency as genuineness* – sticking to behavior that is in line with who one really is. And if leaders are truly genuine, this inner strength and balance will shine through to all those around them, further strengthening the confidence that people have in them.

However, consistent leaders quite consistently fall into a number of pitfalls by exaggerating each of these four qualities. Starting with the last one, consistency as genuineness, this can easily spin into genuine self-centeredness. "Staying close to myself," can quickly begin to mean: "The world should adjust to me." "Not losing myself," rapidly morphs into: "Get lost, I don't feel like doing any effort to adapt myself." Assuming that one is entitled to "be oneself" is a form of egotism that pushes all responsibility for a fruitful relationship on to others. Yet the very nature of leadership is that a person is willing to step forward to engage others to move in a certain direction – hence, take responsibility for establishing a fruitful relationship. Leaders need to connect with others, winning hearts and minds, which is impossible if one is overly self-involved and worried about the stress of having to adjust to the needs of others.

This overemphasis on genuineness isn't always due to self-centeredness, but can also be rooted in an overly static view of one's identity. "I am who I am" is clearly true at this moment, but who says a person can't change and grow?

Who says that one's current authentic self can't learn new leadership styles and become more responsive? The fact that a leadership style doesn't feel authentic and comfortable *yet*, doesn't mean that leaders can't over time adapt and add styles to who they genuinely are.[10] Unfortunately, being consistent actually inhibits learning, as leaders keep on applying their fixed recipes, instead of experimenting with new ones. "Being genuine," therefore, often means "being conservative" and halting personal growth. As Bernard Berenson says in his quote at the outset of this section: "Consistency requires you to be as ignorant today as you were a year ago." Stay in your comfort zone and stop developing.

The same is true for the argument that consistency allows for specialization and building on one's strengths. While it makes sense to use one's strengths wisely and master one's default leadership styles well, consistent leaders can become overly obsessed with further fine-tuning styles they already have at their fingertips, while disregarding potential growth in other styles. Deep specialization might make sense in fields like medicine and engineering, where many specialized tasks exist, or in sports and music, where there is little need for generalists. But when it comes to leadership, there is usually limited need for one trick ponies, because almost every leader needs to deal with different types of people in a wide variety of situations.

Consistent leaders can also exaggerate their advantage of being predictable by becoming overly rigid. Instead of being "recognizably stable," they slide into a "one size fits all" approach to each situation. Instead of listening to the needs of followers and being attentive to the specific circumstances, they bluntly bulldoze over the specifics, imposing their favorite approach time and time again. This is bad enough when it is driven by blindness to the requirements of the situation, but it is often driven by insensitivity and a feeling of superiority. Consistent leaders often exhibit an intolerance towards the annoying people who "don't know their place" and don't fall into line by adjusting themselves to the clear approach of the consistent leader. Many of these leaders believe that their position justifies their demand that all others should do the adjusting and that it is not their duty to cater to the whims of the people around them. They come to believe that their attitude of "it's my way or the highway" is an acceptable manner of dealing with the inconsistency of diverse people and circumstances.

Finally, the advantage of consistency being seen as honesty can also lead to dysfunctional behavior by consistent leaders, particularly where they feel the pressure to live up to their "authentic reputation," even when it doesn't make sense. Many consistent leaders with an outspoken and recognizable style can easily become the prisoner of their own "genuine brand," as people expect them to behave according to their sharp profile. To remain trustworthy and not create any unclear precedents they must engage in foolish consistency, even when adjusting their style would have been more effective. A far darker side of the consistent leadership style is that consistency can actually be used to fake honesty. By acting their part in a very consistent way, leaders can suggest that they are truthful and sincere, while in reality manipulating people. By projecting an authentic image, they can fool people into believing they are acting transparently, while in the mean time playing Machiavellian games. As the old quip goes: "The main thing is honesty. Once you can fake that, you've got it made."

Qualities and pitfalls of the responsive leadership style

> *I cannot give you the formula for success, but I can give you the formula for failure, which is: Try to please everybody.*
>
> Herbert Swope (1882–1958)
> American journalist

Being a responsive leader starts with taking the *initiative*. Instead of waiting for followers to adjust themselves and for the right situation to emerge, responsive leaders take responsibility to ensure attunement. Responsive leaders literally take the lead in the relationship, searching for ways to connect with people and bridge the gap. They step up and don't automatically expect to be followed, but believe that they have to earn acceptance as leader every day, by listening and responding appropriately. As in their private lives, responsive leaders realize that to be successful one has to keep working on one's relationships, never taking the other for granted and never assuming the other should just take you the way you are.

Taking the initiative to achieve fit is a quality in itself, but by embracing this responsibility responsive leaders show an even more important quality – *caring*. By going out of their way to listen to people and by making an effort to "speak the other's language," responsive leaders demonstrate respect and show commitment to making the relationship work. Simply by expressing interest and making obvious that the other is important, a bond of trust can start to be built. By then adjusting their behavior to the needs of followers, responsive leaders show even more that they are willing to keep the interests of followers in mind and invest energy to accommodate them. If these responsive leaders subsequently solicit feedback and react with empathy and engagement, they will be seen as caring and loyal, leading to an even higher degree of trust.

Maybe the most obvious quality of the responsive leadership style is being able to maintain a *dynamic fit* between the leader on the one hand and the followers and circumstances on the other. Responsive leaders not only care about others and take the initiative to respond, but they also have the capacity to actually adjust their leadership behavior to what they see is necessary. Successful responsive leaders generally work hard at mastering a broad repertoire of leadership styles to give them the potential to adjust when needed. They tend to develop multiple leadership styles and practice their ability to smoothly switch between them, thus building leadership style flexibility. At the same time, responsive leaders strive to improve their learning capability, so they have the option of acquiring new styles in future, thus enhancing their leadership style adaptability. Taken together, responsive leaders' flexibility and adaptability make them well-equipped to achieve ongoing fit, while at the same time strengthening their credibility of dealing with changing people and circumstances.

Last but not least, the responsive leadership style not only encourages leaders to adjust for the sake of effectiveness, but also to *learn* for the sake of personal development. After all, being responsive is not only a duty to others and an effective attunement approach, it is also a massive stimulus for personal growth. Instead of staying within the confines of their comfort zone, responsive leaders continuously challenge themselves to learn by forcing themselves to think and respond outside-in. Instead of accepting their current identity as a fixed entity, responsive leaders are willing to stretch their sense of authenticity and become someone broader and richer than they currently are. In other words, they don't see learning as a chore, and definitely not as a necessary evil, but rather as one of the most enriching processes a person can experience. Being a responsive leader is a beautiful way to grow on the job – of learning while earning.

But, of course, responsive leaders also habitually tumble into a number of pitfalls waiting there for the overly enthusiastic adjuster. It starts with the danger that adjusting can be seen as *acting* – saying whatever is needed to get one's way. Behaving differently to different people under different circumstances can be seen as manipulative, whereby one's true intentions are hidden behind whichever mask is acceptable. Responsive leaders can be seen as two-faced, carefully only showing the behavior needed to get the intended result, while concealing what they are really thinking and what they truly have up their sleeves. This can seriously undermine trust in responsive leaders. The more calculated and artificial the adjusted leadership behavior feels to followers, the more they will be reinforced in their sense that the leader is being disingenuous. And in the worst cases followers will be right. Being responsive can not only *seem* fake, but it can actually *be* fake, as responsive leaders indeed deviously say and do whatever is required to achieve their aims. This is leading by being misleading – as a chameleon, taking on any hue to fool others and protect yourself.

Besides seeing adjusting as acting, people can also interpret adjusting as *giving in*. Being responsive to the needs of others can create the impression of being weak-willed and submissive. It can make responsive leaders look like cowards, not taking a stand by "telling people like it is," preferring to tell people what they want to hear. They can appear faint-hearted, not setting a clear direction, but taking an "any way is fine for me" stance, hoping to keep everyone happy. It can seem that responsive leaders are only slavishly pandering to the fickle whims of their followers, instead of actually leading. And often it is true. They not only *seem* timid, but they actually are, as they truly "try to please everybody." As Herbert Swope suggests in the quote at the outset of this section, this is a formula for failure, usually pleasing few, while undercutting one's credibility at the same time. And the more diverse the audience that overly-responsive leaders try to please, the less likely they will be successful.

All the well-intended adjusting done by responsive leaders can also make them *unpredictable* flip-floppers. This is adjusting as "leading by exception" – every situation will require a unique, tailor-made response. This can make it very difficult to guess in advance how leaders will respond, as it will "all

Qualities of Consistent Leadership Style	Qualities of Responsive Leadership Style
1. Gives followers responsibility to adjust	1. Takes responsibility to adjust to followers
2. Builds outspoken, recognizable brand	2. Builds open, accessible profile
3. Fits well to specific situations	3. Fits well to variety of situations
4. Reacts predictably to changing circumstances	4. Adjusts quickly to changing circumstances
5. Focuses learning on deepening repertoire	5. Focuses learning on broadening repertoire
6. Builds credibility by focused competences	6. Builds credibility by flexibility and adaptability
7. Listens carefully to needs of self	7. Listens carefully to needs of others
8. Shows sympathy by being sincere	8. Shows empathy by being caring
9. Strengthens trust by being honest	9. Strengthens trust by showing respect
10. Connects by speaking from the heart	10. Connects by speaking the other's language

Pitfalls of Consistent Leadership Style	Pitfalls of Responsive Leadership Style
1. Blindly ignores the needs of followers	1. Slavishly panders to whims of followers
2. Shows low tolerance for diversity	2. Shows excessive tolerance for diversity
3. Descends into 'It's my way or the highway'	3. Descends into 'Any way is fine for me'
4. Pushes 'one size fits all' solutions	4. Creates inconsistent 'tailor-made' solutions
5. Loses trust by being a blunt bulldozer	5. Loses trust by being unpredictable flipflopper
6. Obsessively focused on own needs	6. Out of touch with own needs
7. Unwilling to leave comfort zone	7. Unwilling to take a stand
8. Rigid behavior feels egoistic	8. Chameleon behavior feels manipulative
9. Seen as genuine, but unsuitable for part	9. Seen as fake, acting a part
10. One trick pony	10. Jack of all trades, but master of none

Figure 12.2 Qualities and pitfalls of the consistent and responsive leadership styles

depend on the circumstances." This inability to anticipate leaders' behaviors can easily trigger uncertainty, insecurity and anxiousness among followers. Leaders can be seen as loose cannons, dangerously erratic and therefore difficult to count on, instead of a reliable safe pair of hands.

Seeming unpredictable, like seeming to act and seeming to give in, chips away at the confidence that people have in responsive leaders. People don't necessarily see leaders' responsiveness as entirely positive. These are pitfalls that are all concerned with how leaders are perceived. But a further pitfall is less about perception and more about capability – acting responsively might actually weaken leaders' ability to build their competences and routines. By constantly adjusting themselves to their followers and the situation, each leader might become a jack of all trades, but a master of none. Instead of concentrating themselves on a limited set of leadership styles close to their inherent talents and becoming extremely good at these, responsive leaders might spread themselves too thinly, developing themselves poorly in all. By striving to have a broad repertoire of leadership styles available to tap into, responsive leaders run the risk of being second-rate at most of them. And if it shows, this too will not strengthen the confidence that people will have in these responsive leaders.

The last key pitfall goes beyond competences to the heart of each leader's identity. If leaders constantly strive for attunement outside-in, there will be an ongoing danger of losing touch with their inner core. They will be tempted to exhibit behavior that is at odds with their values, beliefs, physique and personality. There will be an enduring threat of straying too far from their feelings, ambitions, drives and dreams, resulting in inner strife and stress. If, in their desire to respect the needs of their followers, they don't respect their own, they run the risk of emotional distress. If, in their aspiration to be as flexible as bamboo they forget that bamboo will bend but eventually break, they will run the risk of snapping as well.

Profiling your leadership style

Example is not the main thing in influencing others, it is the only thing.
Albert Schweitzer (1875–1965)
German philosopher, physician and medical missionary

Do you recognize your own leadership style preference? Do you tend to hang out on the side of authenticity, preferring to be as consistent as possible? Or do you have a strong inclination to adjust yourself to the stakeholders and situation around you, attempting to be as responsive as possible? Are you more the type of person who, when a painting needs to be hung up, consistently exhibits a strong preference for a hammer and a nail, or do you first examine the wall, weigh the painting, look at the frame and go to your toolbox to see what's available? And do you also recognize your favorite pitfalls? Are you the person that Maslow meant when he said that: "When all you have is a hammer, everything looks like a nail"?[11] Or are you more often the person whose only consistency is that to every leadership question you answer "it all depends"? Just in case you need a bit of help determining your default style, we again have added a brief leadership style profiler in Figure 12.3.

As for Jeffrey and Claus, who we met at the start of this chapter, have you already determined what you would do? If you were in Claus's shoes as head of HR, what would be your advice to Jeffrey? Should he go for a more consistent leadership style, remaining true to himself, and adjust his management team to his own profile? Or would you advise him to develop a more responsive leadership style, challenging himself to grow into his new role and grow as a person? Going down the consistent leadership route would be easier for him at

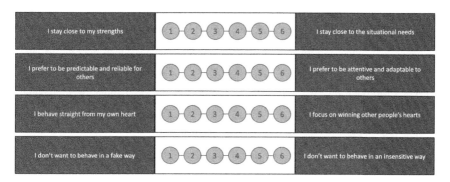

Figure 12.3 Profiling your leadership style: Leadership attunement

the moment, as he is currently consistent by default, not really by choice. On all of the nine other leadership style dimensions he only has access to one of the opposite styles, locking him into being consistent. In other words, in the short run he doesn't really have options, as he has very low leadership agility – he hardly has *the capacity to flexibly switch between leadership styles, and adaptively master new ones, in rapid response to the specific needs of the people and situation they want to influence*. If you advise him to become more responsive in the medium term, that would mean that he would have to improve his leadership agility along some of the other leadership dimensions, to at least have access to some alternative leadership styles and thus have the capacity to be responsive.

Do you see how leadership agility is all about having the *potential* to be responsive? Leaders who are agile don't always have to employ the responsive leadership style, but they do have the capacity to do so if they so choose. Agile leaders can decide that under certain circumstances or in a certain period it is wiser to be consistent, and they might even have a preference for being consistent, but they are not stuck being consistent. Leadership agility means you have the possibility to be responsive and you're not trapped being consistent purely because that's all you're capable of doing.

So, whether you have a preference for the consistent or the responsive leadership style, you might want to be able to have the capacity to switch between them, which means working on your leadership agility – which is exactly the topic of the next chapter.

Notes

1 Libraries have been filled with works examining human psychology from a wide variety of angles, and the field of psychology is deeply divided into many schools of thought, each with their own definitions, concepts and models. This makes any kind of simplification fraught with difficulty and a possible affront to the sensibilities of specialists in the field. Yet, the quality of a good model is that it simplifies in a way that is fit for purpose. This layered model is indeed a highly simplified view of the inner working of people, which skirts around many controversies and disagreements in the field yet we believe is useful to structure our thinking around leadership here.

2 The definition of personality used here is the narrow one, referring to core traits of an individual, such as the "big five" (i.e. openness, conscientiousness, extraversion, agreeableness and neuroticism), as opposed to the broad definition, which includes all feelings, thoughts and behaviors that make up a person (from the Latin, *persona*).

3 Note that others also form an opinion about who we are, which we call our *image*. Both identity and image are subjective interpretations of an individual and can greatly differ from each other and from reality.

4 For a thorough review on the concept of authenticity see Gardner, W.L., Cogliser, C.C., Davis, K.M. and Dickens, M.P. (2011), "Authentic Leadership: A Review of the Literature and Research Agenda," *The Leadership Quarterly*, Vol. 22, No. 6, pp. 1120–1145.

5 We have coined this term with the analogy of meta-communication in mind, which is the act of communicating about communication. Hence, meta-style as the style of dealing with styles.

6 The consistent leadership style as described here largely overlaps with the concept of "authentic leadership," although the latter is more broadly defined. For a good

overview see Gardner, W.L., Avolio, B.J. and Walumbwa, F.O. (eds.) (2005), *Authentic Leadership Theory and Practice: Origins, Effects, and Development*, San Diego: Elsevier.

7 Many writers use the term "authentic leadership" as the opposite of a more narcissistic type of leadership. Being yourself is presented as being the positive opposite of having an inflated ego and being self-centered. E.g. George, B. (2003), *Authentic Leadership: Rediscovering the Secrets to Creating Lasting Value*, New York: John Wiley & Sons. In our view such authors tend to blend authenticity with service and health (i.e. the consistent, servant and virtue-driven leadership styles) into a feel-good mix and contrast this approach with the pitfalls of the responsive, sovereign and value-driven leadership styles. The result is often more ideological than insightful – the "authentic leader" as a modern-day noble savage against the corrupted celebrity CEOs.

8 While these words are fully in line with Darwin's thinking, it seems quite likely that he never wrote this exact sentence. See: http://quoteinvestigator.com/2014/12/19/fittest/

9 The idea of focusing on one's strengths is widespread. One of its earliest proponents was Peter Drucker. See Drucker, P. (1967), *The Effective Executive*, New York: Harper Collins.

10 Ibarra, H. (2015), "The Authenticity Paradox," *Harvard Business Review*, Vol. 93, No. 1–2, pp. 53–59.

11 Maslow, A. (1966), *The Psychology of Science*, New York: Harper & Row, p. 15.

Part VII
Leadership development

13 Developing leadership agility

For a book called *Leadership Agility*, the first 12 chapters have said relatively little about the topic. It has been all about leadership styles, the building blocks of leadership agility. The focus has been on understanding the variety of leadership styles, each with its own inherent qualities and potential pitfalls. Leadership has been brought down off its pedestal and made tangible, by dissecting it along five dimensions, the *leadership roles*, and ten challenges, the *leadership tasks*. We have described how each leadership task has a *leadership paradox* at its heart and that leadership styles are a reflection of emphasizing one side of a leadership paradox over the other.

All along the way during this voyage of discovery past the ten leadership paradoxes and twenty corresponding leadership styles you have been asked to consider which leadership styles you currently have at your disposal and which pitfalls you occasionally tumble into. After discussing each set of opposite leadership styles, we actually pressed you to think which of the two is your "default style" – the style that feels most comfortable and which you prefer to use if at all possible. We encouraged you to recognize your predisposition, not because we wanted to push you into one camp, but to get you to critically reflect on your own inclinations or even biases. At the same time, we emphasized that mastering your default style didn't necessarily mean that the opposite style was not part of your leadership style repertoire.

Now that you have completed your "introductory tour" of all the leadership styles, it is time to move to the issue of leadership agility, and in particular how you might be able to further develop yours. We will take you through this discussion in five steps. First, we will start by reviewing your *present leadership style repertoire* to gain a more nuanced picture of your current profile. This first section is all about determining where you currently stand. Second, we will look at the different *leadership development objectives* that you might want to set for yourself. This section is all about identifying the different types of personal growth that you might want to strive for. In the third section, we will discuss how you need to set *leadership development priorities*, as you can't master every style perfectly and effortlessly switch between all of them. Here the argument will revolve around selecting criteria that will help you to determine which leadership development goals will be most important to you. In the fourth section, we will then go more in depth into *leadership development methods*. Here we will examine which factors commonly inhibit leaders from becoming more agile and then we will present ways to strengthen your leadership agility. Finally, in the last section we will turn to drawing up a practical *Leadership Enhancement Action Plan* (LEAP), to assist you in bringing good intentions into practice.

Your current leadership style repertoire

> *Knowing yourself is the beginning of all wisdom.*
>
> Aristotle (384 BC–322 BC)
> Greek philosopher

At the end of each chapter, you were invited to position your preferred leadership style somewhere along a continuum between two poles. While a valuable initial step in mapping your current leadership style repertoire, this exercise was a bit of a simplification for four reasons:

1. *Emphasis on the poles.* The first limitation in the discussion so far has been that we have necessarily focused on describing the two opposite poles of each continuum, without saying anything about mixed style alternatives in between. We have described "black and white," which is relatively easy and clear, without describing the various "shades of gray" in between, which exist in reality but are much more difficult to distinguish and classify into recognizable categories. At least we have compensated for this "bipolar disorder" by presenting a continuum along which to position your default style instead of only a digital choice between one style or the other. But it is important to emphasize again that the poles are really the extremes – and also their explanations were clearly extreme – while in practice there are many different styles in between that make different combinations of the two sides of each paradox.
2. *Emphasis on discrete position.* A second simplification in the mapping you have done so far is that we have pushed you to plot yourself at one point on each continuum. As we have argued, it is important to acknowledge your default style as the key style that you will use, and misuse, on a regular basis. It is also likely that your default style is the approach at which you are best. Yet, at the same time, only recognizing your default style masks the extent to which you have a broader leadership style repertoire that you can tap into. Knowing the style you prefer doesn't tell us much about your ability and willingness to switch to an alternative style. Therefore, besides knowing your default style along each continuum, we should actually map all the style variations to which you have access.
3. *No mapping of mastery.* While asking you to determine your default style, we further simplified our measurement by not asking how good you think you are at this style. We asked for your preference, not for your level of mastery. Yet, to get a good picture of your current leadership style profile, it is also essential to know how skilled you are at each of the leadership styles.

4. *No mapping of pitfalls.* The fourth simplification that we used in mapping your leadership styles so far is that we didn't ask you to plot the extent to which you fall into a style's pitfalls. However, the frequency with which you exaggerate a style or use it in the wrong situation tells us a lot about your leadership agility, in particular the responsiveness part of agility. Stumbling into a pitfall usually means that someone lacks the ability to quickly tailor behavior to the needs of the situation. Therefore, to get a good picture of your current leadership style profile, it is also essential to map how often you are seduced by each style's "dark side."

To resolve all of these shortcomings, we advise you to take your initial default style measurement and upgrade it into a full-blown leadership style profile. This is best done in three steps. First, to overcome limitations 1 and 2 above, you should take the discrete score you had at the end of each chapter (your default style) and add the range of mixed styles that you believe you also use. In other words, besides identifying your most preferred style, you also want to map the repertoire that you have at your disposal. This step is visualized in Figure 13.1, using the example of Chapter 3 on the supervisory and

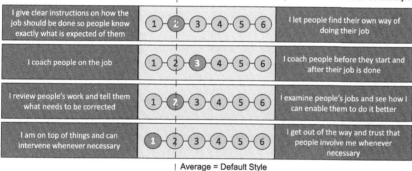

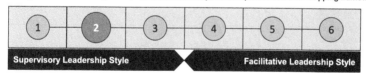

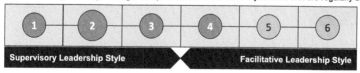

Figure 13.1 Mapping your current leadership style profile: Step 1

facilitative leadership styles. At the top of the figure you will recognize the leadership style mapping statements introduced at the end of the chapter and at the bottom the "translation" into a style repertoire mapping continuum. Note that the range of mixed styles available to the leader in this example is given a different shade to distinguish it from the mixed styles the leader does not use. The person's default style is indicated by its larger size.

Once you have determined your style range along the 1-to-6 continuum, the next step is to estimate how good you are at each of the six. In other words, what is your level of proficiency for each of the style variations? This second step is illustrated in Figure 13.2. For each of the six shades between the supervisory and facilitative leadership styles you need to determine your level of mastery. To avoid making the process unnecessarily complex, we use five levels of skill:

1. *Novice.* You have rarely used this style.
2. *Apprentice.* When you use this style, it feels uncomfortable and not very effective.
3. *Journeyman.* You are proficient at this style and the results are satisfactory.
4. *Professional.* You are good at this style and get the results you intend.
5. *Master.* You are excellent at this style and have little left to learn.

In the example given in Figure 13.2, the person being mapped has a leadership style range of 1 to 4, but clearly doesn't master all to the same extent. This person estimates that she/he is best at her/his default style (2), reaching the level of professional, but believes that styles 1, 3 and 4 are only "available" at a lower level of ability.

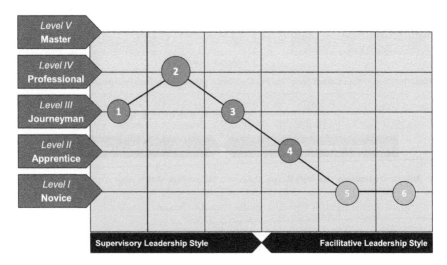

Figure 13.2 Mapping your current leadership style profile: Step 2

The third and last step in drawing up your current leadership style profile is to give an indication of how often you find yourself in each style's pitfalls. So, for each of the style mixes between 1 and 6 you should guesstimate how frequently you overuse or misuse this leadership style. Here we suggest an even simpler measurement scale, namely *occasionally*, *regularly* and *systematically*.

To achieve a full overview of your current leadership style profile, Figure 13.3 needs to be completed for all ten pairs of leadership styles. If you are of a more traditional bent, feel free to do this with pencil and paper (or chisel and clay tablet if you are really old school), but you can also use the Leadership LEAP App that has been designed to accompany this book.

If you really want to arrive at a robust picture of your current leadership profile, you shouldn't only rely on your own assessment of your leadership styles, but should ask for the opinions of the people around you. Remember that in Chapters 1 and 10 we spoke of the leadership circle of people that you want to lead? These people experience your leadership behavior in a particular way and should be able to tell you how your leadership styles are exhibited in reality, not necessarily how you intend them to be. For this reason, receiving 360-degree feedback on your leadership styles is an essential manner by which to check and fine-tune your picture of your current profile.

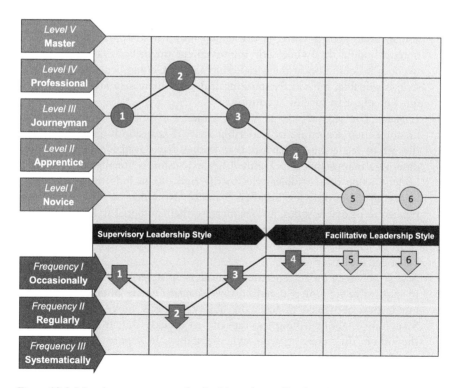

Figure 13.3 Mapping your current leadership style profile: Step 3

Your leadership development objectives

Always dream and shoot higher than you know you can do. Don't bother just to be better than your contemporaries or predecessors. Try to be better than yourself.

William Faulkner (1897–1962)

American writer

Now that you have a clear view of your current leadership style profile, the question is not yet "What do I want to enhance?" but "What forms of enhancement are there?" In other words, it is not yet "Which specific areas do I want to upgrade?" but more generally "How can I upgrade my leadership?" What is leadership development all about and how can I go about becoming a better leader?

When it comes to leadership development objectives, there are five key ways in which leaders can strive to enhance their leadership effectiveness:

1. *Improve.* The first way in which leaders can develop themselves is to get better at what they are already doing. Improvement is about taking a style that the leader already uses and bringing it to a higher level. In Figure 13.1, improvement is literally pushing an existing style higher, to a next level of proficiency. Even people's default styles are often only mastered at a low level, so leaders might want to focus on getting better at existing styles before moving to learning anything new. At the same time, improvement also includes getting better at not falling into a style's pitfalls. It should be noted, though, that while style improvement might boost a leader's effectiveness, it doesn't boost their leadership agility. Getting better at a particular style is valuable, but strictly speaking it doesn't increase a leader's ability to quickly adjust to specific situations.

2. *Expand.* The second way in which leaders can develop themselves is to broaden their repertoire of leadership styles. Expansion is about increasing the set of leadership behaviors that leaders have available to respond to differing circumstances. In Figure 13.3, expansion is literally stretching the leader's scope of accessible styles to the right, to include more facilitative leadership types of styles (numbers 5 and 6). Note that by broadening their repertoire of usable styles, leaders increase their potential style flexibility. If the circumstances change, they have the possibility to use a different style that is better aligned with these conditions. Style expansion thus contributes to enhanced leadership agility.

3. *Switch.* Having a broad repertoire of leadership styles and having the ability to expand to new ones (*leadership style adaptability*) are both very valuable, but leaders also need to have the ability to easily move between them. Switching is about having the capacity to quickly shift from one style to the other, thus creating true style flexibility. In Figure 13.3, switching could be visualized as the lack of barriers between each of the numbered styles – can leaders smoothly slide along the continuum from one side to the other, or does going from one style to the next require a radical switch-over,

involving significant "switching costs" in terms of time and effort. The greater a leader's ability to easily switch between styles, the higher will be that leader's level of agility.

4. *Respond.* With a broad repertoire of mastered styles, between which they can easily switch, leaders almost have all the ingredients needed to be really agile and highly effective. However, there is one last key aspect required to create true agility, which is the ability to quickly know which style is required under specific conditions and to act accordingly. Responsiveness is about rapidly understanding what the circumstances require and tailoring a fitting leadership approach – it is the ability to know which leadership style to pick given the situation and immediately aligning the leadership behavior to match. As with a football player who can kick with both the right and the left foot (*style flexibility*), but needs to quickly know when to use which, a leader also needs to swiftly adjust to the game at hand. This requires going through the cycle of *sensing* what is needed (situational awareness), *making sense* of these signals (situational understanding), *selecting* a fitting response (behavioral determination) and *applying* the appropriate style in practice (behavioral adjustment), all within a short time span. Therefore, developing leadership responsiveness can be just as important to enhancing leaders' agility as developing their style flexibility.

5. *Combine.* There is a fifth and last way in which leaders can further develop themselves, which is to come up with new leadership styles, based on an inventive mix of the two extremes. In Chapter 2, we briefly described that between black and white there is more than only shades of gray. Gray is actually just an unimaginative and boring manner of blending black and white. We suggested that there are many more creative ways of combining the two, as exhibited by the zebra. It turns out that the unique black and white stripes not only look nice, and might confuse predators, but mostly are responsible for triggering small-scale air circulation, thus cooling down the animal. So, combinations are about bringing together elements from the opposite styles in new and inspiring ways. Who says that leaders can only choose between a fixed repertoire of styles? Yes, the paradox at the heart of the styles is fundamental and unchangeable, but there are plenty of ways of combining qualities of the opposite styles to get "the best of both worlds."

In this chapter, we will further explore what it takes to improve, expand, switch and respond. As for combine, that requires some special attention, for which we have designed a separate last chapter.

Your leadership development priorities

The last thing one knows – is what to put first.

Blaise Pascal (1623–1662)
French physicist and philosopher

So, in which leadership style areas do you want to upgrade by improving and expanding, while strengthening your ability to switch and respond? You can't effectively develop yourself along all dimensions and in all ways at the same time, so you'll have to select a number of key topics to focus on first. What will be your leadership development priorities?

Maybe intuitively you already know which two or three leadership styles you want to improve or expand to, and where you need to enhance your switching and responsiveness abilities. But if you prefer to determine your priorities in a more structured manner, it will be useful to review the key criteria that generally come into play when deciding what to assign the highest importance.

Need-based priority-setting

In our view, the best way to start when setting *leadership development priorities* is to consider one's *leadership priorities* in the first place. In other words, where leaders need to develop themselves the most depends on where they need to lead the most. We call people's leadership priorities their *leadership agenda* – the list of crucial issues where leaders believe their personal involvement and effort is needed to reach the intended results. Just as leaders can't develop on all fronts at the same time, neither can they intervene, push and inspire everywhere simultaneously. They need to "pick their battles selectively," identifying where their time, energy and attention are essential to achieve success. We call this leadership agenda the *what of leadership* ("what are the key topics on which leaders should focus"), to differentiate it from the *how of leadership*, the leadership styles they employ to influence others to move.

What leaders have on their agenda will strongly impact which style profile they require to achieve the intended results. This is actually a more sophisticated way of looking at situational leadership – the best suiting leadership style shouldn't *depend on the situation*, but should depend on what leaders want to *achieve given the situation*. Therefore, leaders typically assess the situation, then determine their leadership agenda and then flexibly make use of the leadership styles required to realize their agenda (see Figure 13.4 for an overview). Where their leadership styles are deemed to be insufficient to achieve the envisaged impact, this creates a leadership development priority. This can be labeled a *need-driven* leadership style enhancement stimulus – success in the current leadership setting demands such an upgrade.

It is important to note that leaders should actually draw up their leadership agendas along the same five leadership dimensions as used throughout this book. Leaders will have specific *interpersonal leadership* issues that they want to have high up on their agenda, such as a poorly functioning colleague or a direct report who is unable to deal with increased self-steering. There will also be *organizational leadership* challenges on the agenda, such as low engagement and poor cross-unit cooperation internationally. *Strategic leadership* issues will also be prioritized, such as lagging strategic project execution and the slow response to

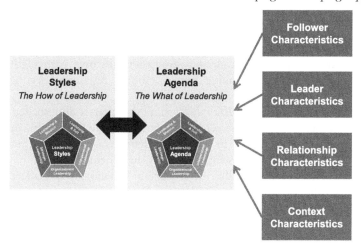

Figure 13.4 Leadership development priorities: Realizing your leadership agenda

a new competitive threat. There might even be a *leadership and purpose* topic on the agenda, such as the need for investment in corporate social responsibility or whether to sell the firm to private equity. And finally, there can also be some *leadership and self* issues that need to be dealt with, such as taking more initiative and gaining more visibility towards younger employees. All of these leadership agenda items will be rooted in a complex web of situational variables, but it is the leader who decides which leadership agenda priorities will be set and therefore which leadership style is required. Of course, the more varied the leadership agenda items and the more diverse the circumstances surrounding each agenda item, the more pressure there will be on the leader to be flexible and adaptive in selecting the most effective leadership style. Moreover, the faster the leadership agenda items change and the more rapid the circumstances surrounding each agenda item shift, the more agile the leader will need to be to remain effective.

To complete this overview of the need-driven side of leadership development priority-setting, it is good to realize that there are hordes of situational variables that leaders need to consider when formulating their leadership agenda. These variables were actually already presented in Figure 2.4 in Chapter 2, as the four categories of conditions that influence the way that leaders and followers interact with one another. These are the four groups of factors that shape "the leadership situation":

1. *Follower characteristics*. Naturally, the first factor determining a leadership situation is the type of people that the leader is trying to lead. These potential followers can vary across a wide spectrum of characteristics (e.g. experience, values, beliefs, history, intentions and expectations) and they can interact as a group in many different ways (e.g. cohesion, trust, rivalries, coalitions and team roles).

2. *Leader characteristics*. Maybe less obviously, the leader is also part of the leadership situation. Each leader will have individual characteristics (e.g. sources of power, track record, capabilities, reputation and presence), but might also be part of a leadership group with its own particularities (e.g. composition, decision-making process, formal responsibilities, ambitions and group culture).
3. *Relationship characteristics*. Each leadership situation is also shaped by the relationships that exist between the leader(s) and the follower(s). Important influencing characteristics include such elements as past and future inter-actions, levels of commitment, credibility and chemistry.
4. *Context characteristics*. Finally, the leadership situation is also affected by a host of other factors in the broader context. These circumstantial elements can be more stable characteristics such as the organizational culture, the industry rules of the game and government regulation, but also include impactful changes, such as shifting market conditions, an organizational crisis and a merger of units.

With so many factors potentially influencing the leadership agenda, it should come as no surprise that drawing up an agenda is a difficult process that can't be automated or even put into a simple flow diagram. Determining one's leadership agenda items requires a qualitative assessment process, not filling in a straightforward checklist. Yet, what can be helpful, once potential agenda items have been identified and need to be prioritized, is the priority-setting grid presented in Figure 13.5.

The priority-setting grid can be used to evaluate all potential leadership agenda items along two key selection criteria. First, leadership issues need to be

Figure 13.5 Priority-setting grid

judged according to their importance, to make sure that challenges that are crucial are prioritized over topics that are less impactful. Second, leadership issues need to be ranked according to the effort required to address them, so that challenges that are easy for the leader to resolve are prioritized over topics that are difficult to tackle. As the names of the four quadrants indicate, generally leaders should focus on the low-hanging fruit first, selectively choosing hard nuts and peanuts to complete their leadership agendas, while avoiding a bite out of a poison fruit. It is useful to note that besides employing this grid to prioritize the leadership agenda items, it can also be used to subsequently prioritize the potential leadership style development items as well.

Resource-based priority-setting

The discussion around setting leadership style development priorities has so far only focused on the "need side" – which styles do leaders need to adequately respond to what they think is important and/or easy in the current leadership situation? However, leaders might not only want to develop styles that are needed, but also styles that build on who they are and who they could be. This line of argumentation runs entirely parallel with the discussion in the previous chapter on the paradox of authenticity and adjustment. Instead of only reasoning that leadership development priorities are driven from the *outside-in*, based on the assumption that leaders need to adjust themselves to the situation they are in, it can be argued that leadership development priorities should be driven from the *inside-out*, based on the assumption that leaders should build on their true selves. Following this inside-out reasoning, leaders should strive to develop leadership styles that fit with their personal profile, leveraging their distinctive strengths and compensating for limiting weaknesses. Leaders should also consider which personal characteristics are easily malleable, allowing for quick growth in terms of style improvement, expansion, switching and responsiveness, and which parts of who they are seem extremely resistant to supporting leadership style change.

In Figure 13.6 this inside-out approach to leadership style development has been added to the outside-in logic that was already introduced in Figure 13.4. To contrast this approach with the need-driven way of thinking, we call it the *resource-driven* approach to leadership style development, as it builds on the personal resources of the leader, as opposed to the situational needs pressing on the leader. This approach starts with an understanding of who the leader genuinely is and then turns to the question of who the leader could become based on these "resources."

Notice that the elements constituting "who the leader genuinely is" were already introduced in the previous chapter. These are the four layers of the framework depicted in Figure 12.1. As was discussed there, people's personality and physique generally only change very gradually over time, which means that it would be unwise to pursue a new leadership style that fits poorly with one's core self. It was also argued that people's values and beliefs are deeply rooted,

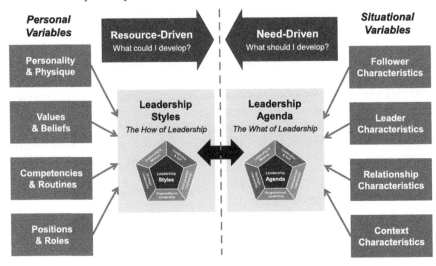

Figure 13.6 Leadership development priorities: Combining need and resource factors

making them highly resistant to alteration. So, here too, it makes more sense to develop leadership styles that are in sync with leaders' attitudes, while avoiding styles that are in conflict with these convictions.

The third layer of the framework is competences and routines, which are a bit less difficult to change and upgrade where necessary. However, it is much easier to build on existing competences and routines than to learn new ones, particularly if these conflict with existing abilities. Therefore, again, enhancing leadership styles that are in line with current strengths will generally lead to better results than selecting styles that need to be rooted in new, potentially contradictory, competences and routines.

The fourth layer, positions and roles, is the most malleable part of a person's self, but also here it makes sense to leverage these as a resource. If leaders have a certain position or play a particular role, this often offers them the opportunity to develop certain leadership styles more readily than others. The position or role can open the possibility to grow by providing access to stimulating people, learning experiences and places to experiment. We usually view a position or role as coming with situational demands, requiring need-driven adjustment, but as described here, positions and roles are also valuable resources, presenting opportunities for leadership style development.

An integrated approach to leadership development priority-setting

Having reviewed the need-side and resource-side factors driving the choice of which leadership styles to further develop, there are two last important factors that need to be added to be complete (both have been added to the final integrated framework presented in Figure 13.7). The first is *leadership ambition* – what are

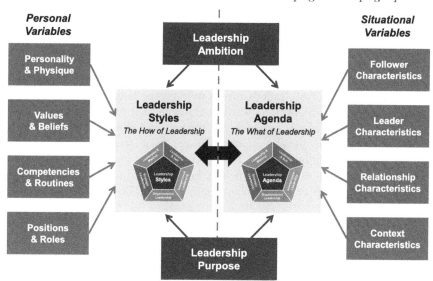

Figure 13.7 Leadership development priorities: An integrated approach

the leader's aspirations for the future? Where does the leader want to be in a few years' time? While the need side emphasized the question "Which styles *should* I develop?" and the resource side asked "Which styles *could* I develop?" the leadership ambition topic raises the question "Which styles do I *want* to develop?" Ambition is about leaders determining where they want to go and "how high they want to jump."

So, leadership ambition is about setting some overarching goals, outlining what type of future state the leader would like to achieve. This can be a concrete plan, but also a big picture vision, as discussed in Chapter 7 (on strategic goal-setting). The ambition can be oriented towards attaining a particular formal position, but can also outline what type of informal roles the leader would like to play in future. But the ambition can also be focused on such things as personal development, intellectual growth, social standing, political influence and contribution to society, to name just a few. In all cases, it is not the current needs and resources that steer leaders' development priorities, but their dreams of what they would like to be.

Strongly linked to where leaders want to go are their underlying reasons for wanting to be leaders in the first place. This is their *leadership purpose* – their fundamental motives for wanting to take a leadership role. While the other factors are all *"what"* issues (What should I do? What could I do? What do I want to do?), leadership purpose is about *"why"* (Why do I feel compelled to step up and go to the trouble of engaging others to move in a certain direction? Why do I see leadership as my responsibility? Why do I even care?). In Chapter 9 it was not the leader's purpose that was discussed, but the organizational purpose; however the conclusion was the same, that having a purpose gives a sense of mission that is a crucial driver in motivating and directing people. If leaders know their purpose, this clearly helps in determining both their leadership agenda priorities and where they want to further enhance their leadership style.

Based on all of the factors depicted in Figure 13.7, each leader will need to select a limited number of leadership style development priorities. In other words, in a few areas the leader's future style profile is intended to be much better than the current profile. We call this intended future state a leader's *stretch profile*. It is the gap between the current and the stretch profile that defines the leadership development challenge. As illustrated in Figure 13.8, this gap can be caused by the wish to improve existing styles and to expand to new ones. Furthermore, there can also be a gap created by the desire to reduce the frequency of falling into certain pitfalls. This we call the leader's *dampened profile*.

Of course, this is a very quantitative way to set one's leadership style development goals and it will not appeal to everybody. Some people might prefer a looser qualitative approach. But for those who favor this more specific and tangible method, because of its rigor, measurability and visual clarity, there is the Leadership LEAP App available that can support drawing up these stretch and dampened profiles for each leadership style.

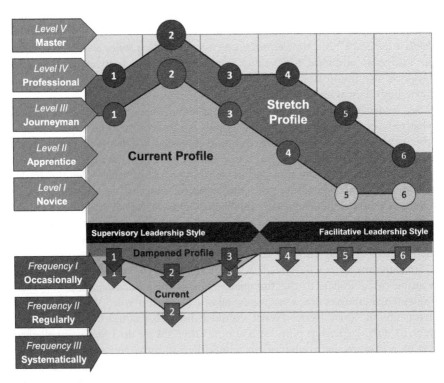

Figure 13.8 Determining your stretch leadership style profile

Your leadership development methods

Greatness, in the last analysis, is largely bravery – courage in escaping from old ideas and old standards and respectable ways of doing things.

James Harvey Robinson (1863–1936)
American historian

With your leadership development priorities set, it is now time for bravery, as Robinson suggests in the above quote. It is time to leave the comfort zone of your existing behaviors and to start doing things that are new. This learning might feel a bit disorienting as you don't know exactly what to do, much as you probably felt while trying to learn a new language while not knowing all of the grammar rules. You might also feel slightly awkward, as you begin to act in ways that you are not used to, much as you felt trying to pronounce difficult foreign words while your mouth wasn't used to creating certain sounds. However, the biggest barrier to leaving your comfort zone is fear – you might dread the thought of making mistakes and looking silly, while having to admit to others that you are not perfect and all-knowing. In learning to speak a foreign language it is this anxiety for losing face that undermines people's confidence and makes them reluctant to try talking to others, while "just doing it" is the only way to learn. So, having the courage to sail beyond your known world to *terra incognita* is indeed important and we will need ways to bolster your courage.

Yet, at the same time, exploring your *terra incognita* can be every appealing. Why linger in your comfort zone, exploiting what you already master, while exploration can bring you new riches, as we discussed for the organizational level in Chapter 8 (the paradox of exploitation and exploration). The voyage of learning new leadership styles, but also improving existing ones and strengthening your switching and responsiveness abilities, builds your leadership capabilities, while the exciting journey can be a reward in itself. So, seeing the benefits of "going where you have never gone before"[1] is just as important as courage. Therefore, we will also need ways to bolster your sense of gain, not only encourage you to overcome your pain.[2]

As learning is fundamentally about changing yourself, it is useful to go back to the "layered individual" framework that was discussed in the previous chapter to reiterate what it is that you are changing when you work on your leadership agility.[3] As was argued there, leadership styles are actually routines, rooted in a variety of competences. The abilities to switch, respond and combine are also found in this layer. For this reason, it can be concluded that all these elements are learnable.

The same framework can also be used to review the four key methods by which people can actually learn and develop themselves as leaders. These four approaches to leadership development have been summarized in Figure 13.9 and will be explored in more detail in the next sections.

Try: Learning-by-experiencing

The first way for you to learn is to seek out new situations that will stimulate you to step up and try out new behaviors. If you want to learn to speak Greek,

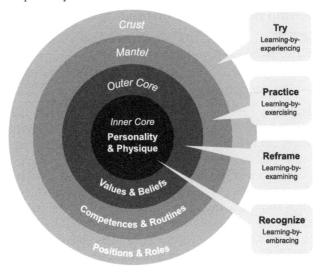

Figure 13.9 Four leadership development methods

pack your bags and go to Greece. If you want to learn to be a good sales-person, find yourself a job that will challenge you to rapidly upgrade your commercial skills. If you want to expand your leadership repertoire to include the federative leadership style, volunteer to lead a cross-functional committee, as you surely will be stretched to grow by the pressures you encounter.

The basic premise of "learning-by-experiencing" is that being thrown into the deep end is a great way to learn to swim.[4] You learn by finding a stimu-lating setting and giving it a try. This means finding a position that you can fulfill or a role that you can play that has a high chance of giving you relevant real-life experience. It is about getting out of your current comfortable set of tasks and taking on a new challenge, but one that you expect will trigger you to come up with new behaviors. Some practical suggestions include:

- *Switching roles.* Maybe the easiest action to take is to trade responsibilities with somebody else on a temporary basis. For example, it can be highly insightful to rotate responsibility for chairing meetings, running certain projects or giving feedback to certain employees. The idea is that by walking in someone else's shoes and experiencing their challenges, you probably need to try out new types of behaviors. Of course, it doesn't have to be a switch, it can also be a new role for which you volunteer or that you proactively start playing on your own initiative.
- *Switching role models.* Instead of actually engaging in a different role your-self, you can also "shadow" someone, to (almost) experience what they are going through in their role themselves. Once you have been inspired by their experiences and their leadership styles, you can turn around and use

their example in your own situation. By using different role models, you can tap into different real-life experiences and copy/adapt what you find to be most useful to grow your own leadership skill set.

- *Switching places.* In a similar vein, it can be instructional to move beyond switching roles, to actually switching places for a while. For example, you might want to go on exchange to one of the other functional departments, business units or country offices for a few weeks to experience firsthand what type of leadership styles are required there. As "where you sit determines where you stand," it pays to sit somewhere else for a while, for example at headquarters instead of at one of the subsidiaries, or on the work floor instead of in the boardroom.

- *Switching jobs.* One step further is to actually move over to a different position on a permanent basis, with your leadership development priorities in mind. So, instead of selecting your next posting on the basis of pay, power or prominence, you can seek out a job that will maximize your leadership learning, exposing you to all the right challenges to make you grow at an accelerated pace.

In all of these examples, the beauty of "switching" is that you not only try out new leadership styles or improve existing ones, but that you force yourself to be responsive to new circumstances and flexibly switch to different styles of leadership. By creating your own situational variety, you build up your own agility. If you switch back and forth between the boardroom and the work floor, or between Miami and Mumbai, and fail to adjust your leadership style, you'll quickly find out that your effectiveness is suboptimal, stimulating you to step up.

However, the key to learning-by-experience is to truly turn an experience into learning. It is all too common for people to do things and to learn nothing from them. Remember the paradox of thought and action in Chapter 11? Plenty of people engage in action, but fail to complete the learning cycle by reflecting on these actions and then drawing conclusions on what worked and what didn't. This means you should invest considerable effort in reaping the learning from experience by reflecting, gathering feedback and interpreting the learning conclusions that should be drawn.

Practice: Learning-by-exercising

The second method at your disposal to enhance your leadership agility is to practice. If you want to learn to speak Greek, find a Greek friend to practice on – a lot. If you want to learn to be a good salesperson, use every sales pitch as an opportunity to exercise your abilities. If you want to expand your leadership repertoire to include the federative leadership style, practice on one of your teams again and again until you get the hang of it.

The basic premise of "learning-by-exercising" is that you can only master a skill or style by doing it over and over again. For a leadership style to be a readily accessible part of your repertoire, it needs to become a well-rehearsed routine, while the underlying competences need to be muscled-up by constant exercise. Practice makes perfect. To achieve mastery of a game on your smartphone might only take weeks of intense practice, but for more complex skills and styles it is more realistic to think in terms of years.[5] To some it might come as a bit of a disappointment to read that leadership development is hard work and requires perseverance, but there is no substitute for exercise.

Of course, you will want to exercise as efficiently and effectively as possible. For this we have a few practical suggestions:

- *Practicing on stage.* The best place to practice is on the job. Every day you spend the majority of your time, attention and energy doing your job, so it makes sense to leverage your daily work as a source of learning. Actually, if we turn it around, how inefficient is it to only "produce outcomes" while you could have "produced learning" at the same time at no extra cost? You also have the advantage that you know your current situation and therefore can probably see where there are opportunities to practice new behaviors. And if you are successful, you will have grown as a leader, while also showing great performance. Yet, many leaders hesitate to practice more on the job because of the aforementioned fear of losing face. This is highly unfortunate, as the fear is often unfounded. On the contrary, people commonly have significant tolerance for leaders who genuinely exert effort to do things better, particularly if these leaders ask for feedback on their own behavior and accept this feedback with humility. By practicing on the job, leaders also give the right example and show that learning and making mistakes are all part of healthy organizational practices.
- *Practicing side-stage.* But if you feel that most teams and units in which you operate are unsafe for practicing your new leadership behaviors, a reasonable alternative is to find a safer "side-stage" – somewhere out of the organizational mainstream, where you have less at stake and are surrounded by people who you trust to give constructive feedback. If this side-stage doesn't yet exist, you can always create one by recruiting people who you think will be good "guinea pigs" for your leadership practicing and with whom you are willing to share your learning goals. You might even be able to make it a win–win by also explicitly supporting them in their personal development objectives.
- *Practicing off stage.* Besides on-the-job learning, you can also speed up your leadership development by practicing off the job, in a training type setting. Just as golf players will practice their swing again and again on a driving range, leaders can practice a leadership style using role play or in a leadership simulation game. It is generally not as life-like as in the real situation, but it has the distinct advantage of being safe and constantly repeatable. The presence of a coach or trainer giving play-by-play feedback can also considerably speed up the learning experience. However, be aware that training is only a useful step up to practicing on stage. As every actor will

tell you, rehearsals are essential, but it's on stage, in front of a sellout crowd, that your skill is truly honed. In the same way, sportspeople will acknowledge that training is very valuable, but you'll never get "into your game" if you don't play regular matches for real.

It is not only off-stage where the feedback of a coach or trainer can strengthen and accelerate the learning process. Also on the job, getting the constructive reflections of a professional specialized in observing leadership behaviors, asking stimulating questions and suggesting alternative approaches can greatly assist in going through the "plan-do-check-act" learning cycle. You must "do," but you would be depriving yourself of valuable help if you didn't get others involved in "check and act."

The broader point is that for practice – but also for the previous topic of "trying" – you are not only *learning-by-doing*, but need to *learn-from-doing*. This means reflecting on your actions and figuring out what worked, what needs to be fine-tuned and what needs to be done entirely differently. For this you need feedback. Obviously, you need to collect this feedback information yourself, by being perceptive to how people respond to your actions, but you also need to ask others to provide you with feedback, based on their perception of what happened. These extra voices not only complement your own observations, adding insights that you hadn't gathered, but also provide contrasting perspectives, often forcing you to reconsider your conclusions. Therefore, it is essential for you to consciously organize your own feedback. You need to "recruit" a circle of people willing to take the time and effort to engage you in a meaningful conversation, sharing what they have observed and how they interpret what they have seen. This circle can include the above-mentioned coach, but should preferably include a variety of perspectives, taking the leadership circle as starting point – your direct reports, peers, outside partners and boss. Not all will be willing and not all will feel safe, but the more angles on your "doing" the better, so getting as many as possible involved in giving feedback in some way will still be to your learning advantage.

Reframe: Learning-by-examining

Both "trying" and "practicing" are based on the premise that "it is easier to act yourself into a new way of thinking than to think yourself into a new way of acting."[6] But sometimes despite all of the trying and practicing leaders find it extremely difficult to structurally upgrade their leadership behavior and this usually points to the fact that they haven't been able to act themselves into a new way of thinking. At the level of their values and beliefs they can't really internalize the thinking underpinning a different leadership style. They rationally understand the opposite style and probably also acknowledge the potential qualities that it could bring, but deep down it conflicts with their convictions. They try the style, but "it doesn't feel right," which generally means it doesn't fit with their worldview and the cognitive dissonance makes them feel uncomfortable.

When this happens, behavioral change can't be triggered at the "more superficial" levels of "position and roles" and "routines and competences," but must be enabled at the deeper level of values and beliefs. It means that someone is stuck in a particular paradigm and is unable to "see" that an alternative way of thinking can also be "true." They are held back by "blocking beliefs" that make it impossible to accept that a different logic can still be logical. Their values and principles have become ideological, blinding them to see that other views also have merits. Therefore, learning new leadership styles will depend on examining their underlying values and beliefs, and then challenging them to consider the alternative logic. This is reframing – looking at the same issue, but by changing the interpretive frame, seeing something differently.[7]

Maybe you immediately recognize one or more leadership styles that really don't fit you and you happily stay on the opposite side of the leadership style continuum. Take one of these for a thought experiment. Ask yourself why you dislike this style and prefer not to use it. If you start thinking about the aspects of this style that you have an aversion to, you will probably come up with many points that are already listed as pitfalls of this style. As illustrated in Figure 13.10, your "allergy" for this style is rooted in your loathing of all of the things that can go wrong when it is used. This is not at all surprising as the pitfalls of style B correspond with the strengths of style A, or stated differently, style A does all of the things right that style B does wrong. If you prefer the autocratic leadership style because of its clear accountability, of course you detest the pitfall of the democratic leadership style, which is a lack of clear accountability. If you prefer the pragmatic leadership style because of its tangible goal-setting, naturally you will dislike the pitfall of the visionary leadership style, which is a lack of tangible goal-setting. This symmetrical link between the strengths of style A and the weaknesses of style B is because A and B are not simply different styles, but opposite styles – they are the two sides of a paradox. They represent diametrically opposed logics that don't fit together and actually contradict one another. So, obviously, you see the downsides of style B because these are all of the downsides of not using style A.

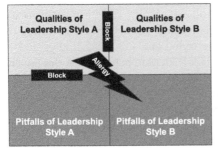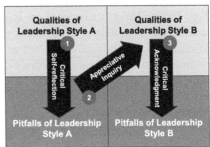

Figure 13.10 Dealing with opposite leadership styles

So, it is easy for you to see the pitfalls of the opposite style, because you are reasoning from the perspective of the qualities of your own style. The more you are a confident believer in the superiority of your preferred style, the more harshly you will judge the pitfalls of the opposite style. If you are convinced that appreciative feedback is the best way to give others inputs, your strong embrace of the encouraging style will make you abhor the pitfalls of the demanding style, which include complaining, blaming and creating fear of failure. But instead of recognizing these negative aspects of the demanding style as only its pitfalls, you will be tempted to react "allergically" to these negative aspects and condemn the entire style as bad. As with a true allergy, it is the overreaction to some of the pitfalls of the opposite leadership style that blocks your ability to appreciate its qualities. And it is inherently difficult to value the qualities of the opposite style in the first place, as its underlying logic is fundamentally inconsistent with your own.

At the same time, leaders' strong conviction that their style is "correct" also blocks their ability to see their own pitfalls. As these leaders are sure that their leadership style represents the best possible approach, they will tend to downplay the pitfalls as normal side effects or they won't even recognize the pitfalls at all. This psychological tendency towards selective perception is often further strengthened by the social tendency to conform to the values and beliefs of the group. The more that leaders are surrounded by people with the same views about the "correct" way of leading, the more they will accept these principles as "self-evident truths," further blocking their ability to see their own pitfalls and appreciate the qualities of the opposite side.

Reframing is about finding a way around these obstacles, to allow you to see the full picture and embrace the opposite style's fundamental principles. It is about helping you to uncover your own blocking beliefs and allergies, so that you can hold two opposite ideas in your mind at the same time, without experiencing cognitive stress.[8] Of course, the easiest approach would be to simply decide to "change your mind." It would then be a matter of reading the appropriate chapter in this book and adapting your values and beliefs to include the premises of the style that you dislike and find hard to master. Yet, we suggest you try the three steps outlined in Figure 13.10, as it is our experience that leaders who struggle to accept the opposite style benefit tremendously from examining what is blocking them:

1. *Critical self-reflection.* The key to challenging your leadership style assumptions is critical self-reflection. It helps to start by recognizing the qualities of your current style, which should be easy, but then to move to identifying the pitfalls of this style, which tends to be much harder. You need to be very tough on yourself to uncover the downsides of your current approach. Put on one of De Bono's black thinking hats[9] and focus on seeing all of the problems that you encounter. Also call on your feedback circle to get their input on all of the shadow sides they see of your leadership approach. It is not the intention to be negative, but you must be

critical, willing to drag all of your shortcomings into the light. The reason is that feeling the pain of your current style creates the opening to seeing the gain of the opposite style. The added advantage is that wholeheartedly acknowledging your pitfalls is the best way of finding a manner to deal with them.

2.   *Appreciative inquiry.* Once the pitfalls of your current style "hurt" enough, you are ready to look for a solution to get out of these pitfalls. This is the moment at which you need to switch from a critical mode of thinking to a more appreciative stance. You need to open-mindedly consider what appeals to you in the opposite style and how it could resolve many of the downsides of your current leadership approach. This "pain-driven" exploration of the qualities of the opposite leadership style generally reaps much more positive insights than viewing this alternative style from a position of moral superiority.

3.   *Critical acknowledgement.* Quickly following step 2, it also helps to vigorously distinguish between the qualities of the opposite style and its pitfalls. Acknowledging the existence of these downsides, but immediately slotting them in the pitfall category, puts them into perspective, while allowing the qualities to shine more on their own.

By going through these three steps you will have completed all quadrants of what we call a leadership style *paradox map*, individualized to fit your own situation. Building up your overview in this order will probably give you the richest and most balanced view possible, helping you to pinpoint where you had some blocking beliefs and see where the opposite style might be of value to you. Moreover, having your personalized paradox map has the additional benefit of assisting you in determining when it might be better to switch from one style to the other.

Recognize: Learning-by-embracing

If after the above reframing you still find it difficult to learn a new leadership style, the source of this inability might lie at the deepest level of who you are, which is your personality and physique. In other words, that leadership style just might be at odds with your fundamental personality traits, making it hard for you to make it work. So, what do you do? At all of the other levels the conclusion was that you have scope to learn and adjust. You can try new positions and roles, you can practice new routines and competences, and you can reframe your values and beliefs. But now at the core of who you are, do we conclude we need to reshape your personality and physique?

Psychologists debate how much of your personality shifts over time after the age of five, but there is little disagreement that it is largely stable, with relatively limited scope for reshaping.[10] Therefore, the opposite is more productive, which is recognizing your fundamental self and embracing it as a given. You have a core that is not malleable that you need to be conscious of and unconditionally accept. If you know your own deeper peculiarities and embrace them, you more quickly learn which leadership styles will never fit you and which you will never be more than average in. This is what we mean by learning-by-embracing – using your self-awareness to determine which leadership styles to enhance and which to ignore because they don't fit. Not only does this self-acceptance help to optimize your leadership style development, but it is probably the most important ingredient of self-confidence,[11] which in itself is essential to being an effective leader.

Your leadership LEAP

> *Plans are nothing. Planning is everything.*
>
> Dwight D. Eisenhower (1890–1969)
> American general and president

With all of your leadership development ingredients now on the table, the last step is to make your learning intentions tangible enough for them to be implemented. This is the moment to use your "pragmatic self-management style" to translate your SMART goals into a concrete plan including what, who, where and how. We call this personal development plan your *Leadership LEAP* – your Leadership Enhancement Action Plan. *Enhancement* refers to all the ways of upgrading your leadership agility discussed before, namely improving, expanding, switching, responding and combining. *Action* points to all of the concrete methods discussed that you have at your disposal to learn, namely trying, practicing, reframing and recognizing. *Plan* indicates that you need to specify how you want to implement these potential actions, detailing milestones and progress tracking, required resources and support, and feedback and rewards.

In Figure 13.11 the five steps that you need to take to arrive at a LEAP are summarized. You will recognize all of them from the discussions earlier in this chapter:

1. *Current leadership profile.* You need to start with a realistic assessment of your current leadership style repertoire on all of the ten style dimensions, mapping which style mixes along each continuum are within your range and what your level of mastery is of each. You also need to guesstimate the extent to which you frequent your style pitfalls. All of this evaluation

Figure 13.11 Steps in making your leadership LEAP

should preferably be done using the inputs from your leadership circle, not only on the basis of self-observation.

2. *Leadership development priorities.* With a clear picture of your current profile, you need to determine which leadership styles have the highest development priority. This short list of development points can be selected on the basis of situational needs, personal strengths, your ambitions for the future and your purpose as leader.

3. *Stretch leadership profile.* On the basis of your selected priorities, you need to draw up your "to be" leadership profile, one to three years into the future, depending on your preferred planning horizon. The gap between your current and this stretch profile needs to be large enough to challenge you to step up, but not too vast, resulting in stress, disappointment and/or resignation.[12]

4. *Leadership development actions.* Once the development gap has been defined, you need to come up with potential learning actions that will help you to achieve your development goals. These actions will likely be a combination of trying, practicing, reframing and recognizing, and should be specific enough that they are actionable.

5. *Leadership development planning.* Finally, the list of potential learning actions that you come up with will need to be operationalized by drawing up a concrete plan. A typical plan will include the following items:

    a. *Milestones and tracking measures.* You should determine when you want to start and finish each action item and how you will measure your progress in achieving your development goals.

    b. *Resources and support requirements.* You should identify whether you need specific resources, such as budget, information and/or time, as well as extra support from a coach, sparring partners and/or your boss.

    c. *Feedback and rewards.* You should also identify how you want to structure your "plan-do-check-act" steering cycle, in particular when and how you want to "check and act" and who needs to be involved in providing the necessary feedback. Last but not least, you should consider how to reward yourself if you achieve your objectives. Of course, the personal growth will be an important reward in itself, but building in extra incentives such as a celebration, recognition and giving yourself the right type of break can work wonders in keeping up your motivation in the long run.

It would go into far too much detail to further describe here what your plan could look like. But if you would like more tangible suggestions, and even a specific format, we again direct you to the Leadership LEAP App that accompanies this book.

Despite the threat of seeming a bit pushy, we do want to reiterate how important it is to engage in this type of planning if you seriously want to work on your leadership agility. You are constantly busy with day-to-day activities, solving problems and contributing to developing the business, developing the organization and developing others. Under these circumstances, it is difficult to keep at least one eye on developing yourself. But you owe it to you.[13] Making a plan forces you to invest time in yourself, helps you to find tangible ways to work on your leadership development and offers you a constant reminder of what you should also be doing. So, making a Leadership LEAP is usually the most important prerequisite for taking a leadership leap, so we warmly encourage you to draw one up.

Notes

1 With a wink to Gene Roddenberry.

2 The approach we suggest here is unabashedly "*voluntaristic.*" We assume that human behavior is not solely determined by external factors and innate programming (the "*deterministic*" view), but that individuals do have a free will and can shape their own actions. Our approach is in line with the *theory of reasoned action*, as put forward by the two leading theorists in the field of behavioral change, Martin Fishbein and Icek Azjen. In a nutshell, they argue that behavioral change is driven by people's intent and limited by the circumstances they do not control. People's intent in turn is influenced by their attitudes (their mindset), the social pressures they perceive (the norms of what they should and should not do) and the extent to which they believe they can influence outcomes (perceived behavioral control). In other words, people's intentions are influenced by a variety of factors, but they still have the "freedom" to make up their own minds.

3 Seeing learning as a multi-layered phenomenon is not new. Our layers roughly correspond with those outlined in Mezirov, J. (2000), *Learning as Transformation*, San Francisco: Jossey-Bass.

4 In the learning literature, experiential learning has a long and rich heritage. One of the godfathers in the field is Jean Piaget and it is worth reading some of his works, such as Piaget, J. and Campbell, R.L. (eds.) (2001), *Studies in Reflection Abstraction*, Hove: Psychology Press.

5 This concept of the "10,000-hour rule" was popularized by Malcolm Gladwell. See Gladwell, M. (2008), *Outliers: The Story of Success*, New York: Little Brown and Company.

6 This quote has been attributed to many different people and we have been unable to establish "the rightful IP owner."

7 The concept of reframing also has deep roots in the psychology literature. One of the intellectual godfathers here is Albert Ellis and his works provide fascinating reading. A good start is Ellis, A. (2001), *Overcoming Destructive Beliefs, Feelings and Behaviors*, New York: Prometheus Books.

8 This is an indirect reference to F. Scott Fitzgerald's famous quote on first-rate intelligence: "The test of a first-rate intelligence is the ability to hold two opposed ideas in mind at the same time and still retain the ability to function."

9 See De Bono, E. (1985), *Six Thinking Hats*, New York: Little Brown and Company.

10 For a good overview of the research and the ongoing debate see Matthews G. Deary, I. and Whiteman, M. (2003), *Personality Traits* (2nd ed.), Cambridge: Cambridge University Press.

11 Usually psychologists point out that self-acceptance leads to self-esteem, which then in turn leads to self-confidence. See James, W. (1984), *Psychology: Briefer Course*, Cambridge: Harvard University Press.

12 This insight was popularized by Lev Vygotsky; see Vygotsky, L.S. (1978), *Mind in Society: Development of Higher Psychological Processes*, Cambridge: Harvard University Press.

13 Note that you not only owe it to yourself, but you also owe it to the others around you: first, because they will all benefit from your increased leadership abilities; but maybe more importantly, because you should be a role model in how to develop leadership. If you don't take your own leadership development seriously, why should they? And even if they wanted to, how would they dare if you don't, and who would they emulate?

14 Mastering leadership agility

"Would you prefer chicken or the vegetarian pasta?" If you've done some economy class flying, you'll have heard that question before. On airlines that's usually the binary choice that you have. Just for fun you should try the comeback line: "Can I have chicken with the pasta?" The answer is usually: "I'm sorry." You need to choose. It's either one or the other, with no combinations possible. This *either-or thinking* frames a situation as a *dilemma* – you need to select between two mutually exclusive options. Sometimes the options are both positive ("Do you want to go to the movies or to the swimming pool?"), but they can also both be negative ("Do you want to pay a fine or engage in a legal battle?"). This is where the expression "horns of a dilemma" comes from – you can decide whether you want to get impaled by the right horn of a charging bull, or run through by the left one.

At moments in this book we almost presented the opposite styles as a dilemma, suggesting you either use the one style or its opposite. But of course, this was for rhetorical purposes and we quickly added that between the two extremes there is plenty of scope for mixing the two into blended styles. We presented the opposite styles along a continuum with a variety of intermediate mixes between the two poles. But we also emphasized that more of one style necessarily results in less of the other, as the two are in conflict with one another. It is like saying that you can spend and you can save, which are each other's opposites but can be balanced at different levels. You can spend 100% and save nothing, spend zero and save everything, and endless mixes in between. This *zero-sum thinking* frames a situation as a *trade-off* – the more you do of the one style, the less you will be able to do of the other. In practice this means trying to find the best point along the trade-off line between the two poles, where the balance of elements from both sides is optimal given the situation.

Considering a continuum of leadership styles along ten dimensions is already challenging enough, so in the previous chapters that's where we left it. But for those who truly want to master leadership agility there is one level of complexity higher that they need to explore. What if challenge and appreciation aren't at odds with one another so you don't have to make a trade-off? Then you could get all of the advantages of challenging and all of the advantages of appreciation, without needing to strike a balance. What if there was no tension between exploitation and exploration? Then you could reap both the benefits of the one and the other at no extra cost. This is what is called *both-and thinking* and it frames the situation as a *paradox*[1] – the two sides seem to contradict each other, but if you look at the tension from a different angle you see ways of creating *positive-sum* combinations.

It is okay to see the ten underlying tensions (e.g. activities and conditions, thought and action) as trade-offs and to focus on developing your leadership agility to switch between the different styles along each continuum. Yet we challenge you to go one step further and to see the tensions as paradoxes (as we have already labeled them). We would like you to embrace the premise that you can combine elements of both sides and arrive at new styles above the trade-off line (see Figure 14.1). We would like to encourage you to be inventive in coming up with *hybrid styles* that combine elements of both sides in order to get the best of both worlds, instead of accepting a compromise somewhere along the trade-off line. If you want to put this mathematically, you are looking to avoid a 5-2 or a 3-4 type blend in favor of a 5-4 or a 3-6 type combination. After all, true mastery of leadership agility involves more than only quickly and graciously switching between your existing leadership styles in response to the needs of the situation. It also involves more than adapting to the changing conditions by expanding your repertoire to include

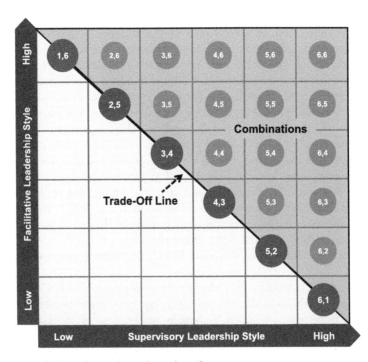

Figure 14.1 Thinking beyond simple trade-offs

leadership styles on the opposite side of the various style dimensions. It includes the ability to come up with specific new combinations that fit different situations even more snugly while achieving even more benefits. One is a real master if the range of possible styles is limitless, as the master painter can create an infinite number of styles with just a few colors and a "master wedding singer" a boundless repertoire of songs with just a few notes.

Mastering combinations

> *The most fatal illusion is the settled point of view. Life is growth and motion; a fixed point of view kills anybody who has one.*
>
> Brooks Atkinson (1894–1984)
> American theater critic and journalist

There is a surprisingly rich literature around paradoxes,[2] sometimes calling them polarities[3] or dilemmas,[4] and usually spurring readers to search for ways to achieve "both-and solutions,"[5] which is varyingly referred to as reconciliation,[6] integration[7] or synthesis.[8] We keep it simple and call all styles above the trade-off line *combinations* – they combine elements of both poles in an attempt to get the best of both worlds. A combination is a hybrid bringing together the positive qualities of both sides. This is the reason why a combination is also called a *synthesis* – it takes elements of the one side (the *thesis*) and of the opposite side (the *antithesis*), and reconfigures them into a new whole. So, while a *mix* of black and white results in a shade of gray, a combination will give you something new such as a chess board or a Charlie Chaplin movie.

There are basically two types of combinations that can be made between opposites, such as between idealism and realism, challenge and appreciation, and direction and participation:

1. *Combinations over time.* Often the easiest combination is to first use one leadership style, soon followed by its opposite, so that the overall style is a hybrid of both. The styles are not mixed but applied sequentially. Take again the example of black and white. If one first uses darkness, then light, then again darkness and then again light, the combination created can be used to establish the identity of a lighthouse or to send Morse code messages at night. Darkness and light are not mixed to create dusk, but artfully combined over time to produce something more meaningful. In the same vein, being able to combine the use of your left and right hand is often used as a metaphor for this skill of bringing together opposites in quick succession. If someone is *ambidextrous*[9] – able to use both hands equally well – they can first use one hand and then the other in remarkably agile ways. Just think of Michael Jordan dribbling, or Lionel Messi shooting with either foot just as well, making combined moves amazingly varied. Leaders can employ similar "combined moves:" for example first showing appreciation and then moving to a challenge; or first challenging, then showing appreciation.

Such combinations can be made in the same conversation, or can be spread over multiple meetings, or even over weeks or months. Likewise, a leader can move from participation to setting direction, followed by more participation, all in the same meeting, or could combine these styles over a period of months, leading a team through a varied decision-making process.

2. *Combinations at the same time.* The more imaginative combinations are where elements of two opposite styles are brought together at the same time. The styles are not mixed but synthesized into something new, just as a child is not the gray compromise between two parents, but a unique combination of their DNA. In such a simultaneous combination, a leader finds a way to cross-pollinate two styles to become, for instance, an idealistic realist, or a realistic idealist. In the case of the paradox of challenge and appreciation, one combination could be to use an "appreciatively challenging" style, in which a person would be challenged to improve but shown great confidence that it can be done ("You need to jump, but I know you can do it"). Another combination could be a "challengingly appreciative" style, showing great appreciation for their potential, thus indirectly challenging a person to live up to the high expectations ("I know you'll be great, it's just a matter of doing it"). Of course, many more combinations of the two opposites are possible, just as zeros and ones can be brought together into an infinite variety of patterns, while never mixing and becoming ½ or ¾.

It was the godfather of creative destruction, Joseph Schumpeter, who argued a century ago that economic innovation is based on new combinations of existing factors.[10] In a similar way, innovative leadership styles are based on new combinations of the existing opposite archetypes. And as with economic innovation, there are endless combinations possible, only limited by the imagination of the person tapping into the basic building blocks.

Mastering combining

> *The intellect has little to do on the road to discovery. There comes a leap in consciousness, call it intuition or what you will, and the solution comes to you and you don't know how or why. All great discoveries are made in this way.*
>
> Albert Einstein (1879–1955)
> German-Swiss-American physicist

Generating new combinations to fit your circumstances will largely be a process of trial and error. Einstein was right that all discoveries require effort and a leap of imagination, not simply filling in a spreadsheet or following "the three steps to success." So, we greatly encourage you to go out and experiment, trying and practicing to see what works for you. There is no substitute for exploring and learning by doing. As Thomas Edison put it: "Genius is one percent inspiration and ninety-nine percent perspiration." Perspiration is unavoidable. You won't master the art of combining sitting behind your desk.

At the same time, it is wise to let yourself be inspired by other people's experiences, so it makes sense to speak to colleagues, find a mentor and read up on the suggestions of others on the Leadership LEAP website. Their ideas won't exactly fit your situation, but they can point your experimentation in a fruitful direction.

What also might help is to follow through on the reframing method discussed in the previous chapter. This approach, illustrated in Figure 13.10, was presented as a way of examining a leadership paradox and open-mindedly being able to see the qualities and pitfalls of the opposite leadership styles. Such a considered understanding of the two poles of a leadership style continuum is a good start if one wants to construct a combination based on the strengths of both archetypical styles. In figure 14-2 an expanded reframing method is presented, building on the analysis of qualities and pitfalls done before. We call this the *double helix* approach, drawing a playful parallel with how two strands of DNA intertwine to create a new being that combines elements of both of its parents. Note that this framework doesn't "calculate" a new combination, but is a method that can assist in bringing about the right state of mind in which a "leap in consciousness" is more easily taken.

As before, the thinking process starts with an open-minded examination of the qualities and pitfalls of a pair of opposite leadership styles. Once the four quadrants have been completed to your satisfaction, the next step is to fully embrace the contradictions, accepting the existence of two partially conflicting logics next to one another.[11] Without wanting to sound woolly, this is not only about intellectually recognizing the validity of both ways of leading, but also about "feeling at ease" with both logics although they are inconsistent with

Figure 14.2 The double helix method

one another. You have to empathize with both worldviews – putting them on and feeling comfortable wearing them – while letting the tension between the two exist, without immediately trying to construct a higher-level logic that explains how the two fit together and are simply complementary. Indeed, the typical mistake is to struggle to hold on to a "clean and tidy," consistent way of thinking, explaining away the tension. Such pacification kills what needs to be a *constructive tension* between two equally valuable perspectives.

Once the contradictions have been fully embraced and you feel the tension between the thesis and the antithesis, then you are ready to engage in a dialogue between the two.[12] This can literally be a dialogue with a person who has the opposite default style, but it can also be an internal dialogue with your inner devil's advocate. In true dialogue style, this conversation is not a debate oriented towards winning the argument, nor a discussion oriented towards establishing a compromise. On the contrary, this dialogue should be focused on exploring possibilities and building on each other. As with the art of cross-fertilization, the dialogue should be directed at establishing the key qualities of both parents that ideally should be passed on to the offspring and which less desirable characteristics should be filtered out.

With this pre-work done, the scene will have been set for Einstein's leap of consciousness. The creative spark is still required to finally generate one or more new combinations, but the creativity-enhancing conditions will be optimal, making the chance of a leap of imagination significantly larger.[13]

The paradox of leadership and followership

> *You will never be a leader unless you first learn to follow and be led.*
> Tiorio (William Boetcker; 1873–1962)
> German-American minister and public speaker

After reading through an entire book structured around ten leadership paradoxes, you might be surprised that there is an eleventh and that it is the most important one for leadership agility. This is the *paradox of leadership and followership*. On the one hand, people in organizations need to step up and exhibit leadership, getting others to follow and move together in a certain direction. Someone needs to initiate, inspire, empower, steer, sway, bridge and nudge, all in order to get others engaged to act in a certain way. Without leadership, organizations would function mechanistically, with decisions made and communicated via the formal channels of hierarchy and motivation stimulated by carrots and sticks linked to key performance indicators. Employees would be human resources to be managed in order to achieve compliance, instead of humans to be engaged in order to achieve commitment.

Yet, organizations also need people to join up and exhibit followership,[14] supporting initiatives and ensuring that movement in a certain direction is realized and sustained. People need to pitch in, putting their weight behind plan execution, offering their cooperation, suggestions and plain hard work. Without followership, organizations would be collections of individuals all pursuing their own agenda and heading off in alternative directions. Or not heading anywhere, just toeing the line, only doing what they would be forced to do.

Clearly, organizations need both leadership and followership even though they are each other's opposites. So, where is the paradox? The challenge is that people need to be leaders and followers *at the same time*.[15] No one leads all people on every topic in all situations, nor should anyone always follow under all conditions. Sometimes you take a leadership role and sometimes a followership one. Sometimes you lead your boss, sometimes you follow; sometimes it is a mix or a combination of the two. Sometimes you lead your colleagues, sometimes someone else is in the lead and sometimes you lead together. The same goes for all relationships around you – it is likely that none is a straightforward leader–follower relationship all the time, but rather a blend of leader- and follower-like behaviors. In other words, no one is permanently "leader" – at most you often play a leadership role. Actually, in this sense the term "leader" is misleading, as it suggests that some people are always leaders while clearly they are also sometimes followers.

Still, you might ask: "Where is the paradox?" Shouldn't people try to lead as much as possible, therefore following as little as necessary? In the trade-off between the two, shouldn't the more talented people emphasize leadership over followership? Isn't leadership in some way superior, more important, or at least more desirable, than followership? Judging by the number of books on the topic of leadership compared to the number of publications on followership, this is a conclusion you might feel compelled to draw. Finding a "followership development program" is definitely much more difficult than locating a program focused on leadership development.

Yet, we believe it is a true paradox, with leadership and followership as opposite, but equally important, behaviors. Hence, the ultimate test of leadership agility is knowing when not to lead but to follow. To be truly agile as an individual in an organizational setting, you should not only have a repertoire of leadership styles that you can quickly and effortlessly tap into, but you should also be able to switch to followership if that is what the situation requires. Moreover, in line with the discussion in this chapter, you should not only strive towards nimbly shifting towards following when necessary, but you should even try to combine leadership and followership, either sequentially or at the same time.

Let us leave you with five arguments why we believe that you would do well to combine leadership and followership. These five reasons for embracing the paradox of leadership and followership can be linked to the five domains of leadership discussed in this book – interpersonal, organizational, strategic, purpose and self. What this suggests is that in each area of leadership there are arguments to be found as to why simultaneous followership will be beneficial. The five arguments, following the order of this book, are these:

- *Interpersonal leadership and followership.* In Chapters 3 and 4 it was argued that it is a task of leaders to steer others and give them feedback. Yet, as every teacher knows, children won't do as you say, but they will do as you do. If you want children to be respectful, don't tell them, show them. We believe the same is true for leaders and followers – don't tell them how to follow, show them how to follow. Don't only lead by steering and giving feedback, but also by showing the way. Show how to be a good follower by doing it yourself. Be the example of how good followers are not passive or slavish, but proactive, cooperative and constructive. Demonstrate that following is not about losing or being submissive, but about building on each other's initiative and being a team player. Be a role model in showing how effective followers support and praise a leader, but also ask tough questions and give challenging feedback. A great side effect of exhibiting this followership behavior is that it also allows others to practice their leadership behaviors, helping them to grow, gain confidence and better understand some of the difficulties that come with being a leader.

- *Organizational leadership and followership.* In Chapters 5 and 6 it was described that it is the task of leaders to build teams and guide decision-making. The argument was that leaders need to help organizations to function effectively and get moving, by ensuring that key decisions are taken and that people pull together into cooperative units to drive implementation. Yet, as every surfer knows, it is much easier to catch a wave than to make a wave. We believe the same is true in organizations – if you want to get things moving, find the waves and ride them. Look for existing initiatives that are moving in the right direction and then throw your weight behind them. Be an earlier follower of other leaders and in turn try to get more people on the bandwagon, to create momentum and really get something moving. Instead of only leading by taking the initiative, selectively following others in order to create "critical mass" can be much more effective. By being the follower of one, you become the leader of many more. Here, too, there are great side effects, such as building team spirit, not becoming too dominant and again showing how to engage in effective followership.

- *Strategic leadership and followership.* In Chapters 7 and 8 it was discussed that it is the task of leaders to set strategic goals and determine strategic priorities. The argument was that someone needs to establish where the organization needs to go and mobilize people to move in that direction. Without a leader making key choices, setting priorities and clarifying the future course of action, organizations would be set adrift and people wouldn't know on what to focus their attention. Yet, as every investor knows, no person or company has a monopoly on good strategic ideas. On the contrary, new perspectives, innovative concepts and disruptive business models often come from unexpected quarters, such as start-ups, industry outsiders or younger employees. Rarely does one person have all the best strategic insights, especially if that person has been an insider for a prolonged period of time. This is why investors spread their bets – they "know that they don't know" whose strategy will be superior. We believe that leaders should think in the same way, embracing the fact that others in the organization will often have better ideas. Moreover, leaders should accept that they generally don't know up front which strategy will be more successful. This means that "leaders" need to be humble, often following other people's strategic insights, backing their initiatives and supporting them in pursuing strategic hunches. Leaders need to distinguish when they know the best way forward and when they "know that they don't know," so they can let others take the lead and support them as best they can.

- *Leadership, followership and purpose.* In Chapters 9 and 10 it was stated that it is the task of leaders to set the purpose of the organization and to inspire people with a sense of mission. It was argued that by clarifying the "why," people would be more engaged in realizing the "what" and the "how." Yet, while leaders should have a purpose, their purpose shouldn't be to lead. Leadership, either sovereign or servant, should be a role played to realize a higher purpose – leadership should be a means towards an end. Leadership should be a tool to achieve something valuable or virtuous, not a purpose in itself. Wanting to be a leader for its own sake is like hoarding money for its own sake, which can easily become an obsession and a driver of moral corruption. Just as money represents power and can go to a person's head, so too leadership is a source of power that can be seductive in its own right, compelling an individual to garner more and more. It is a slippery moral slope from leadership to power tripping. You could say that wanting to be a leader purely for the power that it brings is the key pitfall of leadership – it is the exaggeration, doing too much of a good thing. Therefore, to stay out of this pitfall and avoid the temptation of becoming *power-driven*, leaders should ensure they are *purpose-driven*, following the needs determined by the overarching mission and only using power to achieve these ends. You could say this is a balancing form of followership – submitting to a higher purpose and supporting its realization.

- *Leadership, followership and self.* In Chapters 11 and 12 it was discussed that it is the task of leaders to solve problems and align themselves with the environment in which they need to operate. It was argued that leaders are often role models, so it is important for them to understand how they are seen. But even more fundamentally, leaders need to understand who they are – they need to recognize their character and physique, values and beliefs, competences and routines, and positions and roles. However, knowing yourself is not easy and the longer you stay in the same position and/or role, the more you take the associated competences, routines, values and beliefs for granted. In other words, the longer you play the role of leader, the more you think and act as a leader, but are not aware of it, assuming you are "normal." Being a leader colors your worldview and unknowingly you increasingly see everything from a leadership perspective. Gradually, your ability to empathize with followers withers, making it more and more difficult to truly connect. Obviously, the solution to this potential detachment from the world of followers is to regularly walk a mile in their shoes. If you want to understand followers, you need to be a follower – you need to experience what they experience and feel what they feel. Regularly being a follower is a practical way of deeply understanding others and as a consequence understanding more about yourself. A magnificent side effect is that such followership helps you to remain grounded and humble, while at the same time more appreciative of the power of leadership and more responsible in its use.

Conclusion? Keep on flying economy class every once in a while, even if you can afford first class. And don't settle for the choice of vegetarian pasta or chicken curry – there has to be a way to get chicken with your pasta.

Notes

1 This distinction between dilemma, trade-off and paradox was introduced by Meyer in De Wit, B. and Meyer, R. (1998), *Strategy Synthesis: Resolving Strategy Paradoxes to Achieve Competitive Advantage*, London: International Thomson Publishing.

2 Early authors using the term paradox include Quinn, R.E. (1988), *Beyond Rational Management: Mastering the Paradoxes and Competing Demands of High Performance*, San Francisco: Jossey-Bass; and Poole, M.S. and Van de Ven, A.H. (1989), "Using Paradox to Build Management and Organization Theories," *Academy of Management Review*, Vol. 14, No. 4, pp. 562–578. These were later followed by De Wit, B. and Meyer, R. (1998), *Strategy Synthesis: Resolving Strategy Paradoxes to Achieve Competitive Advantage*, London: International Thomson; and Lewis, M. (2000), "Exploring Paradox: Toward a More Comprehensive Guide," *Academy of Management Review*, Vol. 25, No. 4, pp. 760–776.

3 The term polarity was popularized by Johnson, B. (1996), *Polarity Management*, Amherst: HRD Press Inc.

4 The term dilemma is best known by its use in Hampden-Turner, C. and Trompenaars, F. (1990), *The Seven Cultures of Capitalism*, New York: Doubleday.

5 The distinction between "either-or" and "both-and" solutions was popularized by Collins, J.C. and Porras, J.I. (1994), *Built to Last: Successful Habits of Visionary Companies*, New York: Harper Business.

6 See Hampden-Turner, C. and Trompenaars, F. (1990), op. cit.

7 The term integrative thinking was introduced by Martin, R. (2007), *The Opposable Mind: How Successful Leaders Win through Integrative Thinking*, Cambridge: Harvard Business School Book Press.

8 De Wit, B. and Meyer, R. (1998), op. cit.

9 The term ambidexterity as applied to organizations has been around a while, becoming widely known after the famous article Tushman, M.L. and O'Reilly, C.A. (1996), "Ambidextrous Organizations: Managing Evolutionary and Revolutionary Change," *California Management Review*, Vol. 38, No. 4, pp. 8–30. Since then it has been used almost exclusively in connection with the paradox of exploitation and exploration. Recently there has also been more interest in the leadership side of ambidexterity, but again only linked to exploitation and exploration. See Rosing, K., Frese, M. and Bausch, A. (2011), "Explaining the Heterogeneity of the Leadership–Innovation Relationship: Ambidextrous Leadership," *The Leadership Quarterly*, Vol. 22, No. 5, pp. 956–974.

10 See Schumpeter, J. (1942), *Capitalism, Socialism and Democracy*, New York: Harper and Roe Publishers.

11 The importance of keeping two opposite ideas in one's mind at the same time was recognized as one of the key drivers of creativity by the psychiatrist Albert Rothenberg in the 1970s. On the basis of his research on creative writers and artists he concluded that breaking through accepted wisdom often depended on people's mental ability to entertain multiple logics at the same time. He referred to this type of thinking as the Janusian process, after the Roman god Janus, known for his two opposite faces. See Rothenberg, A. (1990), *Creativity and Madness: New Findings and Old Stereotypes*, Baltimore: Johns Hopkins University Press.

12 The dialogue described here largely follows the method of *dialectical inquiry*. For a good description of this method in a business context see Hampden-Turner, C. (1990), *Charting the Corporate Mind: From Dilemma to Strategy*, Oxford: Basil Blackwell.

13 Our approach largely coincides with the synthesis process described by Sarah Harvey. See Harvey, S. (2014), "Creative Synthesis: Exploring the Process of Extraordinary Group Creativity," *Academy of Management Review*, Vol. 39, No. 3, pp. 324–343.

14 For a good overview of recent research in this area, see: Uhl-Bien, M., Riggio, R.E., Lowe, K.B. and Carsten, M.K. (2014), "Followership Theory: A Review and Research Agenda," *The Leadership Quarterly*, Vol. 25, No. 1, pp. 83–104.

15 This argument is nicely made by Robert Kelley. See Kelly, R.E. (1988), "In Praise of Followers," *Harvard Business Review*, Vol. 66, No. 6, November, pp. 142–148.

Index

For Product Safety Concerns and Information please contact our EU
representative GPSR@taylorandfrancis.com Taylor & Francis Verlag GmbH,
Kaufingerstraße 24, 80331 München, Germany

Printed and bound by CPI Group (UK) Ltd, Croydon, CR0 4YY
08/05/2025
01864429-0001